50 YEARS OF VACATION

Michel P. J. NOBLET

50 Years of Vacation

A lifelong Passion for Excellence in the Hospitality industry

Éditions Mélibée

Éditions Mélibée, 2016
18 place Roguet – 31300 Toulouse

Confiez-nous votre talent :
info@editions-melibee.com – www.editions-melibee.com

With affection
To my parents, Jean and Odette

Acknowledgments

– To my Brother Alain, who with the passion and devotion worthy of a Benedictine monk, played the role of the careful proof-reader.

– To my Partner Hina for her patience and her unconditional help.

– To my Niece Valérie, and to my children for having taken the time to listen to me and understand my motivations.

– To my Friends Danielle and Roger for their recommendations and their huge support.

– To Usman, Stanley and Ameen for their devotion and creativity.

– To my Friend Christine for her enlightened advices and her knack for finding the right formula.

Contents

From Saint Gaudens to Dubai
passing through the rest of the world

Chapter 1

Saint Gaudens

Briefing

Contact moteur…

While I was finishing my game of mini golf in my home town of Saint-Gaudens, Odette, my mother, came to tell me that I had officially passed the entrance examination for the vocational hospitality course in a Toulouse college. This news filled me with joy and I could already feel that my life was taking off in a new direction.

The sacred fire for the hotel industry was starting to set me alight.

I realised just how much this opportunity would help me become emancipated and help me flourish along my path of life. I also understood that I was going to leave my roots in Saint-Gaudens to go and discover the city of Toulouse, the big city where we put on our Sunday best to visit my aunt Jeanne and our cousins, once or twice a year. At that time, Saint-Gaudens was a sub prefecture, of ten thousand inhabitants, of the Haute Garonne department, and was part of the Midi-Pyrenees region.

For the anecdote, this town, which was initially occupied by the Romans, was originally called Mas Saint-Pierre, before taking the name of a young shepherd, Gaudens, martyred by the Visigoths at the end of the fifth century for refusing to renounce his faith.

I was sixteen and my hobbies were somewhat limited in that medieval town. Saint-Gaudens was characterised by its eleventh century Collegiate church; its paper factory; its cellulose factory, which I hated because it triggered my asthma attacks; the market on Thursdays, which was the meeting point for inhabitants of surrounding villages; the Rugby League, where our team stood out by their French championship title; and then the cinema, once a month, in one of the town's movie theatres: the Variétés, the Rex or the Regent. My means of transport was a Peugeot scooter, which I managed to purchase with my savings and a little help from my mum. We were a close-knit family, with two brothers and two sisters, and I can say that we were disciplined in terms of schedules, though these weren't fixed or imposed.

My father, Jean, May God rest his soul in peace, was a native of the overseas department of the Reunion Island, while my mother, Odette, was from the village of Villeneuve de Rivière, a stone's throw away from Saint-Gaudens. My parents managed the Hotel de Bordeaux in Saint-Gaudens and displayed true generosity to accommodate and win the loyalty of the local customers.

I enjoyed helping my parents who worked hard, from morning till night, seven days a week, without ever taking a day off. Once I was back from school, unlike my big brother, Alain, who preferred to hover around, I tried to make myself useful in our modest small hotel-restaurant by playing an active part behind the bar in the café, in the restaurant or looking after the appetisers in the kitchen. One thing I loved doing was chopping parsley! I also enjoyed making the vanilla ice-cream, which I churned in an ice-cream maker. It was another era, where we appreciated the small things in life.

The hotel school in Toulouse.

We're in July 1962. For my family and for myself, one central objective: to organize the start of my school year in September.

This meant: the purchase of a trousseau of professional outfits worn by a cook and a restaurateur, as well as a new suit, shirts and ties.

At the same time, we had to make sure that I had somewhere to live in the big city of Toulouse, issue was solved thanks to one of my aunts who offered me one of her rooms.

Beginning of September, the big day arrived and all of a sudden, coming from my *commingeoise* countryside, I found myself immersed in a new world: Toulouse, also called "the pink city".

Deep down in my heart, and without doubt, I looked at this transition as a springboard for my future since it was matching a liberating fascination for the infinite. My challenge was to prove to myself, as well as to my parents who had given me everything, that I was going to succeed.

Toulouse, 4th city in France, is considered as one of the country's jewels, owing to its history, its character, its charm and also its gastronomy. It stands out by its rich cultural heritage, visible in the old neighbourhoods, but also by its industry, which plays an important role in Europe. It's also a university city. With more than 150,000 students, it is the most important student city in

France, after Paris. When we talk about Toulouse, the typical points of interest are: the museums, the Saint Sernin basilica, the Saint Etienne cathedral, rue Lafayette with its shops and the mythical Wilson square, which converge towards the famous Capitol square, where the town hall and the Capitol theatre (a public establishment) are located.

From day one, I was caught up in an environment which dazzled me with so many unfamiliar things, hence causing a slight dizziness. This said, I was committed and confident in my desire to learn, while discovering the world.

The day after my arrival, I joined the technical school twinned with its training hotel, the Hotel d'Occitanie, newly created and located at number 23 rue du Conservatoire, in Toulouse. Back then, this so-called facility was considered in the country as a pilot institute, which reinforced my ego.

The Toulouse hotel school was originally founded on December 5, 1916 within the framework of trade schools. This anniversary will be celebrated, throughout 2016, by various promotional events. Initially, the school was located in the old historical neighbourhood of Saint Etienne, in rue Croix-Baragnon. It remained there, despite dilapidated and inadequate premises, until 1962 when it was transferred to rue du Conservatoire, in place of the old hotel des Bains.

My Perspective: The Certificate of Professional Competence (Cooking-Pastry Making-Service).

The new structure of the school was organized around two distinct sections, namely:

The first section was aimed at helping students prepare for the vocational diploma in the hotel industry *(Brevet de technicien d'hôtellerie)* over three years. It was based on the basic practices of catering, together with reception and floor management techniques and hotel management.

The second section was aimed at preparing for the Certificate of Professional Competence (*Certificat d'aptitude professionnelle*). It was based on practical and technological catering applied to cooking, to pastry making and to the basics in restaurant services. Its target was to place qualified professionals on the job market –professionals who were immediately operational, and were able to adapt to the sector's evolution and to different forms of catering.

This second option was the basis for my initiatory journey, through my travels over time and the different opportunities that would be offered to me.

When I chose the second option, my father told me:

"You must start with what is hardest, which is gaining solid bases in catering and, therefore, specialising in the culinary art so that you can progress in a practical way."

Today, when we think of "hotel school", even though the foundations of the profession are still the same, more rigorous educational programmes are being specifically developed due to the evolution of international tourism, and the standards and specifications of hotel chains. Additional training modules focus on catering, engineering, dietetics, sciences and techniques in the hotel industry, new technologies, food preservation, management control in a hotel chain, yield management, reservation systems, sales techniques, marketing, etc.

In July 1962, Algeria officially became independent, after a war that had practically lasted for eight years. Many Pied-Noirs were repatriated back to France, which led to an increased presence of new students on university campuses, in colleges, schools and professional institutes, including hotel schools. For instance, in our class, half of the French students were repatriates from Algeria, which was very enriching socially and for our knowledge of others.

My class: "Edouard de Pomiane". According to school tradition, each section of about 60 students was named after someone famous. In our case, the class was called "Edouard de Pomiane" – his real name: Edouard Pozerski. Of Polish origin, son of an immigrant, he settled in Paris after the 1863 revolution. Born in Montmartre, he first went to school in a Polish institute, then to the Condorcet school. A hedonist, Edouard De Pomiane forged a career in biology.

Life at the hotel school was organised around practical exercises and lessons, setting a pace of intense work, and on top we had internships in the trade, allowing students to be confronted with the realities on-the-ground.

Under the supervision of **Mr. Aurière**, the principal, considered as "Mr. Courtesy", discipline was extremely strict. Our education was practically military. Our clothes had to be immaculate, a strict haircut, short nails, we had to be clean shaven, our shoes polished, we had to wear a tie and respect the disciplinary rules.

Every week, we had a capital of 13 points. The principle was draconian. Making noise during study time cost 2 points, arriving late was 3 points, forgetting your set of knives for cooking or pastry practice cost 3 points, misbehaving equalled 5 points, etc.

If we had lost 11 points on Friday, we had to stay at school on Saturday.

If we had lost 13 points on Friday, we had to stay on Saturday and Sunday.

Too many negative points during one term, the parents and the student were called in by the principal.

If a student relapsed, he could be expelled from school.

A word to the wise, once we were punished a couple of times, which happened to me, it was best to think twice.

I always had in mind the experience of my previous schooling at the Valentine College, located 10 kilometres from Saint-Gaudens. Every day, I rode that distance first by bike, then by scooter. But what I remember, with a certain sourness, is that my school career there was simply catastrophic.

In contrast, at the hotel school in Toulouse, I shined, positioning myself amongst my classes' top three students throughout the years. In actual fact, I was in my element. I enjoyed the school environment with my classmates, but also with our teachers who were true professionals striving to convey their love of the profession and who knew how to listen to their students.

In fact, I stayed in touch with some of them during several years.

Chapter 2
Paris, July 1965
On the take-off runway

During my schooling, I successively completed three intern-ships, which shaped my personality and revealed who I was.

My first internship: Residencia in the Lavandou (July / August 1963)

As a four-star establishment, it was both a dream destination and a perfect place for an outright exploitation of young trainees, and this from dawn till dusk.

In the morning, on the double from six am, with breakfast room service until eleven. At half past twelve, we had to be ready for lunch service *à la carte*, or service at the client's table, or in other words "*alla grande*". At three pm, a three-hour break allowing us to crash, not on the beach with my hair in the sand, but on my bed, in order to be in tune for the dinner service that started at half seven and generally finished around eleven pm.

One peculiarity: I shared a Spartan room with no running water nor toilet in the hotel's basement with one of the employees. The owner of the hotel, called Bianchini, also saved on personnel's meals. Invariably, for lunch and dinner, we ate some sort of small sausages with pasta, or pasta with small sausages.

One day, halfway through this so-called lunch, permanent employees of the hotel called the owner and declared that if the food conditions were not improved immediately, customer service would no longer be carried out. Fifteen minutes later, we were served steaks and French fries.

An interesting experience for my friend Lejeune, also an intern, and myself who were both discovering the world. Having said that, a week later, the cycle of small sausages and pasta had started again.

As it was the summer period, the hotel was fully booked, which meant that our kind owner didn't give us any days off. He however made up for it at the end of the internship, paid on a monthly basis of 150 francs at the time (i.e. 23 euros)!

Fortunately, some of our guests, who mostly stayed in the hotel between one and three weeks, showed their generosity with good tips. Concerning tips, one of the customers I had the honour to serve, was on holiday with her husband. One day, she came alone to the restaurant and slipped a fifty franc note in my jacket pocket!!!

She asked me to bring some fruit salad and a jug of fresh orange juice up to her suite.

Fifteen minutes later, I rang her doorbell and what did I see? Horror and disbelief! The client, totally naked, asked me to put the tray down on the console and ordered me to join her on the sofa. At that moment, I simultaneously thought about her husband, about Bianchini, about my career and about my parents, who would have been told:

– Your son has been expelled from school due to his disgraceful conduct which has affected the reputation of our institute.

I was devastated by the pain and the ecstasy of committing an irredeemable act. In the end, despite being scared, I perked up imagining my classmates' faces when, once back at school, I would tell them about this peculiar experience in the hotel industry, along with some juicy details.

My second internship: at l'hôtel des Etoiles in Courchevel (from the 22nd of December to the 4th of January 1964).

My friend Sylvain and I were volunteers for a paid internship in Savoie, for 15 days.

The hotel, built in 1950, was full. The customers were relatively well off.

As far as accommodation was concerned, we were extremely well housed and shared a room with two beds and all the necessary comfort.

On a professional level, our first task started at eight am and consisted in removing all the snow from the large terrace, very popular with guests for relaxation after a morning of skiing or hiking.

That job took us between one and two hours, depending on the thickness of the snow layer. Then, we would set up the dining room for lunch service.

As the customers stayed there for the entire holiday season, the restaurant manager allocated tables according to the customers' desiderata or affinities for such or such spot, or to be more exact, near Robert Hossein's table, –a screenwriter, film director and producer, in brief, one of the giants of French cinema or near the table of a CEO of a multinational or of a TV presenter.

I was assigned by Mr. Aldo, the maître d'hôtel, a sector or more precisely a square including 6 or 7 tables. They were located at the back of the restaurant, with the particularity of being near the access door to the cafeteria, kitchen and dishwashing services.

My friend Sylvain was responsible for the sector next to mine. Together, we worked as one to answer, in the best possible way, our respective customers' needs. The other sectors were under the responsibility of professional waiters, seasonal employees who worked 4 months on the French Riviera and 4 months in mountain resorts. But the atmosphere was pleasant and, as trainees from a hotel school, we were respected.

In my work zone, midday and evening, I had the privilege of serving the CEO of a large company of luxury products who was staying at the hotel with his wife and his two adorable children. Their table was located in the restaurant's left corner, which allowed them to have a broadview of the room.

One evening, when he and his wife were finishing their meal, the CEO asked me, in an amused way:

– Michel, why do you and your friend Sylvain hide the dishes, meant to be returned to the kitchen, under the service console table?

Very embarrassed, I confided in him:

– In fact, at the end of the service, we like to treat ourselves to a little snack.

Once again, he retorted:

– I bet the hotel boss, whom I've known for years, plays the smart guy with the personnel's meals.

He wasn't wrong, like at the Residencia, both owners had something in common regarding restrictions for their employees' meals. Amazingly, the kind CEO informed us that, from the following evening, he no longer wanted to see us hiding the dishes to be returned, either under or in the console table. He wanted us to dine together at his table, after the service. He forced us to order *à la carte* and on his account. Imagine the owner's face. He couldn't do anything about it, as the customer is King.

Three or four days later, the CEO, who was evidently making the most of his stay, had a request that seemed completely unreal to us, young interns. Namely to lend him our room, for two or three hours, for a date.

Fair enough, we thought: "Let's do it, we've come this far!"

Meanwhile, Mrs. Good Wife was enjoying the snowy slopes with the children!

On the day of their departure, the fourth of January, there were two events.

The first one was Robert Hossein and his partner's extreme kindness as they invited the entire staff, to one of the lounges adjoining the bar, to share a huge cake as thanks for the quality of the service and the special attentions they had received. That little reception was wonderful, festive and completely sincere, through their words and friendly attitude.

The second event involved the CEO and his family. They thanked us with much kindness, acknowledgments that were tinged with emotion and gratitude. In return for our devotion, Sylvain and I received two leather bags containing the equivalent of 500 francs in one franc coins!

That kind of situation was never mentioned in the style and teaching at the hotel school.

I made it to the finals, my Certificate of Professional Competence for the kitchen and restaurant room. At the end of my third school year, I had to face the period of oral and written exams, and the practical test in table-service and kitchen.

For a week, I strived to do my best, thinking about my parents who were extremely proud of my academic career at the hotel school and about my future, which was also at stake.

What we dreaded the most, in this compulsory phase, was the cooking or pastry part. Based on an imposed menu, we had to write the supplies' requisition slip or *bon d'économat* according to the traditional expression and to estimate its cost.

The products were then given to us in accordance with our order and after, it was time for us to get to work to impress a jury composed of the best chefs from the Toulouse region.

The dishes I had to prepare were first a plate of fillet of sole *bonne femme,* followed by a *tournedos forestière* (a fillet steak with mixed vegetables). After having detailed, estimated and obtained the ingredients, I was off for a rock-and-roll session where I had to associate the practical aspect, the setting-up, cleanliness, while always having a clear working space. Of course, we had to respect a given time in order to serve the guests at the right moment.

Amusing anecdote: after fifteen minute of solid work, one of the chefs from the jury came to see me and asked:

– How's your dad and how's business at your hotel in Saint-Gaudens?

Dumbfounded, I answered that he was doing very well and I thanked him. Then he gave me a hand stirring the vegetables for the *forestière* garnish!

In short, all those great professionals were kind and friendly. In fact I think that they would have preferred to be cooking than playing the role of hard-line experts. As a result, my colleagues and I were able to do our work without any stress, to the satisfaction of the members of the jury and the restaurant guests.

As far as the table-service was concerned, I had to serve two tables of four and the honourable guests were members of the Toulouse high bourgeoisie, as well as teachers from our school, under the control of Mr. Pujol, the restaurant master, who was supervising my work.

The highlight of my service, for which I received congratulations from Mr. Pujol and from the maîtres d'hôtel who coordinated the service between the restaurant and the kitchen, was the dessert, consisting of sorbets, *plombière* ice-cream and a brioche. This famous tall brioche, presented as a cylinder, couldn't stand vertically on its own on the presentation plate. To resolve this, I had found a foolproof system. I took the liberty of carrying two dishes with my left arm, which isn't spectacular in itself, except that instead of having the brioche lying on the plate, I held it vertically by inserting my left thumb in the brioche, which was hidden by my waiter's napkin.

Distraught, the pastry chef told me:

– Young man, you're crazy! It's going to topple over as soon as you go through the swing doors, between the kitchen and the restaurant.

Confident, I replied:

– Don't worry chef, everything is under control.

And off I went, kicking one of the swing doors to the restaurant with a thundering "watch out ahead". All this drew the attention of Maître Pujol, colleagues who were also passing the test and the maître d'hôtel who quickly said:

– Put it down Noblet, put it down, put it down.

Finally, for the show of the day, I presented the ice-creams with the brioche to each guest. In the end, Mr. Pujol told me:

– Noblet, you're really special, but you'll explain your trick to me later.

A few days later, while I was in my bedroom in Saint-Gaudens, my dad came to see me waving the newspaper "La dépêche du midi" and proudly announced that I had passed the two exams for the Certificates of Professional Competence for restaurant service and kitchen. With tears in his eyes, he said:

– Now, my boy, you have a job and you can express yourself professionally and your future lies ahead of you.

For him, the fact that I had graduated from the famous hotel school of Toulouse was an achievement and a success from the perspective of our little town of Saint-Gaudens; but also from the point of view of his status of President of the hoteliers' association for the Comminges region. And so, in the café, my dad was asking his friends, with a hint of haughtiness: "Have you heard the news?"

My third internship: le Café de la Paix, Place de l'Opéra, Paris. My passion for the hotel industry had caught fire.

Two months later, after the usual recommendations from my mother and father, I left my provincial town to complete my last internship at the Café de la Paix, following an application I had sent at the beginning of the year.

Arriving at the Austerlitz station early in the morning, I realised that I was giving a new dimension to my destiny. I was literally throwing myself with apprehension into another world, a world that I was going to devour, hoping to succeed and demonstrate my determination and my passion in this exciting adventure.

My internship form stipulated that I was to be housed at the Grand hotel, rue Scribe, and that I was to complete my cooking internship at the Café de la Paix, Place de l'Opéra.

Both addresses matched the same building, similar to an island surrounded by the Place de l'Opéra, boulevard des Capucines, rue Scribe and rue Auber.

I would later learn that the two prestigious businesses belonged to the Chapotin family.

Reaching the hotel reception, I was told that I had to go through the staff entrance to fill a registration form disclosing my identity.

Then, a staff member, in charge of the timeclock and overall security, took me to my room located under the hotel's rafters. Years ago, this was the messengers' floor (*étage des courriers*), used by drivers and servants. The room was small but very comfortable.

At that time, I was serene and started to define my action plan.

It was nine o'clock in the morning and I had the whole day ahead of me. First thing: to find a way to call my parents to reassure them about my journey and my safe arrival at the hotel. Then, breakfast at a café and locate my whereabouts in relation to my workplace since, the next day, I had to meet Mr. Georges Buffeteau, head chef and France's Best Work (*Meilleur Ouvrier de France*), who worked at the famous Café de la Paix, the mythical café for Americans and for foreigners in general.

The Café de la Paix has been the most famous meeting point for over one hundred and twenty years. The most famous artists have painted it, all the greatest names have stopped there.

I walked around to get my bearings and to become acquainted with the capital city. I walked till evening through the boulevard des Italiens, la rue Lafayette, la rue de l'Opéra, les Tuileries, la place de la Concorde...

When I got back to the hotel, even though I was exhausted, I was delighted and confident for my first interview that was to take place the following morning.

At the appointed hour, I went to the staff entrance of the Café de la Paix, rue Auber, and all of a sudden, I found myself in the lair of the establishment, in the basement.

I had never imagined that a kitchen could be below ground. Once there, I found a very special environment where everyone is running like in a ballet, cooks on one side, and waiters on the other.

I finally met Mr. Buffeteau who received me with much kindness, asking if I had settled nicely in the hotel and explaining the procedure for uniforms' collection, for my locker, the work schedules and what he was expecting from me during my two-month internship.

After donning my work uniform, he told me that the Café de la Paix had several points of sale, namely the gourmet restaurant, the Café Pacific where 600 to 800 covers were served daily depending on the season, the reception rooms and the bar, where Mr. **Alberto** worked as head barman.

For the anecdote, at that time, Alberto was considered as a reference in Paris. A key figure, as regular clients came to him either to hear about the latest gossip, to get a specific service or to find out the names of the best placed horses in the Arc de Triomphe Grand Prix, or any other tips.

Alberto's principle was to pay his assistant barman a twenty franc tip in advance, at the start of their service, and all the tips made during the service were for him.

In the cooks' and pastry chefs' brigade, there were about sixty of us. All of a sudden, I felt dizzy. In the Hotel de Bordeaux in Saint-Gaudens, we had the cook, Henri, and a waiter called Benjamin, who was part of our family. What a transition!

In order to make a successful start and to understand how things worked in Paris, Mr. Buffeteau included me in the brigade from the Café Pacific and assured me that if all went well, he would later include me in the gourmet restaurant brigade.

In that kitchen, which was considered as a satellite of the main kitchen, there were only five of us: the chef who announced the incoming orders from the waiters or maîtres d'hôtel, a station chef combining the work of an *entremetier* (vegetables in hotel jargon) and sauce maker, the grill chef (grillardin), a kitchen help and myself, in charge of soups and appetisers.

The space was confined, rational and limited to one person in each section. In my work area, everything was calculated to the nearest millimetre, from the place where the bain-marie stood, to keep the soups warm, to the cold section with all the necessary ingredients to prepare the nicoise salads, the shrimp cocktails, the plates of smoked salmon, the club sandwiches…

My first service, or the attack on fort Alamo. During my first service, I did indeed feel like I was under attack at Fort Alamo as orders kept coming in, announced by the chef who acted as the announcer. He was broadcasting as follows:

"Here goes, so three covers, one farmer soup, one plate of crudités, one club sandwich, followed by one mushroom omelette and a medium rare grilled filet with thin-cut French fries."

Thirty seconds later: "here goes, so five covers, three gazpachos, one tartare, one Vichyssoise soup, one shrimp cocktail, followed by a grilled andouillette mustard sauce, two entrecote steaks with marchand wine sauce, one medium rare, the other well done."

Forty five seconds later: "here goes, so two covers for Mr. and Mrs. Chapotin, one plain consommé, one croque-monsieur, followed by a sole meunière with boiled potatoes and one calf's kidney à la crème…"

On average, we served between 600 and 800 covers per day. In that context, there was no time to fool around.

The waiters, who were paid on service charge and looking for super tips, were constantly harassing us about everything, especially me, because for most orders, the first course was coming from my station. Consequently, we had to produce rapidly, very rapidly to satisfy them.

After three days of baptism of fire, I found my rhythm and my bearings and I enjoyed going faster and faster under the watchful supervision of the chef, who controlled everything.

Mr. Buffeteau was right when he said "Paris is different from the province". Here, you must go fast, very fast."

My transfer to the main kitchen, pantry station, under the supervision of Chef Buisson. Three weeks later, while I was in my element, I was transferred to the main kitchen to work the evening service during two or three weeks. I gladly accepted and found myself in the pantry section under the guidance of the station chef, Jean, to guarantee the set-up and basic preparations for all kitchen services.

What did that consist of?

Slicing the legs and thighs, racks, strip loins, filets, ribs, etc. of a side of beef, veal or lamb.

Preparing the Parma ham, which had to be boned, rolled and bound; the cold soups (Gazpacho, Vichyssoise), the thousands of canapés for the cocktails, etc.

In fact, the pantry station was the nerve centre of the kitchen organisation. All the food stuffs, vegetables, fruit, meat, poultry, fish etc. unavoidably passed through that station to be stored, then worked on accordingly.

As I worked at night, our job was also to ensure the evening service, which also included a second service related to the release of the Opera. Indeed, many Opera-goers came to treat themselves to some soup or a simple snack at the Café de la Paix before heading back to their hotel or their Parisian home.

In fact, this created another rush, as customers wanted to be served rapidly.

In-between the traditional evening service and the release of the Opera, we had a forty to fifty minute break, which allowed us to eat.

The night chef was Mr. Buisson, a man who had always lived in Paris and who considered people who lived below the Loire as provincials.

He called me *"mon bonhomme"* (my chap) but, through his quirky traits, he was a good guy. At break time, as we were only five cooks, he always said:

– Indulge yourselves and take what you like.

As far as our meals were concerned, we were perfectly organised with my friend Laurier, who was in charge of the vegetables and the sauces for the service. Our menus could vary from one day to the next.

One of the deals that we had made was a double entrecote, grilled or pan-fried, with a mountain of French fries against a platter of oysters dressed by the oyster seller at his counter.

We enjoyed "our order" in the pantry's second cold room, amongst the meat carcasses, because we had to be careful not to be caught red-handed by potential visitors from outside the kitchen brigade.

It was a well-oiled system. While Laurier prepared the double entrecote, I prepared the buttered toasts, the shallot vinegar and the bottle of lemonade. At the expected signal, the oysters that had already been opened arrived in a crate covered in seaweed and the same crate left in the opposite direction with the double entrecote and French fries.

From time to time, we would restrict ourselves to a bowl full of ice-cream, which must have been the equivalent of about twelve scoops of ice-cream of various flavours.

The idea was to break into the temple of *patisserie* of the Café de la Paix. During the day, there were around twenty pastry chefs who strived to make all sorts of pastries, creams and ice-creams. The ice-cream zone was unique and heavenly, where one could find many different ice-creams.

Armed with a glass bowl and an ice-cream scoop each, Laurier and I happily dug in the midst of a firework display of colours, exotic flavours, in the trays of vanilla, strawberry, kiwi, passion fruit, pistachio, caramel, chocolate, etc., ice-creams. To look nice, we generously sprinkled the whole lot with little chocolate and nougatine sticks and, as a final touch, we added a good dose of whipped cream to top it all off.

It was heaven, but things could get even better, namely the special "tsunami" raid on the fridges in the mini-pastry zone. The refrigerated cabinets had two super imposed fridges that we called *timbres* in French (literally "stamps"). As the daytime pastry chefs always prepared for the following day, these famous *timbres* were packed with mini-pastries that were nicely aligned on trays and on different levels.

Always remaining practical, the attack strategy was always the same. Laurier would take the top *timbre*, as he was the tallest, and in fifteen minutes, we both had stuffed our faces with forty or so mini-pastries, such as chocolate and vanilla eclairs, millefeuilles, baba savarins with pastry cream, the famous chocolate operas and various fruit tarts.

Our rhythm worked like a metronome: one mini pastry equalled one bite without batting an eyelid. To hide our misdeeds, we were wise enough to turn the trays around so that the pastry brigade wouldn't notice anything. At that time, we were only nineteen, without any weight problem.

Chef Buffeteau's assessment after completion of the internship. As my internship was coming to an end, Mr. Buffeteau invited me in his office, which was entirely glazed, with a panoramic view on his kingdom. He wanted to hire me on a full-time basis as second commis chef, with a salary of five hundred francs, the equivalent of eighty euros today, but with the obligation of renting my own accommodation. After expressing my warm thanks for his confidence, I suddenly realised that I was going to enter the workforce, and in Paris of all places.

What made me even keener was that I had been noticed for my work by one of the most famous chefs of Paris. On my internship record, his evaluations were as follows:

- Presentation: spotless appearance
- Courtesy: very good education
- Clothing and body cleanliness: very clean

- Exactitude at work: punctual
- Obedience: perfect
- Goodwill: very serious and very diligent
- Improvements made during the internship: excellent aptitudes for teamwork, has all the assets to become a chef.
- Signature: George Buffeteau, head Chef.

Furthermore, he offered me to work day shifts with Mr. Charles, regarded as Paris' best sauce chef.

I was positively thrilled and quickly told my parents at the end of the service. On hearing the news, they decided to come and see me a few days later.

The characteristic of Mr. Charles, who was in his sixties, was that he wasn't always even-tempered, with himself and with others, especially with Mr. Buffeteau, a man who was far more modern and progressive regarding the evolution of cooking.

Mr. Charles, as we were to call him, and not chef, was the kitchen "prima donna" working in the traditional way, by respecting the standards of Auguste Escoffier, the chefs' king.

After two or three days, I was in the old man's good books and I can say that we got on well. I was supposed to start at eight in the morning but I was so passionate about my work, I always arrived at seven o'clock, hence an hour before the other commis and station chefs. This allowed me to prepare the classic setting-up for the sauces. In other words, the necessary equipment to cook, which I took directly from the dishwashing area: the pots we called russian, the large cooking pots and the smaller ones, a big bain-marie, the spatulas and whisks to whip the sauces.

I also prepared all the bases: the *Orly sauce* (a tomato sauce), the chopping of the fine herbs, tarragon, parsley, chives, garlic, etc. And icing on the cake: covered with crushed ice, in one of the sinks, a bottle of white wine, one litre bottle of beer and a bottle of lemonade for myself.

When Mr. Charles arrived and saw my organisation, he was always appreciative and complimented me by saying:

– Well done, my chef. He never called me by my name.

Before we started working, the ceremony was always the same.

– So Mr. Charles, what will you start with today? A little glass of white wine or of beer?

Having said that, once the engine was started, we got on with the serious business by consulting the order forms for the receptions, business lunches and dinners.

There wasn't a minute to waste until lunch, with the whole kitchen brigade surrounding Chef Buffeteau in an immutable protocol order: the chefs, the assistant chefs, the first commis chefs, the second commis chefs and the apprentices.

The meals were copious, washed down with mineral water, beer and lemonade. According to the calendar, we respected the different religious faiths for the staff meals.

Half an hour later, uproar for the service. Mr. Charles and I were ready for the orders' on slaught which were always punctuated by a "very neat" added on by Mr. Buffeteau or possibly by a sous-chef.

From Mr. Charles, we had to "steal the expertise" as he never gave any details about his recipes. Since I spent a lot of time observing, in the evenings, once back in my little bedroom, I carefully wrote down in a notebook all the details I was able to gather during the day.

Occasionally, after the service, part of the brigade met at the corner café for a drink. The atmosphere was warm and relaxed. It was out of the question for the commis chef to pay, a matter of principle in this large brigade where everyone respected everyone.

I lived in rue Tiquetonne, a street perpendicular to Saint Denis, a hotspot for prostitution, where I inevitably came across the ladies of the night who tirelessly asked me whether I wished to follow them ("*Tu viens chéri?*"). My room was rather Spartan, with just a small sink. As my finances were limited, I worked extras in Les Halles, which were practically fifty meters away from where I lived.

For twenty francs a night, plus a free snack, usually at the Pied de cochon or some other brasserie, I carried, during part of the night, dozens and dozens of crates of vegetables between the delivery truck and the stall-keepers in Les Halles.

Even though it was tough, I liked that job, done in the noisy, teeming and festive atmosphere of Paris, the true Paris.

With this additional financial resource, I could treat myself, not to a lady of the night, but to a discovery of Paris and its surroundings, and to enjoy club sandwiches or milkshakes at the Renault pub on the Champs-Elysées with my friend George, who sadly did not succumb to the charms of Paris' frantic life; as in the end, he chose to take refuge in his native province of Languedoc.

I dedicated my day off to either roaming around, willing to learn and discover the world, or doing laps in the Deligny swimming pool.

The extras at *La Grille*.

One day, one of the sous-chefs of the Café de le Paix told me that if I wanted to work as an extra on my day off, I had to report to the association of Paris cooks, which was commonly called "*La Grille*". Wishing to experiment, I went to *La Grille*, where a whole group of people were already present.

After having waited for a few minutes, a fat man introduced himself by announcing the work available on that day. After a few announcements for station chefs, he asked:

– For Le Sébastopol brasserie, one commis chef.

I immediately raised my hand and disclosed my identity. Forty five minutes later, I was at the location. After having introduced myself, the head cashier said: "Come this way, young man."

Suddenly, he opened the trap-door under his seat and invited me to go down the stairs, while closing it behind me. The stairs were rather steep and in the darkness I heard:

– Are you the commis chef? And I answered: Yes sir.

He then replied:

– There is no Sir here, you call me Chef. Understood?

He showed me where I could get changed and then I set to work. In fact, the job was rather centred on peeling and cooking French fries and preparing the side garnishes for the fish and the meat.

The saucy, or rather dramatic side of my time in that sordid kitchen was that, right in the middle of the service, the so-called chef asked me to go and fetch a large pot of mashed potatoes under his desk.

In my mind, his desk was similar to Mr. Buffeteau's. Yet the desk in question was a plain wooden table, equivalent to a school desk, and the pot of mashed potatoes was on the floor, between the four legs. When I pulled the heavy pot towards me, one of the pot's handles hit one of the legs of this Imperial desk, which was then thrown off balance, and by extension, the desk drawer ended up right in the middle of the mash. Tough luck as among the rubber and pencils there was also a Waterman inkwell which merrily emptied itself into the highly culinary preparation, thus becoming a work of art with meanders of ink forming in the midst of this epicurean scenery.

Simultaneously, I heard the chef, on the verge of having a stroke and yelling:

– This is sabotage, you're good-for-nothing! Where are you coming from?

While trying to salvage some of the mash, I apologized, and once he recovered, the famous chef forgave me, saying that such things could happen in this job but that one had to be careful. Having said that, I never went back to *La Grille*. In fact, I realised that, despite everything, it was interesting to become aware of certain realities existing within the catering industry.

Mr. Buffeteau, my Supreme Leader. One day, Mr. Buffeteau invited me to attend the Arpajon culinary fair where the Café de la Paix was presenting sweet masterpieces and dishes, cooked and very artistically decorated.

That day, I took a lot of pictures to complete my album, which I would use wisely in due time.

Mr. Buffeteau, who knew everybody, introduced me as if I'd been working for him for years. After having had lunch in one of the fair restaurants, we learnt that the Café de la Paix had been brilliantly rewarded with two gold and three silver medals for the works presented.

At that moment, I understood that Mr. Buffeteau had his own special way of motivating his teams, while promoting the image and the prestige of the Café de la Paix enterprise.

I learnt a lot from him, and I am indebted to him for having given me a leg up, for his support, his leadership and his charisma.

I was honoured and privileged to work with him for over six months. But one day, with a heavy heart, I informed him of my desire to expand my knowledge and my professional experience by benefiting from an opportunity at La Tour Eiffel, as first commis chef at the gourmet restaurant. He didn't want to understand my reasons. At the end of the service, he summoned me and tried to reason with me.

Sadly for him, my decision was clear and definitive. Money wasn't really the issue, the true reason was that I wanted to move forward, to refine my knowledge while discovering a different world.

He had understood that I didn't want to confine myself to just one prestigious company and that my path of knowledge was under way for the best, because I was hungry to see more and especially to succeed everywhere. We parted on good terms, while making the promise to stay in touch.

Chapter 3
Paris, April 1966
Take-off

On April the 1st 1966, I made my entrance in what is known as the symbol of Paris, one of the most visited historical monuments in France.

People from around the world come to discover this extraordinary creation by Gustave Eiffel, built for the 1889 World Fair, which also symbolises the hundredth anniversary of the French Revolution of 1789. So many stories and emotions.

The lift to rise up in the world of haute cuisine. The particularity of the Eiffel Tower was that we depended on the lifts. The first lift at seven am was reserved for suppliers, delivering the necessary goods for the Tour Eiffel restaurants and bars.

The second trip, still with the same lift, was at exactly half past eight, and was reserved exclusively for the staff.

For customers, the lifts ran from ten in the morning. If by misfortune we were not punctual, we were good for the "pedibus cum jambis" via the stairs. When this happened to us and the bigwig or the kitchen chef was waiting for us at the top, on the last step, we learned our lesson and, usually, didn't do it again.

When you climb on foot, the first spiral staircase from the ground floor to halfway up, the stairs have a long tilt which make them relatively easy to climb. It becomes tough when you start the second spiral staircase, with a 45 degrees tilt!

Once at the top, half-dead, we would hear the top chef say, in a sarcastic way:

– Are you ok, young man? To help you recover, and instead of taking a break, you'll be in charge of cutting stalks off the runner beans, there are ten crates waiting for you in the pantry!

The experience at the Eiffel Tower was interesting and complementary to the one at the Café de la Paix.

I learnt new recipes from the sous-chef who was also France's Best Worker, MOF as we call it. Practically, I was in charge of the sauce station, where one of the flagship garnishes was the *sarladaises*, sautéed potatoes with truffles! In this restaurant, my work was relatively simple, because most clients were foreigners who appreciated the selection menus, as opposed to ordering *à la carte*.

What I did find unusual and curious –but apparently considered as a tradition– was that at the end of each service, the pantry chef asked everyone (even the commis), what meal for two we wanted to take home. The requests usually varied between two steaks, two fish fillets, cold meats, half a chicken, etc.

The relevant packs were systematically left, at the end of the service, in each fridge or *timbre* of the concerned party.

As I was a bachelor, this issue did not arise for me as I didn't cook in my room. One day, the General Manager, Mr. Pignare, asked the security service to check all the cooks' bags as they exited the lift. As a result, three employees were dismissed. Most of the others, or more precisely those who had been there a long time, had their own tricks.

That's how I learnt what pilfering meant and the cost of food for a catering company. Having said that, currently, with the strict cost controls, that sort of practice is gone, especially in renowned companies where everything is calculated down to the last penny.

My passage in that world only lasted three months.

Chapter 4

Beaulieu sur Mer, October 1966

Five star service on board

Recommended by George Buffeteau, I had the privilege of being hired on the French Riviera in the legendary hotel, La Réserve de Beaulieu, managed by the aptly named **Mr. Potfer** (iron pot in French). He was a strict and eminently respected man in the luxury hotel industry on the French Riviera.

Mr. **Pierre Pernet**, the head Chef, also *France's Best Worker*, offered me a salary of 700 francs, with room and board, for the position of first commis pantry. To ensure the transition and recharge my batteries, I spent a few days with my family in Saint-Gaudens. My parents were delighted by this new work opportunity in this Mecca of the hotel industry on the French Riviera.

Founded in 1880, La Réserve de Beaulieu is a palace with 50 suites and apartments with living rooms, which has managed, early on, to acquire a high reputation among all the European courts and the international high society. Alongside monarchs and princes of royal blood, the whole aristocracy of finance, arts, literature and politics could be found here, attracted to this key place of gastronomy. This establishment belonged to the Laroche family.

We had an elaborate menu made of original recipes devised by **Mr. Pernet**, but also classics from the regional cuisine.

Nonetheless, most clients, whose influence extended throughout the world, preferred to express their immediate desires directly to the maître d'hôtel, rather than choosing à la carte. In the kitchen, aside from the base elements, all the preparations were made on the spot, which meant that we had to have a practical mind.

Under the leadership of Mr. Pierre Pernet, there were eighteen of us, working in an extraordinary work environment. The top chef Pernet, who had a contagious charisma, taught us the love of the trade and every minute spent in his presence was a motivation to always learn more.

My experience at La Réserve lasted three years, where, thanks to my will power and determination, I was able to evolve in every kitchen role, starting with the pantry, entremets, the grill, the rotisserie, to finally reach the position of station chef sauces.

Since gastronomy was the flagship of La Réserve de Beaulieu, everything had to be perfect. Each dish leaving for the restaurant had to be decorated and was, naturally, systematically controlled by Mr. Pernet.

At the time, in the world of catering, it was usually said that there were always tensions between the kitchen brigade and the restaurant staff. At La Réserve, this wasn't the case, as both brigades respected each other and knew that they were complementary to obtain, in the end, the customers' and management's satisfaction.

Naturally, this could only be possible thanks to the intelligence of two main actors: **Mr. Bessey**, the restaurant manager, and Mr. Pernet. These true professionals often combined their talents to bring a special touch to a preparation or to the elaboration of a recipe or of a presentation in order to impress a particular customer.

At the end of the season, as a token of the restaurant staff's gratitude towards the kitchen brigade, Mr. Bessey thanked Mr. Pernet for his support and gave him an envelope containing thirty thousand francs, which he royally handed over in full to Mr. Picard, the sous-chef, responsible for ensuring an equitable distribution between all the brigade's members.

On the subject of money, one day Mr. Pernet informed me that Mr. **Potfer** wanted to see me in his office immediately. As you can imagine, I was surprised as this was the first time I was experiencing this kind of situation. Intimidated, I went to see the big boss, who welcomed me kindly and in a simple and straightforward manner, thanked me for my excellent work and my ability to work long hours. He gave me a five hundred franc note, which I refused by telling him that I was happy to be part of La Réserve staff, where I was learning a lot.

While insisting that I keep the note, he asked me what my projects were for the future. Such a sensitive issue for me, but at the same time, it was the opportunity to express myself directly. So, spontaneously, I told him that I wanted to go to England to learn English and therefore pursue an international career.

He listened to me carefully and said:

– You're right, it's important to move forward. For my part, I'm ready to help you and to find you a job in London. On one condition: that you stay until the end of next season.

We certainly had a deal, but Mr. Pernet, who was old school, only half approved what I said, but the dice was cast for my next challenge, to take up in a few months' time.

At that time, I was in love with a young woman called Michèle, who lived practically opposite La Réserve de Beaulieu. We saw each other every day, and after passing my driver's licence, I bought a Renault 4L, which allowed us to travel along the French Riviera, alternating with Italy – distance of only a few kilometres. I can say that, during that time, we could have created a magazine about the motels or little hotels, because from Menton to Cannes, we knew nearly all of them to host our naughty getaways.

Alongside the nooky, I had to handle my job at La Réserve de Beaulieu, which was hard work.

With the bigwig, we had to give 100% every day, but personally I was learning something new daily. Mr. Pernet was a permanent inspiration to me, which resulted in demonstrations of savoir-faire in all culinary areas and classical standards. The problem was that we had to follow his pace and he was working fast in his own way. At the beginning of the much-touted last season, he called me in his office and told that, from that day on, I would be working as station chef sauces with Mr. Picard, the deputy kitchen chef. It felt like a dream and, for the first time, I sensed that my career in the hotel industry was taking a whole new dimension.

Under Mr. Pernet mentoring, I became one of France's youngest station chefs in a two-Michelin star restaurant, and was admitted to the prestigious Auguste Escoffier fraternity.

Nonetheless I redoubled my efforts to exceed my masters' expectations. With two colleagues, Jean Paul Buisse and Jean Paul Bonin, who later became the head Chef at Le Crillon in Paris, we worked during off-duty hours on projects, decorating dishes and culinary pieces. One evening, after the service, which usually ended around eleven o'clock, we loaded in my Renault 4L our masterpiece, a culinary spectacle on the theme of hunting, of a size of one meter forty by ninety centimetres! We drove all night to drop our work in time for the culinary exhibition of Arpajon, to have a cup of coffee there before immediately driving back to La Réserve de Beaulieu for lunch service, like nothing ever happened. Later that evening, we heard that our creation had won the gold medal in its category.

At the time, we didn't think about media impact. We simply did it for our own personal pleasure.

La Réserve de Beaulieu was a mini-palace that could be qualified today as a Boutique Palace. It was the place to be, just like the Negresco in Nice or the Martinez in Cannes, not to mention the palaces of the Principality of Monaco.

Some of the clients' antics. La Réserve had its summer months' aficionados who came to stay for three or four weeks. Odd events would often happen.

I remember Mr. Schlesinger who, in a moment of childish folly with his little circle, amused himself by spraying the hotel's palm trees with magnums of champagne!

Or this other original character who, on a fifteenth of August at precisely one pm, was served some choucroute by the swimming-pool with friends. Of course, at the end of this orgiastic feast, he and his guests threw themselves into the water.

Another anecdote, even more delightful, involves the Duchess of Alembert who ordered a tea-steak for her tiny dog. In this instance, the tea-steak was a beef aiguillette, cut into thin slices, then cooked quickly on the hot plates, expressly with no oil (due to cholesterol). Then, with a press, the juice of these slices had to be extracted and collected in a tea cup to finally be served by the maître d'hôtel to the little dog, gently waiting next to his mistress. I must specify that the tea-steak had to be served lukewarm!!!

Chapter 5

London, November 1968

New direction

As promised, at the end of the season, **Mr. Potfer** confirmed my employment at the Rubens Hotel on Buckingham Palace Road in London, part of the Grand Metropolitan Hotels group. I was expected there within a month.

Here we go, my journey was going on. For the first time in my life, I was moving to an unknown destination, which I already loved.

In fact, I was not asking myself any questions, because, as usual, I had to prove to my future boss, and to myself, that I was going to do the utmost to get the expected satisfaction from the Rubens Hotel, but also with respect to Mr. Potfer, so disappointment was out of the question.

And so I set off for London with my 4L. I eagerly enjoyed every landscape, the French national roads, as highways did not exist yet, then the ferry crossing to discover a new horizon, keeping in mind that I had to drive on the left, which wasn't easy at first.

The Rubens Hotel, incredibly well located in the West-end, near Victoria Station and Queen Elisabeth's palace, had a good reputation. 189 elegantly decorated rooms in the Flemish style, its lounges, its bar and its restaurant where we offered à la carte and a daily menu.

To give me time to find accommodation, I stayed in one of the hotel rooms for three days. It was the first time in my life that I stayed in an actual hotel, and this meant that I was able to familiarize myself with the workplace. I was surprised to discover that the entire housekeeping staff was of African origin. This caught my attention. Somehow, I found this strange, but why not after all, because as a Frenchman, I was also an immigrant.

Station chef in England. The day after my arrival, after completing the necessary formalities at the personnel department and after introducing myself to the General Manager, I was operational in the kitchen, as station chef.

I must say, the French kitchen chef had limited experience in the area of gastronomy and, in some ways, had a complex towards my experience at the Café de la Paix, La Tour Eiffel and La Réserve de Beaulieu.

To make the soup, the *entremetier*, or if you prefer the person in charge of soups and vegetables, poured, in a large cooking pot of boiling water, one or two boxes of vegetable powder, depending on the desired quantity, added some salt and pepper, stirred the whole thing and the soup of the day was ready to be served!

Strangely, I was discovering a different world, allowing me to learn about the English practical side for the culinary art, revealing a certain subtlety.

The deputy kitchen chef, Derrick, an Englishman, could eat a sandwich filled with French fries for lunch! The kitchen brigade was very cosmopolitan: Polish, Spanish, Italian, German, English and French. All these people spoke in broken English, which could make communication sometimes quite chaotic.

As far as accommodation was concerned, I finally found a small bedroom of 9 square meters, due North, with a sliding window, without water or toilet, for five pounds a week, while my weekly salary was fifteen pounds. When I was using the bathroom on the landing, I had to make sure I had enough coins, because water and electricity, even in the bedroom, had to be paid for via a meter. For instance, to fill the sink with water, I had to put three pence; for a half-full bath, two shillings; for half an hour electricity, one shilling.

As the room was orientated due North with only one window without shutter (at the time in England there weren't any shutters in the houses), in winter my room felt like a fridge, if not a freezer. To the extent that I was sleeping with a balaclava, pyjamas, a tracksuit, in a sleeping bag, covered by a pathetic blanket.

In the morning, I had to put coins in the meter to connect a small heater, which provided a bit of heat. Having said this, if I was too close to the appliance, it burnt my legs, and if I was moving too far, I could not feel anything. In such a situation, I had to have a practical mind to get dressed and rush with coins to the bathroom, hoping it was free.

In the hotel, one thing amused me: occasionally, the General Manager, called **Martin** and who spoke a bit of French, asked me to prepare a typical French meal for him and his guests, which made the kitchen chef insanely jealous.

While alternating between my English classes and sightseeing tours of London and surroundings, I got a call from the kitchen sous chef of the Dorchester, a former employee of La Réserve de Beaulieu, who offered me a position as second deputy kitchen chef with a salary of sixty pounds per week, which was equivalent to four times my current salary.

After a day spent thinking about it, faithful and loyal towards Mr. Potfer, I declined the offer. I was actually free but, in my mind, to leave after only five months wasn't correct towards the Rubens Hotel. This event allowed me to question myself.

Ex abrupto, I move from the kitchen to the reception. I decided to meet the General Manager to ask him for a transfer from the kitchen department, where I was not learning anything, to the hotel reception. Although surprised by my request, he understood the motivation that drove me on my career development plan within the hospitality industry.

A week later, I was working at the reception desk, with the compulsory suit: black jacket, trousers with black and grey stripes, white shirt and black tie, for a salary of only ten pounds per week, as I had no experience and was starting over.

I was conscious of the financial sacrifice but happy to have the opportunity to discover and learn something else; for me, the transition was irrevocable and there would be no turning back to the kitchen.

My new function was very time-consuming. I had to learn everything, room bookings, planning, customer reception, invoicing, etc.

Having said that, the automatisms acquired at the Hotel de Bordeaux with my parents helped me a lot.

The way to treat a customer is ultimately the same in France or in England. I learnt a lot from my mistakes, but my Italian boss had the style and class to provide a training support in any given situation.

One of the difficulties I encountered at the beginning was invoicing, done on a huge NCR cash register with mechanical keys, which I had to press hard to ensure the operations were recorded. An extra difficulty: I was faced with the English monetary system. I had to juggle with penny, three pence, one shilling, half crowns, pounds or guineas. This exercise wasn't easy, especially at the end of the day, when we had to do the bank reconciliation, taking into account the currency exchanges.

To improve myself, I didn't hesitate to spend more time with my morning or evening colleagues, in order to understand all the workings and subtleties of the reception and of the cash register, which was highly appreciated by the hotel hierarchy.

My life in London with Michèle. In May 1969, we got married in the South West of France to make our relationship official. We then settled in 66 Lupus Street, in the Victoria neighbourhood in London.

As our finances were limited, we lived in a simple basement room with a view on a poorly maintained small garden and minimum comfort. For the storage of our personal belongings, it was quite peculiar, as we only had a small cupboard, where the coat-hangers hung side-ways, which did not allow us to hang all our clothes. This forced us to have a rotation between summer and winter clothes, according to the season, with the others put away in boxes under the bed. The unavoidable meter, where we had to put shillings to have some water and electricity was in our room.

We both worked in the hotel industry: me at the Grand Metropolitan Rubens Hotel and Michèle at the Grand Metropolitan Park Lane.We had the privilege of being fed during our respective service period. However, in this new simple life, we were happy with what we had and were particularly proud to have got off the beaten track, with the feeling that expatriation and new experiences were synonym of success and fulfilment for the future.

During our linguistic, professional, tourist and "gourmet" stay, we particularly enjoyed the fish and chips served in a newspaper cone, and the steak and kidney pie from the takeaways. No kidding, fish and chips really belong to the heritage of English cuisine!

During my stay, I found a way to pass my driving licence with my 4L car, epic test taken in the Wimbledon borough.

After the traditional Highway Code questions that I had learnt by heart, the inspector invited me to drive and told me that when he hit the dashboard with his folder, I had to stop the car straight away, in emergency. After two minutes of driving, the inspector hit the dashboard with such a force that it startled me. I stopped the car immediately, but, for him, it was too late. So, with an "I am afraid you failed", I had to take the test again the following month. The following month, the same exercise with another inspector who, when he hit the dashboard with his folder, also hit the windscreen with his face. Out of the corner of my eye, I had anticipated the manoeuvre and had hit the brakes as he'd asked me to, in emergency. Unfortunately for him, safety belts didn't exist yet!

While rubbing his face, the inspector gratified me with a "well done, Sir" and told me that I would receive my driving licence by post. Although I could drive with my international driving licence, I saw this operation as a victory.

During our off-days, we visited one tourist and historical attraction after another, such as Tower Bridge, St Paul's Cathedral, Westminster Palace, Big Ben, Buckingham Palace, Westminster Abbey, the Houses of Parliament, Windsor Castle, etc. The museums: the British Museum and Madame Tussauds, the markets and the most popular parks in London, such as Hyde Park, Battersea, where I parked my car, and Kensington Gardens. We were on the move and we always wanted to know more.

Although everything had been going perfectly well for several months, we decided to move back to France and settle down in Paris. With this plan in mind, I wrote a cover letter to the General Manager of the Grand Hotel in Paris, highlighting my professional experience in France, particularly at the Café de la Paix, which was part of their organisation, at La Réserve de Beaulieu, along with my London experience. For her part, Michèle got in touch with her former boss, who was in charge of a hotel project at the Gare d'Orsay in Paris.

Chapter 6

Paris, May 1970

Stopover for VIPs

I finally received a letter from Mr. **Vernay** asking me to come and see him for an interview the following week. He was the General Manager of the Grand Hotel, the Meurice, the Prince de Galles and the Café de la Paix in Paris.

Motivated and resolute, I confirmed at once and a few days later, off I went by train, then on a ferry to Calais and another train to Paris.

This time, I didn't go in through the service entrance, but through the Grand Hotel front door and proudly went to see the concierge to inform him about my appointment with Mr. Vernay. Immediately, the concierge called a groom who took me directly to Mr. Vernay's office, who received me warmly and asked if my trip had gone smoothly.

Something curious caught my attention in his impressive office as, on one of the radiators, a pair of bathing trunks had been put out to dry!

I later learnt that Mr. Vernay regularly went swimming at the Port Royal pool on the Seine river to keep fit.

The interview started off well, as he complimented me on my writing and my letter's presentation, which, to be honest, had both been done by my wife.

Getting into the heart of the matter, he asked me what my aspirations were in the hotel industry, then followed up on technology, catering and food cost in the United States. Paying close attention I wondered into what trap I had run, because I had never heard of that sort of terminology. However, I had to hold on and gamble on what I had gleaned from French gastronomy, France's influence around the world, expectations from American customers when staying in France; all of this through my experience at the Café de la Paix, La Tour Eiffel, La Réserve de Beaulieu and an English hotel chain, the Grand Metropolitan Group, with 25 hotels in London, not forgetting that I was also a hotelier's son.

After forty five minutes of friendly discussion, he asked me to prepare a three/four page report on food cost. Seeing me to the door, Mr. Vernay demanded, despite my refusal, that I give him the receipts of my travel expenses, which the hotel cashier reimbursed.

On the way back to England, I relished the time spent with that gentleman who had welcomed me with such simplicity and humility. I also realised than in life, if one wants to succeed, one must take on responsibilities and risks.

A few days later, after searching everywhere with my wife's help, we managed to write a report of several pages on the food cost system, which didn't exist in Europe yet.

The food cost is an American concept that later spread to hotel chains and is an integral part of the uniform system of accounts for hotels.

Two weeks later, I received a letter from Mr. Mario Dell Antonia, Deputy General Manager of the Grand Hotel, offering me the position of Executive Assistant Manager at the Grand Hotel and a month later, he received me in his office at the Grand Hotel to explain the nature of my future job.

Our sub-directorate, a large laboratory for the scientific organisation of work. In the sub-directorate office, which was located next to Mr. **Dell Antonia's**, there were four of us: **Jean-Paul Lafay**, Management Assistant, who later became the General Manager of the Bristol in Paris; **Annie Sourdeau**, Human Resources Manager; **Brigitte Lamy**, Executive Secretary; and myself, Executive Assistant.

The Grand Hotel sub-directorate was in fact the central pillar of the hotel organisation, where we coordinated all the hotel administrative functions. We were the point of contact between the heads of department: finance, commercial, purchasing, reception, concierge service, catering, room service, technical, security, and many more. The task was difficult but rewarding, as under the responsibility of Mr. Dell Antonia, Jean-Paul and I were always on the front line. All the files had to be prepared and approved by Mr. Dell Antonia, then handed over to the hotel General Manager to be signed.

When there was a board meeting with the CEO, Mr. **Radius**, we had to be well organised, as there was no room for error. The respective signature books, according to the agenda, had to be perfectly presented and in a specific order.

For instance, for the refurbishment of a suite or other, the cheque on the top of the pile could not be signed if one of the following documents was missing: the scope of work, the quote, the order form, the delivery receipt, the invoice, or the authorisation for payment. Each document had to be perfectly lined up and the whole thing had to be stapled with utmost care.

In front of the CEO's seat, as a ritual, we placed a pen-case with three ballpoint pens: one blue, one black and one red, besides a rubber and a pencil!

Of course, logistics had to follow a prescribed manner for the hot and cold drinks' service. One day we were almost hit by a revolution in the hotel because one of the order forms had been misplaced. Madame **Sching,** one of the top management éminence grise, made such a fuss, blaming X or Y. Jean-Paul and I were concerned, as we were facing a global tragedy, which ended with the acceptance of a copy taken from the order book stub.

In the organisation of the Grand Hotel, the Meurice, the Prince de Galles and the Café de la Paix Company, there was a technical department, extremely rare occurrence, which included a team of upholsterers. All the carpets in the different facilities had to be laid by that team. Moreover, the MET department (*méthode étude et travaux* – method, survey and works) provided all the surveys and follow-up of renovation and maintenance works, specific purchases, in order to potentially increase the performance or profitability in a specific department, or even the creation of a new form for the requirements of any department. No less than fifty employees in those two departments!

We had to constantly apply the principles of the Scientific Organisation of Labour, based on the analysis prior to any organization action and we were required to attend training sessions to perfect our knowledge.

This way, any innovation, such as a simple printout, had to have the MET director's, Mr. **Humblot's,** approval – another top management éminence grise.

With Jean-Paul, my colleague, we made countless round trips between the MET office and our own, to each time hear the same track:

– I cannot accept your proposal because of a lack of reflection, and other blah, blah, blah.

Mr. Humblot was a real nightmare for everyone. He liked to repeat this Descartes principle:

"It would be better never to think or seek the truth about anything than doing so without method, because it is obvious that studies without order and obscure meditations disturb the natural limits and blind the mind, and whoever gets used to walking in the darkness, weakens his sight to the extent that he can no longer bear the daylight."

Deep inside, we criticized Humblot, but on the principle, he was quite right in his approach and pedagogy to do things correctly, which ultimately would be of productive interest for the hotel.

For all phone calls, whether it was an external or internal call, we had to go through the switchboard and very often through Madame **Chenevé**, the chief operator. This lady, who was always elegant, was also an éminence grise of the top management. So she was perfectly aware of everything that was going on in the hotel, as she had the privilege to listen to all our conversations!

The Grand Hotel, the largest hotel in France, historic Paris landmark, was built during the reign of Napoleon III in 1862.

Over the years, it became the hotel of the most important figures of the diplomatic, political and artistic worlds, such as Offenbach, Churchill, Eisenhower and many more!

It was honoured to employ staff with many years of experience. It was particularly the case for all the heads of departments and services who were respected by the owners, the hotel, and who proudly represented the name of the Grand Hotel.

The shambles of May 1968 events. However, in life things always evolve and can express themselves violently, like the events that took place in May 1968 with the students and the working class.

All of a sudden, these events took a worrying turn. Beyond the usual salary demands, there was a whole register of disputes about the calling into question of the Gaullist government, which had been in place for a decade, about the structural difficulties, about the democratisation of the universities, the rejection of capitalism by the Marxist, leftist, Trotskyist, Maoist parties, etc.

All this led to a general and wildcat strike, the most significant one of the twentieth century, with 7 million strikers on the streets. That strike, which took an insurrectional turn, mobilized all nation's professional circles, leading to the paralysis of France for several long weeks. The government, totally overwhelmed by this alarming situation, had to make huge concessions to curb the movement.

There was the dissolution of the National Assembly on May the 30th 1968, followed in April 1969 by a referendum on regionalization, on the role of the Senate and the departure of the General de Gaulle. The French said NO to General de Gaulle, which forced him to definitely leave power.

The events of May 68 in France also challenged the consumerist society, a socio-cultural conflict and an accentuation of activism against the public and political sphere.

This context of the "French trouble" had repercussions over the following months and years, and regrettably affected the Grand Hotel de Paris, symbol of the hotel industry in France. And so, for two weeks, the trade unions spoke out by negotiating with the hotel management to obtain additional benefits related to wages, while organizing daily protests in and around the hotel, chanting anarchist slogans dictated by the labour federation, with a lot of banners. During these events, followed by 80% of the staff, the general management took the following decisions:

- The minimum service would be guaranteed by the executives and the department managers.
- No booking to be recorded.
- Increased hotel security, etc.

We practically had to do everything ourselves. With my colleagues, who had also volunteered, I could be working at the concierge service in the morning, with the head concierge who was called **Pierre Porte** – an extraordinary guy who by himself embodied an encyclopaedia, combined with the Who's Who, which he practically knew by heart. In his lodge, there was money everywhere in the drawers for shows, excursions, horse races, plane bookings, car rentals, call girls, tennis tournaments (Roland Garros and Wimbledon).While in the afternoon, I could be acting as an elevator operator or assigned to make the beds. On this topic,

I learnt the technique of how to make a bed in less than two minutes.

As we had to stay in the hotel for the entire duration of the strike, we didn't have a free minute to go out, even though the hotel was only operating at 20% occupancy.

What was extraordinary, was that some customers, who were there for extended stays, supported the hotel management, and as they didn't want to leave the hotel, they didn't mind making their own bed or getting clean sheets and clean towels from housekeeping. I reckoned that some customers had never had the opportunity to make a bed before.

We had an elderly customer who stayed at the hotel all year round and who castigated the strikers by telling them that they should be ashamed to be on strike, in her view unpopular. "From now on, I shall no longer give any tips," she said!

In short, that experience, which ended in a conflict of interest between the two trade unions, the CGT and the FO, resulted in a compromise in the form of protocols between the parties and especially, the management's gratitude for the non-striker volunteers who had maintained the hotel's activities and ensured security.

The aftermath of 68 wasn't easy. There was distrust in the companies with the trade unions, driven by their federations, and in particular the collusion between the French Communist Party (PCF) and the General Confederation of Workers (CGT).

Despite everyone's efforts for diplomacy, the team spirit had changed in the relations between management and staff.

One fine day in October 1971, I was in the office when I received a personal phone call from Mr. **Pierre Monet**. I knew the name, I had heard of him, but didn't manage to identify him at the moment of the call.

He immediately told me that he would like to meet me for a job opportunity, and suggested that I meet him directly in his office, at the Air France headquarters, for an interview.

Two days later, I went to the Air France headquarters, located on square Max Hymans in Montparnasse. The reception attendant knew that I was coming. He told me which floor to go to with the lift. Mr. Monet met me and I immediately recognised his face. He was the former General Manager of the Intercontinental Hotel in Paris. His welcome was extremely courteous and pleasant.

After the usual questions about my career path in the hotel industry, he offered me, on behalf of the hotel company HFI, Hôtel France International, subsidiary of the Air France Group, the leadership of three hotel units in the National Park of Niokolo Koba, seven hundred kilometres from Dakar, the capital of Senegal.

My net monthly income would be 125,000 francs CFA, equivalent to 2,500 French francs and 75,000 francs CFA – 1,500 French francs – for my wife, who would be responsible for the secretarial work, bookings, etc., and to these conditions, he added a plane ticket per year, food and accommodation.

He concluded by asking "Are you interested?"

My answer: "Thank you for this opportunity, but could I have a case file?"

His answer: "If I give you a case file, you will never leave!"

My answer: "Then under these circumstances, Mr. Monet, I accept!"

When I got home that evening, I proudly told my wife: "Honey, I have news for you, we're leaving for Africa in a month!"

Once she had recovered from the surprise, and after being told the facts, we were very happy about the prospect of discovering the African continent and being adventurers in the bush, and especially getting away from the strikes, the trade unions and the general uneasiness and non-productive environment.

Chapter 7
Dakar/Simenti, November 1971
Diversion

Senegal, homeland to the Poet-President Leopold Sedar Senghor. One month later, we were on an Air Afrique DC 10, on our way to Senegal, home to the Poet-President His Excellency Leopold Sedar Senghor, former Minister and Member of the French Academy.

Our enthusiasm and our craving for new destinations was at the top. Our respective families shared our appetite for discovering the world.

At the Dakar-Yoff airport, it was a complete immersion in an incredible hubbub, a firework of colours, real kaleidoscope between the extremely coloured women's boubous, the exoticism, the atmosphere of the airport, the musky aromas and the hecklings between the arriving passengers and those welcoming them.

Strangely, I already felt part of this movement and fervour, which I had imagined. I saw a sign "Mr. Michel Noblet" emerging from the bustling crowd. Simultaneously, I heard a generous "Welcome to Senegal, Mr. and Mrs. Noblet" uttered by **Roger Cassir,** the Deputy General Manager of HFI Senegal, who has been a good friend ever since, along with his wife Danièle.

So off we went to the N'Gor hotel, which was located at the far end of the Cap-Vert peninsula, in the N'Gor bay, in the heart of a ten hectare park where we would spend a week before driving to the National Park of Niokolo Koba.

The day after our arrival, we met the N'Gor Hotel General Manager, Mr. **Leygues,** who was also responsible for two other hotels, adjacent to the N'Gor: the N'Gor Village, with its 220 rooms and additional 150 bungalows, and the Diarama Hotel, with 220 rooms, whose opening was scheduled for a few months later.

This huge complex, key for the tour operators, travel agencies and Dakar wealthy clientele, had a unique location overlooking the sea, with a dozen restaurants, its bars, its two nightclubs, its sports facilities and the famous activity hut, which had the reputation of being the largest in Africa.

My mission in the National Park of Nikola Koba. The General Manager, Mr. **Leygues**, in the presence of **Roger Cassir**, who used to work for Hilton, gave me a great deal of details about my mission.

The instructions were as follows:
– You are the General Manager of three hotels belonging to the Senegalese government, and under HFI management. There is the Simenti with 50 rooms and 20 straw huts, which is the central element of your organisation; then there is the Badi village, with its

35 huts, which is 30 kilometres away from Simenti; and Niokolo, with its 25 bungalows, which is some 80 kilometres away from Simenti.

— From a hierarchical point of view, you're reporting to Roger Cassir.

— The rainy season is now over, so you have 15 days to recruit the personnel and make all three units operational.

— You have a Peugeot pick up at your disposal and a driver called Camara who knows the area perfectly.

— Before leaving Dakar, you will have to stock up on food and drinks for your hotels, and to do so, the N'Gor Finance Director will lend you five hundred thousand CFA francs that you will use as working capital.

— You will stay 6 months in your job, meaning during the whole tourist season or, in other words, until the next rainy season.

— Moreover, as there is no telephone connection, you will be in daily radio contact with the N'Gor Hotel for two time exposures of fifteen minutes, morning and evening.

— Be careful on the road, because from the check-point onwards, which is three hundred fifty kilometres away, it's all laterite.

— I wish you and your wife good luck and don't hesitate to discuss the details with Roger Cassir.

After this interview conducted in a hurry, my wife and I decided to review Mr. Leygues' instructions and we implemented an action plan that would start on the following day. After that, Roger invited us for lunch in the executives' cafeteria who were all French surrounded by their families.

After having been introduced by Roger to all these people, we had the impression of being labelled as the "crackpots" who had come to manage a hotel deep in the bush.

It was, for Michèle and me, our second expatriation. We felt embarrassed as we noticed a lot of arrogance in the remarks and exclamations of these Europeans towards the Senegalese.

We also thought that some of them would have been better off staying in their own country, rather than criticizing and expressing judgments on locals' behaviour or on their way of working. Michèle and I felt a dislike for some people who thought they were in a conquered land, and therefore, we were yearning to discover our new universe, in order to live our Senegalese experience to its fullest.

Two "Toubabs" in Dakar. The following morning, Camara, the driver, made us discover the capital of Senegal, bit by bit, as we made the necessary purchases. It was a real immersion and the best way to soak up the city's atmosphere.

Within a few hours, we discovered:

– The big market of Sandaga, for its fruit and vegetables, its meat and fish, where the "doudous" (sales women) always kept a watchful eye on their children, sleeping peacefully in an infernal noise, in the midst of myriads of flies.

– The covered market of Kermel, for European food supplies and the flower saleswomen who entice you with their overflowing sensuality.

– The fish market and the arrival of fishermen who offered thiof, captain fish, shark, prawns, shellfish, skipjack, red mullet, etc.

– And finally, the craft market of Soumbedioune, the ideal place to buy souvenirs.

To end this highly instructive day, we decided to discover the Senegalese cuisine in a restaurant only frequented by locals. Camara, initially surprised by our request, asked us:

– Are you sure? Wouldn't you rather have lunch in a place for toubabs (white people)?

In fact, we wanted to taste one of the traditional dishes. To our great satisfaction, it was the "thieboudienne", considered as the national dish. Even though the so-called restaurant was nothing more than a shack with metallic slabs on top, on solid ground and with incredibly mismatched furniture, we were the kings of the world. In terms of taste, the thieboudienne was simply divine.

The Senegalese thieboudienne is served in a colourful aluminium basin, with fish rice and is eaten with your fingers. The recipe of this national dish: fresh fish, usually thiof, which looks like grouper, molluscs and rice cooked with manioc, pumpkin, cabbage, carrots, aubergines, parsley, tomato purée, fresh chilli peppers, garlic and onions.

After this feast, Camara took us back to the hotel and before leaving us, he whispered:

– You and Madam, you are very different from the other toubabs.

Departing for the great adventure. Three days later, an eight tonne delivery truck was ready for the journey that would take twenty four hours. The following day was for us synonym of great start for an adventure that promised to be exceptional.

In my mind, I was not asking myself any questions because I firmly believed that the experience we were going to live would be unique, with ups and downs undoubtedly, but isn't that part of life?

The next morning, at five o'clock sharp, we were off with Camara to the Niokolo Koba National Park, passing through the towns and villages of Rufisque, Diourbel, Kaolak, Kefrine and

Tambacounda. From Kefrine, things got more complicated: firstly because the car clutch died, forcing Camara to keep driving without stopping as it would be difficult to restart the car. Whenever we drove through small towns, we had to scream through the window so were allowed to pass. Secondly, from Kefrine, the road was no longer paved, which forced us to drive on laterite, with our windows closed. Laterite roads are rust coloured, made out of iron, bauxite and illite. Under the cumulative effect of the excessive heat in the summer and rains in the winter, of the wind and truck transits, the road surface had become little waves. This required to drive fast to avoid the vibrations and the noise giving the impression that the car was going to disintegrate. Camara was an expert driver in this hostile environment, while managing to avoid potholes and ruts caused by the last rains.

Once in Tambacounda, the administrative centre of Eastern Senegal, we headed to the only hotel in town, which was in fact the station hotel, though no train ever passed. The hotel, which was important in the region, was characterized by its lack of customers and the fact that there was no water. As we wanted to take a shower, the receptionist brought us water in two containers, a watering can and a bucket. He asked me to choose which one I wanted. Surprised, I said: "But I want both".

He answered: – "But boss, it's one or the other because I also need water to cook!"

Later on, we were invited for lunch by Mr. Velasco, an Italian businessman who owned a trade where you could buy all products of first necessity, such as flour, sugar, tomato paste, groundnut oil, sweets, etc.

During the conversation, he told me that we were the only toubabs living in the area and that we could consider his home as ours. By late afternoon, we proceeded towards our final leg of the trip, Simenti.

The Niokolo Koba Park listed as UNESCO World Heritage. At the entrance of the park, where we were expected, we were told to be extremely careful, thus the ban to get out of the car because of the wildlife. The park stretches out for nine thousand square kilometres and was located between the borders of Gambia, Guinea-Bissau, Guinea Conakry and Mali. It is part of Eastern Senegal. Fully protected from poachers by guards, it includes more than eighty species of mammals, hundreds of bird species, reptiles, amphibians and a lot of fish species – including the famous Silurus.

We had only just entered the park when we saw a black panther, which quietly moved on. Spellbound, we opened our eyes even wider and tried to spot other animals.

An hour later, we arrived at the Simenti hotel. It was pitch-dark. Suddenly, we realised that we already had some visitors as two cars with diplomatic license plates were in the parking lot. We saw shadows and men came to greet us. Four men introduced themselves as Russian diplomats and told us that they wanted to stay for the night, with dinner, if possible. Meanwhile, dozens of Senegalese came to offer their services to work at the hotel and, finally, a park ranger, called Doukouré, came to meet and welcome us with a large smile. He then gave us a box of Petit Lu biscuits containing the hotel keys, without any labels!.

At that moment, and despite the seven hundred kilometres we'd just travelled, I realised that I had to deal with an unusual situation. At this point, I was the only one who could decide, while forgetting where I came from, from the Grand Hotel on Place de l'Opéra, in Paris.

And so, in such circumstances, I had to keep a practical mind and communicate logically. Equipped with torches and the biscuit box to open the doors, off we went to visit the premises with the Russian diplomats, Doukouré and our future employees.

My first objective was to open and ventilate the bedrooms for our first clients, then find a place to house the employees, and finally to put our personal belongings in our staff bedroom, adjacent to the infirmary. All this took at least one hour, as finding the right key in the midst of hundreds was quite a rock and roll.

Next, what to do about dinner? The answer was found in the hotel store, where there was indescribable stuff. As the generator was only going to be activated the following morning by a technician from Tambacounda, we couldn't cook anything. We settled for cans of cassoulet, heated on makeshift campfire in the middle of a courtyard. Our diplomats were delighted by our resourcefulness. The little bit of bread that was left in the car, the cassoulet washed down with the vodka offered by our customers, all this made up for a very successful welcome dinner.

As our African friends were no fans of beans cooked in goose fat and of vodka, because of their religion, they fell back on a load of dry biscuits, complemented with pureed tomato sauce. The night was short because we were woken up by hippos snorting in the Gambia River below the hotel.

The visit of the Simenti hotel in broad daylight allowed me to develop, with my wife and a man named Daouda who spoke good French, a roadmap with six points:

1. Restore the hotel to working order by cleaning it thoroughly.
2. Restart the generator.
3. Assess the employees based on their capacities.

4. Once the generator is operational, ensure the radio link with the N'Gor hotel.

5. Delivery of the cargo truck coming from Dakar.

6. Set up the administration, the bookings' planning, the product's definition, combined with the other two hotel operations of Badi and Niokolo, the definition of catering standards, personnel training, etc.

To be credible in the field, I didn't hesitate to carry beds and give the maximum of myself to lead by example. The employees, who needed to work to feed their families, displayed unswerving ardour and dedication. The team spirit already worked well and late that night, the hotel was relatively in working order.

The next morning, I was awoken as usual by the hippos, but also by something more subtle that struck me: the smell of baked bread. One of the employees, Mamadou, a true force of nature, was a baker by trade. Early that morning, he had drawn from the company store some of the previous year's stock of flour and yeast and had simply made some baguettes. To do so, he had used as mould a corrugated metal sheet, used to cover roofs. He had then reactivated the earth oven in the courtyard, between the kitchen and the restaurant.

This world and this new environment delighted me perfectly. Paris, and even Dakar, were already far away, and our immersion, faster than planned, enabled us to understand that the human being, as long as he forgets his ego, can easily fit in any situation.

These employees who, risking their lives, had walked through the bush with all the implied dangers, were more than just employees, they were colleagues who were going to contribute to the success of the Niokolo Koba hotels.

We didn't know each other but I already had the feeling and the conviction that our collaboration would be perfect, because I needed them and they needed us. I always kept in mind that we weren't at home and therefore, we had to respect them and we had to adapt to this new environment, with its habits and customs.

A few days later, I had the privilege of welcoming a Mr. Giraux, the Park Director, and self-proclaimed "Colonel", with fake stripes on his safari jacket. A man complexed by his short stature and who was full of himself. He was to be called on the radio, and by his entourage, "Authority Koba".

The koba in Senegal is the antelope, but on the radio waves, there were different names for the people involved: Authority Koba; Pink Koba, his wife; Patapares Koba, one of the park's entrances; central Koba in Dakar; and white Koba, myself.

Twice a day, for fifteen minutes, I was in radio contact, either with central Koba to be informed about rooms' bookings (where we were, there was no telephone nor telex), or with one of the other Kobas.

Our conversations were like in the army:

– Hello, hello, white Koba from Authority Koba, hello, hello, white Koba from Authority Koba, how do you read me?

– Hello, I read you 3 out of 5, Authority Koba; hello, hello, how do you read me now?

– Hello, hello, I read you loud and clear, over.

– Hello, hello, I'm informing you of the arrival of tourists who have just passed through Patapares, over.

– Hello, message well received, Authority Koba, over, etc.

It was quite weird because often we could not understand a thing, as the connection was so bad.

One day, an inspector of the Tambacounda Post and Telecommunications came to bring me the official Post Office stamp and informed me that I had become Simenti official postman. My salary would be two thousand CFA francs per month, forty French francs, or the equivalent, at the time, of 6 US dollars. All of a sudden, I found myself with a second job, which I delegated to the hotel receptionist.

The Badi Marabout. Early January 1972, four weeks after our arrival in the park, Roger Cassir and his wife Danielle brought from Dakar a Renault 4L van, while I had asked for a Land Cruiser, far more appropriate for bush tracks; fire extinguishers and a calculator, because my wife was doing all the accounting manually since our arrival!

The calculator was a Facit, essentially used by bankers to add and subtract in good time. The machine was working with a winding handle, and you had to be really talented. After having inputted the numbers, for an addition you had to wind the handle forwards; however, to subtract, you had to wind backwards. For a division, wind twice forwards and twice backwards. To generate the income account at the end of the month, you had to be courageous and reckless, and remain cool at the risk of throwing the calculator in the Gambia River.

During one of our private trips with Roger, his wife and mine, we went to visit the park and pay a courtesy visit to the Badi village chief, also the village marabout. I usually brought with me fresh bread, groundnut oil, tea, sugar and collyrium for his eyes, as the chief had problems with his eyesight. The chief and his wives always welcomed us warmly. He enjoyed offering us honey that he kept religiously in a basin under a pallet. He was so reputed as a Marabout that, according to the legend, even President Senghor himself came to consult him.

One day he told me:

– The tribe would like to offer you three drums, or tam-tams, but you must choose the tree so we can shape them.

In the end, I didn't choose the tree, but by my next visit, the three drums, called "djembes", with different sounds, were completed.

On the way back from Simenti, the four of us were standing at the back of the vehicle and were cheerfully singing "*Nini Peau de Chien*"[1], when a tree branch hit Roger in the face, throwing his glasses to the ground. Both lenses were smashed, but this didn't stop Roger from putting his glasses calmly back on and to continue singing "*A la bastille on aime bien Nini Peau de Chien, etc.*" Good old Roger!

The Méridien Hotels Company. The adventure goes on.

During the three days we spent together, Roger informed me that since the 1st of January, HFI (*Hôtel France International*) had merged with the Hôtels Relais Aériens established in Western Africa, and so the Méridien Hotels Company was born, which meant that our employment contract was going to progress.

We were entering History. By merging two of its hotel subsidiaries, Air France created both the Méridien Company and its first Méridien hotel in Paris. A hotel with 1,023 rooms, one of the largest in Europe. This construction met a specific need, namely to satisfy the requirements of an international frequent flyers' clientele (businessmen or tourists) at a time when accommodation opportunities in Paris were insufficient and unsuitable.

---

1. Song written by a French songwriter, Aristide Bruant.

This news suited me completely: as Méridien would undoubtedly have an even bigger international dimension, thanks to Air France's numerous stopovers around the world. The adventure continued…

Bassari show for French soldiers. Two weeks later, all three hotels were up and ready for the season. In view of the bookings registered by N'Gor Dakar, the occupancy rate wasn't very promising and I had to pay the wages and the suppliers at the end of the month, which meant that we would have to juggle with the cash flow. With Velasco, for example, I didn't have any problem as he agreed to defer my payments.

Two months later, a miracle happened with the arrival of a real colonel of the French army, assisted by two other officers, who had asked to see me.

The objective of their visit was to book half of the available rooms for two months for French soldiers based in Dakar. They would come and spend three days' leave with their families in the Niokolo Park in shift, at the French government's expenses!

At the end of the day, we had signed an agreement. The programme devised for our dear soldiers was as follows:

When the French army's DC8 flew over the hotel, we had to go and greet the soldiers and their families at the Simenti airport, an airport in name only as the runway was made of laterite, and the terminal was a hut with four walls and a wobbly counter, half eaten by termites. With my wife, we organised a unique reception, with the Bassari folkloric group doing a welcome show for a few minutes. The soldiers and their families were then leaving for the hotel by pick-up.

Once the registration formalities completed, our visitors in casual dress (no way wearing a uniform when one is on leave at the taxpayer's expense), had lunch on the restaurant terrace, where our "tourists" could enjoy the show of hippos, crocodiles and baboons on the opposite bank.

In the afternoon, excursion in the park, led by our guide, Mr. Dartevelle, worry wart about departures and arrivals. Born in Besancon, his role was to take tourists, with an African guide, to discover wildlife. In the evening, barbecue.

The second day, excursion and picnic at Niokolo. In the evening, a Bassari event, which was their stay's ultimate highlight. I had discovered these famous Bassaris, of Peul origin, non-Muslim, on the plateau in the Mount Assirik area in Eastern Senegal, very close to Guinea. Hunters, farmers, blacksmiths, potters and basket makers, they had agreed, provided a special deal (a small financial compensation and some red wine!!!) so that they could warm up before their spectacle!

Their unique show was based on their village initiation rites. The men wore a woven penis sheath decorated with a triangle of antelope skin. They wore masks made out of tree bark and fibres, copper bracelets with bells on their wrists and ankles, and to emphasize a certain elegance, a porcupine quill in their noses and necklaces made out of lion claws.

Women wore a fabric cache-sex, embroidered with pearls, and a belt made with rings of bronze, copper and pearls, bracelets on their arms and ankles. Once they were dressed and before the show, men and women formed a circle and drank copious amounts of red wine which, I must say, had heated up all day long in two hundred litre metallic casks supplied by the French army.

Their performance, at the end of the meal, was truly remarkable, vibrant and impressive with their distinctive dances, to the sound of bells and men's guttural sounds, who were hitting the ground with their spears. The tourists were thrilled and at the end of the show, everyone was joining the dancers by moving around a big fire. Our program was working perfectly, until the day our generator started showing signs of fatigue. Being obliged to inform by radio the "real colonel", with whom we got on well, he replied "message received and we're taking action immediately."

Unbelievable but true, by the end of the afternoon, an army DC8 landed at the airport, with as cargo a brand-new diesel generator intended for our hotel.

The two military engineers, who had been dispatched for the occasion, dissembled our generator during the night, which, in their opinion, was not suitable for the weather conditions. They replaced it with the new one. It was the relief of my life, because without electricity, there was no air conditioning, no refrigeration and especially no water, as we were pumping, stocking and filtering water every day from the Gambia River. Which just shows that the army brings good things, especially as we were never charged for the generator. Whatever that means!!!

Apart from the army, our tourism clientele was either from Europe, or nationals and expatriates. From time to time, we had super VIPs who were mainly diplomats invited by the Senegalese government. Often, when there were too many excursions, I turned into a driver and guide, explaining and showing customers, lions, elephants, buffalos, giraffes, baboons, rhinos…

When I arrived in the park, I had no prior knowledge of the African fauna and flora, but after three or four weeks, I could play the part of an "expert", explaining what was what, particularly the fairly diversified flora:

The baobab tree with multiple uses in pharmacopeia – its leaves for the preparation of tisanes, its bark to make ropes and handicrafts. The kapok tree used to make pirogues and kitchen utensils. Or even the borassus, acacias, palm trees, bougainvillea, mango trees, lemongrass, etc.

There were also little-known animals, such as the Lord Derby eland, the wild dog, which could be very dangerous because they hunted in packs, the warthog, the "*guib harnache*" (bushbuck), the kob, etc.

What I enjoyed the most, was to take some VIP ladies, a "pain in the butt" due to their behaviour observed at the hotel, for an excursion in the bush. They would turn up all dolled up, bright red lipstick, hair lacquered, sexy outfit, as if they had a romantic date.

The scenario never changed: we left with two cars, the first one, driven by me, was showing the way, and the second one with the "pains in the ass". When the track became dusty, I accelerated a great deal for a few meters and then, all of a sudden, I hit the brakes as if there was an obstacle on the road. The speed and the sudden stopping of the car caused a thick cloud of dust that hit the ladies straight in the face. This, repeated two or three times before heading back to the hotel, had a "Belphegorian" and terrifying effect. The ladies benefited from an African cosmetic mask free of charge. Usually, the next day, they stayed idle by the hotel pool.

Ten young lions from captivity to their natural habitat. Mid-March 1972, "Authority Koba", with his usual arrogance, told me that there was going to be an extraordinary international campaign to promote the park. French and Senegalese Medias and TVs would come to cover the reintegration in their natural habitat of ten lions from Thoiry, born in captivity, and coming by plane in two weeks.

As we were providing the reception, we had to put the right organization in place.

On D-day, in front of the ten wooden lion cages, everyone was there to watch the show. Especially the French Consul, the Senegalese dignitaries (including the region's traditional leader), the owner of the Thoiry castle and its animal park, Authority Koba and the park rangers, my wife and myself.

At the signal, the cages were opened by the rangers and then, stupefaction: the lions didn't want to come out of their cages, because, for years, all they had experienced was confinement. This forced the park rangers to pull the lions by their tails, or simply turn the cages over, but the lions still wouldn't move.

Authority Koba grew impatient, because the scoop for the media had misfired. He gave the rangers this definitive order:

– For the love of God, kick them in the ass!

It was virtually a caricature of communication, because the lions simply didn't want to leave the human environment!

At last, after much effort, they disappeared into thin air. A few days later, it was clear that the insertion of the Thoiry lions in their natural habitat was a total failure. These young lions had no killing experience to feed themselves, so they hung around villages. This terrorised the villagers. Authority Koba and his henchmen were forced to get the lions back, isolate them in a large secured enclosure where, every day, rangers brought them a living goat or donkey, to get them used to and forced them to kill to feed themselves. Personally, I was shocked by this situation to the extent that I sent a film to the Ministry of Tourism and to the Animal Welfare Secretariat, which created a significant controversy within the government.

Simenti in flames. In April, we operated the business at cruising speed. The Ministry of Tourism, to whom we reported back in his capacity as owner, was pleased with the operational and financial results, until the day the disaster occurred.

After going to the market and having lunch with Mr. Velasco, he noisily woke me from my nap:

– Mr. Noblet, Simenti is on fire, I have just received the information by radio after a flyover by an Air Senegal plane. Quick, hurry up!

With Camara, we left at once and like a rocket back to the hotel. The first thing that I saw were all my belongings, retrieved by the staff and scattered on the ground, my wife in tears and then, the apocalyptic vision of the hotel.

All the straw huts, where the staff lived, had gone up in flames, the large restaurant/bar hut completely destroyed, the walls of the main building, where the radio was located, totally charred.

Once the shocking effect had faded, I asked Doukouré, the head ranger, the cause of this disaster. He explained that every year, during the dry season, under Authority Koba's instructions, they had to burn different zones of the bush to regenerate the soil. Unfortunately, the fire, apparently under control, was swept by a sudden violent wind towards the Simenti zone.

At the same time, he told me that an official delegation from the Ministry of Tourism, including a radio engineer from N'Gor and Roger Cassir, would come the following day to assess the damage. In situations like this one, I had to be up to it because everything rested on my shoulders.

The personnel, completely distraught, was waiting for my instructions. My first order was to make sure that no one touched anything, because we had to write an accident report and attach pictures, then we had to worry about the logistics for the few customers remaining and relocate them, with the staff, in the two other hotels, the Badi and Niokolo.

The next day, an Air Senegal Dove landed. My wife and I greeted the delegation, which would only be staying for the day. After the overall assessment in the presence of all parties, with the exception of Authority Koba who had disappeared, and for good reason, an action plan was put in place. Mr. N'Gueye, the radio technician, was in charge of re-establishing the connection. Mr. Meguard, N'Gor chief engineer, took pictures and notes to take all the necessary measures later with his team in Dakar. Roger Cassir ensured the coordination of the information with head office in Paris. The Ministry of Tourism representatives, who recorded the extent of the damage, assured me of their full logistical and financial support to repair the hotel as soon as possible.

On the bright side, the generator and the cold rooms were not damaged, which allowed our chef Ali to prepare a convivial meal for our guests. To top it all off, I found, in the middle of the rubble and ashes, three bottles of red wine totally scorched, which I tasted and served to our guests. The result of our wine tasting was divine, because it was in fact a young Bordeaux wine that had aged thirty years in five minutes!

Once the delegation had left, apart from N'Gueye, who had to stay a couple of days longer, I asked Camara to warn the Bassaris and invite them to rebuild the large hut. This was done within ten days!

One evening, N'Gueye told me that I needed to have some sort of protection and warmly recommended that I wear a belt of charms (*grigris*) against the worst dangers. He added:

– With this belt, you will be invincible against the lion and against that stupid Giraux, who calls himself "Authority Koba". He won't be able to do anything against you or against any other disruptive element …

A month later, N'Gueye offered me the belt with its little bulges containing the charms (*grigris*). The belt must have brought me good luck, as nothing unfortunate happened until the end of my stay in Niokolo Koba.

After those six months, which were revealing for me in terms of human experience, my wife and I left the Niokolo Koba Park saddened. We left true friends behind us: the staff, the rangers, the Bassaris, the Marabout and his entourage. Paradoxically, we were also happy to have played a role in the tourism development of Eastern Senegal. With our heads full of memories, we made a wish that one day, we would go back there, to be able to tell to our grand-children this story:

"*Simenti m'était conté*", because there was still so much more to say…

Chapter 8
Dakar/N'Gor, September 1972
Overbooked on board

Back-to-back in N'Gor. September 1972, back to civilisation with road traffic, pollution, noisy environment; the transition was tough. After giving our report and a review of our financial and operational activity, Mr. **Leygues**, General Manager of Méridien Hotels in Senegal, decided to give me the position of General Manager of the N'Gor tourist village, consisting of 160 bungalows (half of which with air conditioning), the famous large animation hut, unique in Africa, its restaurant, bar and shops. International tour operators' representatives were using some of these bungalows both as offices and as accommodation.

My wife was lucky to be appointed Assistant to the Finance Director for all three hotels: the N'Gor, the Diarama opening one month later, and the tourist village of N'Gor. The latter functioned essentially with the tour operators, mainly European ones, such as Jet Tours, Kuoni, Franco Rosso, Air tours, Thomas Cook, etc.

In principle, customers stayed a whole week. The specific term, in tourism jargon, was the back-to-back, meaning one group leaving, another one arriving. Since we used pre-booking and pre-allotment of the rooms, the keys were given directly to guests, which saved time.

Every week, there was a huge volume of arrivals and departures. The bungalows, with and without air conditioning, were awarded randomly, which often created a shouting match at the reception. Some clever customers had previously run into leaving customers who had told them "Ask for bungalow X or Y because it has air conditioning, or another one because it is well positioned near the sea or near the animation hut". This meant that some arrived at reception requesting bungalow X or Y.

Sometimes, a customer accepted the key to his bungalow and then came back running to the reception shouting: "My bungalow has no AC!" He was then told that nothing could be done in the immediate future. He then shouted even louder, saying: "You don't realise, we are in Africa, and air-conditioning is a necessity. I'm going to die from heat!"

For the "commedia dell'arte", I must say that the Italians were the best. We had to convince them that, at this time of year, air-conditioning was not necessary because of the trade winds providing a light breeze and moreover, cool evenings. For the most recalcitrant, we offered to find a solution within twenty four hours.

Usually they didn't come back as they understood that air-conditioning was not imperative. From time to time, to satisfy the still frustrated customer, an air-conditioned bungalow was allocated to him. A short time later, we would see that same customer wandering around with a scarf round his neck and a little cardigan because, after using too much air-conditioning, he had become sick.

All these situations could have been avoided if the tour operators had mentioned the seasonal weather conditions in their brochures and that we had bungalows with and without air-conditioning.

Every night, after a dinner enhanced by a giant buffet with Senegalese specialities, pieces of beef, méchouis, grilled food, salads, fish and seafood of the day and an avalanche of deserts and ice-creams, it was party time in the animation hut, under Mr. Ruffier's magic wand. Mr. Ruffier used to work for Club Med and had the skill and the style to create a very hot atmosphere with African dances to the sound of infectious drums, folk troops and games. And until dawn, the local and international clientele were dancing on beats as languid as crazy and fast.

With the exception of the departure day for some and arrival day for the others, the atmosphere in my holiday village was generally good-natured and a team spirit prevailed.

The financial results were in line with budget target, which reassured the hotel owner. Unfortunately, an unthinkable situation occurred in the reservations centre, which had always worked with a manual system, i.e. with a pencil and a rubber!!! Overnight, a new, far more sophisticated, practical and modern system was established. The consequence was that, despite a sustained training, given by the Paris team, the reservations manager for the three hotel units completely lost it. Instead of only transferring the bookings already recorded, he combined both old and new bookings. This resulted in a double booking, thus more or less one thousand rooms per day instead of the 550 available in the three hotel units.

This situation, certainly unique in the hotel industry, had devastating and catastrophic impacts for the N'Gor hotels' and the chain' reputation. To tackle the situation, a crisis unit was set up, under the General Manager's responsibility, Mr. Leygues, to find solutions for the current and future arrivals.

As far as I was concerned, my holiday village only had 160 bungalows, so we had to find an extra 140 rooms on the market for the following week. This situation was totally surreal and beyond all imagination.

The client, who arrived with a voucher in due form, was told:

– Due to a technical problem in the reservation centre and because there has been a double booking, we regret to inform you that an alternative solution has been found at such and such location. The fees and compensation will obviously be at the N'Gor hotels' expense.

Most of the hotels in Dakar were full, due to the tourist season. The alternatives that we offered were diverse, varied and surprising. The customer, who had bought a dream holiday in a hotel by the sea under coconut palms, could end up in the Filfilli ranch 20 kilometres away, or in Saint-Louis in the North, or on a docked ship that had come from Marseille, or even worse, in a private clinic bedroom!

It was so disastrous that the Ministry of Tourism issued instructions to the tour operators and the airline companies Air France and Air Afrique, not to bring any more tourists to Dakar.

Extraordinary situation, an Alitalia charter plane with 150 Italian tourists on board, who had booked a week holiday at the N'Gor hotels, were diverted during the flight, in the middle of the Atlantic Ocean, to the Méridien hotel in Guadeloupe.

This unspeakable disaster lasted eight to ten days and ended with a significant compensation paid by the company, and the eviction of the reservations manager and the General Manager.

Off to explore Senegal. Although my job was demanding and exciting, it gave good times: for instance, being able to discover Senegal from every angle, mainly on my days off.

In this respect, we discovered and enjoyed Senegal Teranga, meaning land of welcome in Wolof. This country is characterized by a multitude of natural environments and historical sites.

Senegal, a symbol of hospitality, of give-and-take, is a crossroad of ethnic groups and traditions, the land of the Wolofs, the Peul and Toucouleur pastoralists, herdsmen from the Senegal River valley, the Soninke, the Jolas from Casamance, the Serrekes and the Mandinka.

The city of Saint-Louis is rich in history, located between a river and the ocean, with its many typical houses from the colonial era, with wooden balconies and wrought iron railings.

The must-visit places are the Governor's Palace, opposite Place Faidherbe, named after the famous colonial governor; the langue de Barbarie, inhabited by a community of fishermen; and to the North, about an hour's drive from Saint-Louis, the National Bird Park, one of the largest ornithological reserves in the world, with its entire colonies of pelicans, flamingos, egrets, etc.

You should know that national parks and nature reserves account for 9% of the national territory, allowing residents to explore and appreciate an exceptional country through the diversity of its tourist attractions.

When you are a resident, there is a compulsory excursion to do to the Gorée Island, a historic world heritage site, located 20 minutes away from the African continent by boat or pirogue. This landscape exerts a fascination that you can feel when visiting every corner of the peaceful island. The House of Slaves still retains all the poignant reality of the hundreds of thousands Africans, enslaved and embarked in Gorée for the New World.

Also worth discovering is Casamance, which is named after the Casamance River, located in the south-west of Senegal, between Gambia and Guinea-Bissau. Casamance is considered as one the most beautiful regions in West Africa, with its beaches, its lush vegetation surrounding rice fields and mangroves. The city of Ziguinchor is characterised by its colonial historic centre and its tourist shops and restaurants. As a ritual, on Sundays, we went with friends to Cap Skirring, our favourite place for barbecues, where we grilled flattened lamb meatballs flavoured with coriander, cumin and pepper, served with tabbouleh and mixed salads. All this in an exception summer setting, in which we practised water sports, fishing, not to mention lazing around under the palm trees.

In my environment at the N'Gor tourist village, the relations with employees, and sometimes their families, got us involved in special events in their village, such as the Tabaski-Eid El Kabir, highlight of the religious and cultural life in Senegal. But the most important event was that my wife Michèle was a few weeks pregnant, forcing us, with delight, to organize a special space in our bungalow.

In fact it was a waste of time, as on May the 29th 1973, my birthday, the new acting General Manager offered me, on head office's instructions, an appointment in Abidjan, capital of Ivory Coast, for a six month interim between the departure of the General Manager and the arrival of the new one. The position in question was at the Cocody Relais Hotel, formerly under the control of Relais Aériens, a subsidary of Air France, and, by extension, part of the Méridien portfolio.

Chapter 9
Abidjan, February 1973
Technical stopover

Pierre Quentin, General Manager of the Relais de Cocody, whom I was to replace in June 1973, welcomed us at the Abidjan airport.

An insidious viral hepatitis B. On our way to the hotel, something happened inside me, because suddenly I felt extremely tired, with an urge to vomit. Once at the hotel, we settled in a splendid bungalow. We were then supposed to have lunch with Pierre Quentin and his wife in the hotel restaurant. Unfortunately, I was feeling so tired that I was incapable of getting out of bed and I had to be excused. The next day, my condition had worsened and the doctor, we called for, immediately diagnosed a viral hepatitis B and suggested that I go back to France at once, to avoid serious risks. He was surprised when I told him that it was impossible, as I had come to make a replacement for my company. "It's your responsibility", he replied. He gave me a prescription for drugs to be taken immediately, while specifying that this was a serious illness and that it would take me at least six months to be completely cured. The medical treatment consisted of two injections, noon and night, with a whole series of pills to be ingested at regular intervals.

Despite the seriousness of my condition due to the weight loss and my body competing with 'Menton lemons' colour, the instructions handover took place with Pierre, who had to be back in France a week later. Remaining consistent with myself, I decided to inform head office about my health condition by telex. Curiously, there was no reaction. With Pierre gone, I was in charge of a rather distrustful team, with the exception of the French chef who had been transferred from Méridien Dakar three weeks earlier. The Relais de Cocody hotel was very well located in the residential neighbourhood of Cocody, overlooking the Cocody lagoon. Furthermore, we were 200 meters away from Hotel Ivoire, the flagship of the African hotel industry, with its numerous restaurants, bars, shops, conference centre, casino, bowling alleys and sports facilities. It wasn't very far from the residence of the Head of State, His Excellency President Félix Houphouët-Boigny, father of the nation.

At first a French protectorate in 1843, Ivory Coast became a French colony in 1893. It only gained its independence in August 1960. Its economy, mainly based on coffee, cocoa, and wood production, enjoyed exceptional growth.

My hotel, which consisted of a hundred or so rooms with 30 bungalows, a restaurant, a snack-bar by the pool, a meeting room and a huge park, was positioned on the market as a business hotel for short and long stays. Business was relatively good and, curiously, we realized a higher turnover from catering than accommodation.

What made the difference was the catering service and the large volume of banquets and events we organised in the park.

Long live the kimkiliba. My treatment continued but my physical condition was not improving as I continued to lose weight. It was impossible for me to swallow anything and the sight of food made me want to vomit immediately.

To encourage me, the chef made me fat-free vegetable broths. I couldn't take more than ten steps without having to sit down. To retrieve a file from the other side of my office, I had to sit for a while on one of the visitors' armchairs, take the file from the cupboard, then sit down again on one of the armchairs, before reaching my seat behind the desk. In one month, I lost 14 kilos. One morning, as I was looking at the clientele's outstanding payments, my attention was drawn to Mr. Boubacar's account, who was there for a long stay and owed the hotel a substantial amount. I immediately called the front office manager, Célestin, and asked for explanation:

– He's a regular customer, blah, blah, blah, etc., he told me.

My answer was:

– Please ask Mr. Boubacar to come and see me.

That evening, Mr. Boubacar came to see me and while handing me the check of what was due, and after the usual greetings, he asked:

– What is wrong, my friend, are you unwell?

After explaining my condition, he answered:

– You are mad, you shouldn't be working.

Point blank, he advised me to try the local medicine. "Tell your people to buy some kimkiliba at the Treichville market, which you can drink in any form – tisane, broth, cold, lukewarm or hot." He carried on:

– This kimkiliba will allow your body to free itself of all impurities.

I followed his advice by drinking decalitres of kimkiliba and one week later, my health was improving day by day, until a full recovery in two weeks!

And on 20 August 1973, our son Ralph was born at the Clinique du Plateau, in Abidjan. A birth celebrated with champagne and petits fours. A month later, with family and friends, we properly celebrated Ralph's birth around a lovely table: foie gras, vol-au-vent, stuffed chicken with truffles, French cheeses and, to finish off, a "Welcome Ralph" cake, with gourmet frivolities. All this accompanied by Laurent Perrier champagne. The hepatitis was gone thanks to Boubacar and the kimkiliba. Long live the kimkiliba!

The arrival of the baby was an event in our respective families, because on Michèle's side, there were only girls, and on my side, my elder brother, Alain, also had a daughter, Valérie. So our lineage was guaranteed with Ralph.

When I told my mother Ralph's name on the phone, she was surprised and said:

– How are you going to call the little one?

My answer: "Ralph".

– What? Do you think that it's a nice name?

– It's a very nice first name, all the more since his second name is Jean, for dad, and the third, Robert, for Michèle's father.

– All right then, in that case, Ralph isn't so bad!

In the hotel, Ralph was the darling of the female staff, and it has never changed since, where women are concerned, which shows that living in Africa has its good points. They all wanted to hold him in their arms. We were spoiled for choice for baby-sitting.

A cocktail reception for 5,000 lawyers! During my stay, an incredible business event took place. One day, I received a call from the Supreme Court of Justice inviting me to meet Mr. Amoakon, their president (In Ivory Coast, the Supreme Court of Justice is the highest authority in the justice system). The next day, he received me in person in his office and right away asked me to make a proposal for the closing night for 5,000 lawyers, coming from all over the world to participate in a symposium organised by the Ivory Coast government.

Two days later, the President invited me to visit him. He wanted to tell me that my proposal was the most attractive one, compared to those from Hotel du Parc and Hotel Ivoire. While thanking him warmly for his confidence I asked him the location of the event.

It will be at Cocody university campus!

– Your Excellency, I know the location but given the amount of food that will be displayed on the buffet, we risk being vandalized by the surrounding villagers. Therefore, it would be desirable to have adequate security to prevent any disruption.

– I understand your concern, Mr. Director.

At the same time, he called the Minister of the Armed Forces to explain the situation. Turning towards me, he said:

– The Minister suggests a company of two hundred men, does that suit you?

– Perfect, Your Excellency.

Back at the hotel, I invited my top management to join me in my office: André, the head Chef; Quentin, the Restaurant Director; Sangaré, the Maintenance Director; and Zoumana, the Finance Director. I told them the good news, a 15 million CFA deal, twice as much in old French francs, a staggering amount of money for our small company.

We had ten days to be ready. The only downside was that our equipment could only guarantee receptions of around 1,000 people. As we were wide off the mark, I plucked up the courage to call my colleague from Hotel du Parc and asked him to lend me one hundred trays, as well as tripods for the buffets. His answer:

– You've got a nerve. Not only do you pinch the business, but you also ask us for equipment.

– Yes but I owe you one, as usual

Finally, I got my one hundred trays and tripods, which delighted me.

Second episode, Hotel Ivoire. I called Diab, the Catering Director, who was legally the trade union representative for the four and five star hotels in Abidjan. I asked him if he would be kind enough to lend me sixty chafing dishes, which are silver bain-maries with a lid.

I understood, by the way he reacted, that he was angry because he knew it was for the lawyers. For him, I sidestepped the issue:

– Mr. Diab, would you please, with your name and your reputation on the market, especially with your brothers from the Relais de Cocody who love you and look up to you with great respect, sixty little chafing dishes for the Hotel Ivoire, it is not much. Of course, as we are neighbours, I owe you one, blah, blah, blah.

In the end, he said:

– Mr. Noblet, I'll do it for you, because my comrades and I appreciate the way you work with Africans. Tell your chauffeur to go to the service entrance.

I finally had the basics to organise the reception. Our organisation, tiny in comparison with Hotel Ivoire and Hotel du Parc mammoths, started to take shape and to fall into place three days before the event.

André, the chef, an Africa veteran, easily managed with his brigade who worked night and day. To ensure his team was always in good shape, he gave them a "magic potion" to help them carry on. He made his cooks and kitchen helps line up and, with a tablespoon, he told each one: "Open your mouth!"

Everyone received their dose of God knows what, it was a secret. Still, on D day, everything was ready in due time as regards to the cooking.

The morning of the reception, Quentin and his team set up the trays with tripods on a surface equivalent to the perimeter of a football field, as well as the tables for the VIPs. Meanwhile, Sangaré put up a huge podium in the middle of the ground, together with a sound system, so that the folk groups could perform.

As everything had to be in place by seven thirty pm, the catering and kitchen teams began putting the buffet out at around six pm. At quarter past six, as if by magic, the rain started. Quentin and André asked me what they should do. My reply:

– We go on guys, and find the way to cover the buffets with tablecloths and banana leaves.

All of a sudden, at seven pm, I saw army trucks turn up and an officer introduced himself:

– Mr. Director, I am Colonel Coulibaly and I'm at your service for the safety of the reception.

– Thank you for your assistance, Colonel, which will be invaluable. How many men do you have under your command?

– There are two hundred of us!

– Very well Colonel, as you can see the field is rectangular, so I suggest that you put fifty soldiers on each side, to ensure security of the buffet. If your security service is perfect, your contingent may enjoy the buffet once the guests have left the reception, and I will personally offer you a case of whisky.

– Under those conditions, you can count on me, Mr. Director.

I immediately felt reassured, especially as the rain had stopped around 7.15 pm.

At seven forty five pm, His Excellency the President of the Supreme Court and his entourage came to make sure we were ready to welcome the guests. At eight pm, a stream of Mercedes, with chauffeurs, dropped off hundreds and hundreds of magistrates at the entrance of the reception, where a special welcome was organized by an ethnic group and with a lot of tam-tams. The party looked promising, as the President of the Supreme Court enjoyed welcoming his colleagues and having the VIPs escorted by voluptuous creatures to the top tables.

The staging of the reception under the stars was magical. The field lighting was centred on the buffet and the large podium, which meant that you couldn't see anything beyond the buffet.

In the midst of the tam tams' sound, we could hear very strange noises and sounds, such as "ow, ouch, crack, bang" and angry shouts in Baoulé that I didn't understand. In fact, the beatings confirmed that security was in action.

In the middle of the dinner, the traditional dances were in full swing with the Mande tribe of the north-west with the Malinkés, the Voltaic tribe of the north-east with the Senufos, the Kru tribe of the south-west with the Bétés and the Guérets, and finally the Akan tribe of the south-east with the Baoulés.

When this grand reception came to an end, Quentin, who had been dedicated exclusively to the VIPs, asked me to join the president of the Supreme Court at his table. He got up and congratulated me for the perfect organisation of the reception and asked me:

– Mr. Director, what was the quotation for this reception?

– Mr. President, our proposal was for fifteen million CFA.

He then gave me three bricks of bank notes wrapped in newspaper!

– Here you are, Mr. Director, with my thanks for this excellent work that honours Ivory Coast.

I had fifteen million CFA wrapped in newspaper in my hands and thousands of people around me. I immediately called Zoumana, the financier, to place the money in the hotel safe. Once the reception over, the soldiers cleaned the plates in ten minutes and Colonel Coulibaly received his case of whisky with a smile, while hoping to have again the privilege to guarantee security for a future reception.

End of November, I received a phone call from Mr. **Jacques Carpentier**, former General Manager of Hotel Ivoire and newly hired by the Méridien Hotel Company as Vice-president of hotel operations at head office. He informed me of his imminent visit to supervise the instructions' handover between myself and **François Prévost**, the new hotel General Manager.

I had great pleasure of welcoming Jacques Carpentier. He was considered as a star at Hotel Ivoire, whose operator was the Intercontinental Group. Jacques had played an important role in its influence. Everything goes back to 1963. That year, His Excellency President Houphouët-Boigny asked the Romanian-Israeli architect Moshe Mayer to build Hotel Ivoire, a five-star hotel in the bourgeois neighbourhood of Cocody.

By creating this symbolic and unique hotel on the African continent, President Houphouët-Boigny dreamed of a Riviera overlooking the Ebrié lagoon. Hotel Ivoire, inaugurated in 1969, was a must for the men in high places, politicians but also artists such as Claude François, Stevie Wonder and later, Michael Jackson.

The instructions' handover was an interesting and instructive exercise for me, giving me the opportunity to appreciate Jacques' charisma and professionalism.

A week later, with my little family, we said good bye to Ivory Coast. After a mandatory detour to introduce our offspring to our respective families, Paris was reaching out to me again, for a new challenge: Executive Assistant Manager at Méridien Paris hotel, regarded as one of the Best hotels in Europe, operational since April 1972.

Chapter 10
Paris, March 1974
Destination Méridien Maillot City

In the early 1970s, hotel capacities in Paris were limited. With the emergence of big jumbo jets (Boeing 747), Air France began the construction of the first high-capacity hotel in the capital. That's how Méridien Etoile was launched, joined after by the Méridien chain development abroad, in the main Air France stopovers.

I arrived in Paris on 8th March 1974, the day the Charles de Gaulle airport was inaugurated. There I was, at Méridien Paris, the largest hotel in France, located on a rapidly expanding economic axis: La Défense, Porte-Maillot, Arc de Triomphe and the Champs-Elysées, meaning in the heart of the business district, on the right bank. Officially open early 1972, it was the first prestigious hotel of the company and, in a way, a strong symbol of the Air France Group.

In Méridien Etoile, there was a harmony between comfort and modernism: 1,023 elegant rooms and suites, its restaurants –"Le Clos Longchamp", jewel of the Parisian gastronomy; its coffee shop "L'Arlequin"; its Japanese restaurant "Le Yamato"; its bar "Le Rendez-vous"; its nightclub "L'Ecume des nuits"; its conference centre and all the multilingual secretarial services, etc.

A few moments later, I was in the General Manager's office, Mr. **Ernst Etter**, a Swiss national. An icon in the hotel industry, he was admittedly old enough to retire, but he symbolised the prestige of the hotel business by his worldwide experience with major hotel groups such as Hilton, Sheraton and Intercontinental. He received me very kindly and gave me considerable detail about the nature of the job I had to perform.

Generally speaking, my job consisted of being an interface between the hotel clientele and management. Under my authority, I had three other executive assistants, among them my future boss, **Bernard Lambert**, who became in 1997 President of Méridien Hotels. Later, I enjoyed teasing him by saying "Don't forget that I used to be your boss!"

This hotel, with its 1,023 rooms, was a real city: between 1,500 and 3,000 customers per day if you took into account the restaurants' and banquets' clients; as well as staff members, who could come close to 1,000 people with the casuals, because there was always something going on at Méridien Etoile.

Once I got into the swing of things, I really loved my job which allowed me to keep an international outlook by staying in contact with a clientele coming from all over the world for tourism, for business, for a conference or an exhibition, or simply because they were airline companies' crews in transit, and accommodated by us.

You had to keep an eye on everything. One day, while I was talking with the head of security, Mr. Chazot, a former intelligence service executive, we saw a well-dressed man carrying a TV and walking towards the main exit. When we intercepted him, he casually told us that he was taking the TV from his room to be repaired outside the hotel!!!

Chazot asked him to follow us into one of the reception offices. After consulting the police file, he turned out to be wanted by the National Police, which came to pick him up half an hour later.

Another day, Lambert and I had locked a room, on the 8th floor, with a female customer inside. Despite the cashier's and reception's successive reminders, the client in question could not settle her bill, which amounted to several thousand francs. Finally, the next day, a man, looking like a Mafioso, came to pay in cash his protégée's bill, who, we gathered from intelligence, was on file as a high-flying prostitute and worked in all major Parisian hotels. The payer was none other than her pimp.

On two occasions, macabre episodes, desperate people rented a room to commit suicide. They threw themselves into the void of the hotel's central atrium. Moment of total panic for the witnesses who needed psychological help.

Thankfully, I experienced more invigorating, even lyrical moments. Like the day **Mr. Etter**, the General Manager, invited the management team to come and see him play the organ in Notre-Dame de Paris.

Mr. Etter was one of the very few people authorised to play in Notre-Dame de Paris. We were captivated by his talent. Our bachelor boss was a member of the prestigious hotel business' aristocracy. He played his representational role perfectly when he was in the presence of well-known figures, of members of the jet-set or of journalists. When he was leading a board meeting, it was always great art, full of respect but also of firmness while explaining the logic of his reasoning.

During the first semester of 1974, France experienced a political upheaval with the death, on April the 2nd, of President Georges Pompidou who had kept his illness secret until the last moment. As provided by the constitution, he was deputized by the President of the Senate, Mr. Alain Poher.

It was also the "May of the banks", when all the major French banks were on strike. On May the 10th, the whole country participated in the televised debate between the two rounds, the famous face-to-face and cult sentence of Valéry Giscard d'Estaing to François Mitterrand: "You do not have a monopoly over the heart, Monsieur Mitterrand."

On May the 19th, Valéry Giscard d'Estaing (nicknamed VGE) won the presidential election with a close score of 50.8% of cast votes, and on the 27th, Jacques Chirac became Prime Minister.

VGE, who had a liberal vision of society, had laws passed for the lowering of the civil and voting majority to 18 years, for the decriminalisation of abortion and the authorisation of divorce by mutual consent. He also created a Ministry for Women's Affairs, but, unfortunately, he had to face the economic difficulties affecting France at the end of the Glorious Thirty.

Managing the hotel's banquets and conferences. Early September, Mr. Etter asked me to take over the management of the hotel's banquets and conferences, on basis of my experience in catering, and following the resignation of Mr. Vaudan, an American who was previously in charge.

I gladly accepted this new opportunity, knowing very well that the catering department was a big contributor to the hotel's global turnover.

I found myself in a huge office to receive with dignity the organisers of national or international events. My team consisted of seasoned maîtres d'hôtel, barmen, handymen, lighting and sound technicians and secretaries. Business was relatively good, between the cocktails for 2,000 people, the business lunches and dinners, and the international conferences. We were operational from dawn till dusk, and often until late at night.

In terms of monthly salary, it was the height of luxury, because the staff in our department was given 15% of the service. Our salary was based on the "mass and points" principle, which meant that I had, with the head concierge, the highest salary in the hotel, in my capacity as department head. From one month to the next, my salary had increased five-fold! Which led to much jealousy within the hotel. But, at that time, this principle was applied in all the major hotels in Paris, in conformity with the collective agreement.

Meanwhile, Méridien Hotels were being opened, one after another, thanks to **Jean Bertelet** who, as Development Director, was free to sign management contracts in the name of the hotel chain. Distinguished hotelier and former General Manager of the legendary hotel "Le Saint-Georges" in Beirut, Bertelet's name was linked to several prestigious hotels, such as the Méridien in Rio and in Salvador de Bahia. And, of course, thanks to the Air France Group, he was playing an important role in the group's expansion.

Mr. **Pierre Monet**, who had hired me for Africa, was appointed General Manager of Méridien Nice. Méridien was taking off internationally and had started playing with the big boys, namely Hilton, Intercontinental or Sheraton.

As the days went by, I integrated new management techniques based on the uniform system of accounts for hotels, an American system. In other words, the company's definitions and objectives, the quest for efficiency in every field by combining them in order to optimise the margin rates in the different hotel's departments.

With 1,023 rooms, the financial ratios can quickly move positively or negatively, so the notion of profit had its importance daily. In other words, the profit compensates the risks taken by Air France and its shareholders, and according to market conditions and the quality of hotel management, the profit is more or less important. It can even turn into a loss, which causes endless dramas with senior management and the company's head office.

Unconventional clients. One day, as I was leaving my office to go home, someone knocked on my door. While apologizing, this respectable gentleman asked if I could give him a few moments. I invited him to sit down and asked him the purpose of his visit. He introduced himself as the Vice-President of a multinational company specialised in high-end electronics and audio-visual aids from The Netherlands. To my surprise, I found out that he perfectly knew our events' rooms. He asked me if the Renoir and Matisse salons were available for three full days in three weeks' time. I checked the general planning and confirmed that the requested space was indeed available. That gentleman was delighted and explained in greater detail what he had in mind, namely the organisation of an aperitif, followed by dinner for all Vice-Presidents of their prestigious brand who were coming from the United States, Europe, Africa, the Middle East, Asia and the Pacific – i.e. six people!

I was surprised by his request, since the Renoir salon could seat 1,200 people for a meal and the Matisse 350 people. The client had a very clear scenario in mind: since he was the inviting power, he wanted to impress his colleagues.

His scenario was as follows:

First day: Set-up of the event's organisation with the client's own technicians.

Second day: The event itself.

Third day: Put the salons back in their initial state.

He confirmed that his company would pay for the three days on the basis of maximum occupancy, which reassured me and led me to think that the achieved turnover for only six covers would exceed the world statistics in the hotel industry. The next morning, while signing the contract for the event, the client gave me a 50% deposit, amounting to forty thousand dollars.

On D-day, the six guests were greeted and announced by a master of ceremonies, in a 17th century outfit, at the entrance of the salons, then escorted by charming hostesses to the Matisse salon, which had been decorated in an Art deco style for the occasion, with a central pivoting podium, which allowed guests to appreciate a streaming slide show presenting the group's latest creations.

These gentlemen were comfortably seated in modern Art deco armchairs, enjoying caviar canapés, lobster and foie gras, washed down with vintage champagne, whisky and VSOP cognac.

For dinner, the six lucky guests went through a tunnel, created for the occasion, linking the Matisse and the Renoir salons, where there was a round table for six, surrounded by a floor-to-ceiling circular screen. Outside of this artificial arrangement, a dozen technicians busied themselves with the light and sound, carrying out an overhead projection on the screen. For the time, we were in the domain of pure fiction.

The table had been adorned by a world-class decorator. In front of each guest, on a little screen – technology oblige – on which they could read the menu, devised by Gaston Lenôtre!

The menu was a real invitation to travel, with specialities, presentations and a unique refinement from every continent. The service was provided by waitresses in "Crazy Horse" style, all with the same pink haircut and wearing the bare minimum. During dinner, and between the courses, there was a personalised show for our guests' own pleasure: close-up act, juggler, ventriloquist and strip-tease. The diner went on in the hotel nightclub "L'Ecume des nuits", where our VIPs enjoyed, in good company, other sweet delights. I must say that it was the first time in my life that I organized such an event with no responsibility at all, besides issuing an invoice and a receipt for 80,000 dollars!!!

On another day, I received the visit of a Mr. Sabbagh who organised social caterings on the Paris market place. He called me "Mr. Noblet, my friend" and later "my brother". He made me an offer:

– We could work together to organize events on Saturdays and Sundays. Since your salons are empty on weekends, I have the opportunity to organize Bar Mitzvahs and weddings for the Jewish community. One condition: the banquets' kitchen must be completely sanitized, the dishes and plates must be boiled and the work tables and stoves must be covered with aluminium foil to avoid all contamination, and besides, all this must be carried out under the supervision of a rabbi!

– No problem, Mr. Sabbagh. I'm used to it and we will be happy to welcome you!

By doing this business, my monthly budget was exceeded, much to the delight of my management, who was pleased to have our thousands of square meters made profitable over the weekend.

Promoted Catering Director. On another day, as usual, before starting my duty, I went by the General Management's secretariat to collect my memos and mail. On that occasion, I felt a certain turmoil coming from Mr. Etter's office and heard the voice of the Personnel Director, Mr. Sayes. Moments later, like all the staff members, we learnt that the Catering Director had been fired on the spot for gross misconduct – he had been caught by a housekeeper while making love with a hotel customer!

After consulting me, Mr. Etter sent out a memo to all staff, with a copy to head office, announcing my promotion as Catering Director.

As my employment status had changed, I was no longer paid on the basis of mass and points, but received a remuneration that was a third of the banquets' and events' salary. But being the Catering Director of one of the largest hotels in Europe and having the responsibility for a department of five hundred people was very motivating.

And on the 31st of October 1975, my daughter Nadège Odette Gisèle was born at the Neuilly hospital, she had wanted to discover the world earlier than scheduled, four weeks in advance. Additional motivation. This adorable little thing was the total opposite of Ralph. He was the chill one, who slept like a log but was resisting food. Nadège, on the other hand, was opposed to sleeping but had a good appetite.

When coming home late at night, due to my job, Nadège expressed herself with her vocal cords, which forced me to lie down next to her bed to rock her, while trying to get some sleep because I was dead tired. Michèle was too because, with two small children, there was enough to keep her busy all day.

Besides the oil crisis and the economic difficulties due to the slump in industrial output, the National Assembly came to prominence by passing the Veil law, related to the termination of pregnancy. In November 1975, the number of unemployed in France exceeded one million, and the following month, during a televised address, President Giscard d'Estaing spoke of France as a "medium-sized power", which caused scandal as he broke away from the Gaullist vision symbolised by the famous phrase: "France is only truly itself at the forefront."

My ocean liner, France. Despite the crisis, I developed my department with great resolve, putting in place commercial action plans, restructuring services and developing synergies with other department heads. My hobby horse: a special PR plan to position the hotel as a must in the Paris marketplace.

I considered the hotel as an ocean liner, much like the "France", flagship of the long distance navigation in France.

For me, a hotel is a place where the hotelier sells dreams to customers. We go to a hotel to be welcomed, to be called by our name, to appreciate the ambient warmth, to be received by perfectly-dressed personnels with quality uniforms and perfect attire, for quality background music, refined and perfect decoration, but also for the floral arrangements that must charm, to be served with care and professionalism, while bearing in mind that it's the customer who pays your salary and that same guest will give either a good or a bad publicity to your hotel.

But in a hotel with 1,023 rooms, what makes the difference are the specific high-end events, enabling the hotel to position itself on the market as a destination where there's always something going on.

The "Dolce Vita" parties. In the office adjacent to mine, officiated Mrs. **Lucia Chauvin**, the Public Relations Director and former PR at Air France. Lucia, whom I adored, could organise a press conference with the backing of television in no time thanks to her business relations or simply organise a very special lunch or dinner for the hotel General Manager with, if need be, influential business men or women, nationally or internationally.

Lucia was also responsible for communication, where she excelled, because she mastered six or seven different languages. The only difficulty between us was that we both wanted to impress our ideas or our touch on prestigious events. In the end, she was giving up because I was right about particular approach. She would then leave the discussion, like a diva, to go and take shelter in the General Manager's office. Many times the latter was forced to reconcile us, usually over a drink at the bar, "Rendez-vous", where our dear Lucia particularly enjoyed Chivas Régal whisky…

With her, my team's and the technical service's managers, I enjoyed creating events of all sorts, whether it was a gourmet week of French regions or of other countries.

For example, the ski resort "La Clusaz" at Méridien Paris. For the occasion, we created a ski slope in the hotel's huge atrium, where you could see famous French skiers perform, such as Jean-Claude Killy and Annie Famose, among others. Also a full-scale chalet in the hotel lobby, with its cow, Marguerite, who was taken to graze in a nearby park. Boxing matches in the hotel's ballrooms, where guests came in evening dress for a prestigious dinner with free-flowing champagne to watch epic fights, like Bouttier-Monzon. There were also surreal Russian parties in the nightclub "L'Ecume des nuits". The host, Albert Nayafe from Radio Europe, our driving force to draw the Parisian jet-set, invited, at regular intervals, his violinist friends from the famous "Rasputin restaurant" to welcome our hand-picked guests.

Invariably, the soirée deteriorated in the early hours with the traditional "nasdarovia", tiny glasses drunk bottoms up, then smashed on the ground. Conclusion: hundreds of broken glasses strewn here and there on the floor.

Albert Nayafe, of Slavic origins, was a great guy of superior intelligence. What's more, he had an incredible address book, including the biggest names, even as far as Monaco. He also had a knack to mesmerise the clientele that he wanted for a particular evening and to create an atmosphere from another world.

One day, as I was entering the hotel through the main door at around six am, Albert, a flute of champagne in the hand, wrapped in a bathrobe, came to greet me dramatically in the hotel lobby. We had to part with him a few weeks later, at the request of our legal advisers, because of an external affair that could have had harmful consequences for our hotel. Aside from the fact that we had to restock on glasses regularly, Albert was a fascinating guy, full of ideas. The coordination meetings he took part in were never dull. 3-4 weeks later, he was replaced by one of his colleagues from Radio Europe, Patrice Patoloff, who was working very professionally, though without Albert's exuberant side.

August 1976, we were feeling the impact of the economic crisis. Business was not very good. Furthermore, anger was welling up among the hotel trade unions. All this distressed Mr. Etter, a man of great talent but not really a fighting boss. The hotel board of directors decided to replace him by Mr. **Daniel Gillot**, also a man of experience but with a completely different profile from

Mr. Etter's. He was a well-organized man, self-assured, rational and close to his staff.

On a political level, Jacques Chirac resigned on August the 25th 1976 from his position as Prime Minister, and was replaced by Raymond Barre. The latter inherited a lacklustre economic situation. He declared on that matter: "Easy times are over."

He then launched a plan to fight inflation, established a price freeze until the end of the year, reduced VAT by two percentage points in return for a calendar of contractual negotiations on wages.

On November the 5th, Jacques Chirac, re-elected deputy of the Corrèze region, announced the creation of a new party, the RPR (*Rassemblement Pour la République* – The rally for the Republic) replacing the UDR (*Union des Démocrates pour la République* – Union of Democrats for the Republic).

A month later, while I was talking with Mr. Sayes, the Personnel Director, the head of the CGT in the hotel proudly announced:

– Gentlemen, I officially inform you that, from now on, the hotel is on strike.

Major uproar among the senior management. The Maintenance Director rushed to the technical control room and barricaded himself inside to ensure no one could sabotage the hotel's technical installations.

On the operational departments' side, under Gillot's leadership, we had to know who was on strike and who we could count on to ensure minimum service to our customers.

I must admit that my experience at the Grand Hotel was very beneficial in this area. All the trade unions wanted to send a strong message to the government: to hit the symbol of the hotel industry in France and the national company Air France, the hotel's owner, while voicing their wage demands.

The strike, which dragged on, took a tragic turn when, one evening, there was a firemen's intervention to put out a fire in one of the hotel's rooms. This ended in a summary judgement against the strikers, who were supposed to guarantee the hotel's security.

The strikers, who were held responsible, were summoned the next day by the Public Prosecutor. The following evening, Mr. **Ceccaldi**, the Méridien Paris' president, who had been kept informed of the events hour by hour by Gillot, invited the heads of departments in his office around ten pm. Ceccaldi, a Corsican whom we called "the Che", dressed in black trousers and a black polo shirt, told us that from the following morning, around 6 am, we would evacuate the strikers from the hotel. He then told me:

– Noblet, you will direct a company of the riot squad (*CRS*), which will be hiding in the hotel's coach courtyard, and you will lead them to the first basement, get them inside the hotel through the reinforced door, which gives access to the equipment rooms, because, as you know, that's where the hard core strikers are confined.

The next morning, at five thirty am, I went to the coach courtyard where, to my astonishment, the riot squad was already waiting for me. An officer with a three-coloured (French) scarf introduced himself.

At 6 am sharp, the commando followed me and, when we got to the reinforced door, events followed in quick succession. The officer knocked on the door stating his name:

– I am officer XYZ, representative of the Ministry of the Interior. I urge you to open this door.

– Go to hell.

Second warning.

Same answer.

At the third warning, the officer told his men:

– Gentlemen, go ahead.

The twenty members of the riot police simultaneously pulled down their helmet visors, then with a special battering ram, they broke down the door, not without difficulty. From then on, we witnessed the strikers' scattering, evaporating into thin air, like sparrows.

What a surprise! The strikers had organised a true siege to hold for weeks owing to their organisation. Camp beds just about everywhere, fridges stuffed with food and drinks, tables, card games, a whole paraphernalia to design banners with claims, megaphones, etc.

While the hotel was coming back to life, a few moments later, as if nothing had happened, I saw a commando of sturdy men, dressed in jeans and black polo shirts, turn up on Che's and Gillot's request, with some unusual tools, crowbars wrapped in newspaper. One of them told me: "It's discrete and very effective when you get hit on the side of your face." Their goal was to prevent the strikers from coming back.

This strike had disastrous consequences on the resumption of the hotel activity between the non-strikers and the strikers, who kept a low profile; some were justifying themselves by saying "It was not my fault, I was forced into it… blah, blah, blah." As they say, the Calm after the Storm. We had to rise above and end the distrust on both sides. As head of department, I had to put into perspective our objectives, question ourselves in order to bounce back, make up for lost time and money, and maximise our financial results. The hotel was part of the company's heritage, so a simple gap in the hotel's occupation rate or the number of covers could have serious consequences on the net operational profit.

Back then, we spoke about "RBE" (*résultat brut d'exploitation*) whereas in the international jargon, we talked about "GOP" (gross operating profit), which is the same thing. Invariably every week, we had a meeting, with the Che and Gillot, about the hotel's financial situation compared to budget targets. We often had to take quite aggressive decisions because, to listen to the Che, we had to keep reducing our payroll, which wasn't easy. Our operational problems didn't affect him at all, because his only objective was to present balanced figures to Air France head office.

Between finance and operations, in every field, there will always be a world of difference. So, for each meeting, I had to suggest solid arguments, based on figures and statistics. Gillot, my fellow Directors (rooms division, commercial, technical, personnel, and myself for catering) we literally went to war to face the Che. Deep down in his heart, the Che knew perfectly well that we were doing our utmost to make the hotel profitable, but his obsessional problem was the expenses related to payroll and the loan the company had to reimburse, which were too high. So, what's to be done?

Jazz at the "Rendez-vous". One morning, in October 1976 at around eleven am, Galapides, nicknamed Moustache, a famous jazz drummer, Maxim Saury, a great clarinettist, and myself were having a cup of coffee at the "Rendez-vous" bar, talking about life and things. In a stroke of genius, Moustache said:

– It would be fun to play jazz in this bar. No?

That sentence was the start of an incredible and unprecedented business for Méridien Paris and in France.

Initially, we had decided to give it a try, for one week, with an orchestra of four musicians. Moustache asked me to set up a small podium with some lighting. Since my events' budget had shrunk away to nothing due to the crisis, the compensation I offered was only a meal, plus a bottle of whisky.

In spite of a disastrous first week, we decided to continue for a whole month under the same conditions, to involve our PR department, under Lucia Chauvin's leadership, and to enlarge the podium with more seats and more lighting. Magic happened, the Paris right bank jazz was becoming a reality. The Méridien Paris jazz club was asserting itself day after day.

At the end of the third week, Moustache, the musicians' leader, came to see me to chew the fat and said:

– Things are starting to gel. I suggest we continue, while alternating every month with a European orchestra, then the following month with an orchestra from New Orleans. What do you think?

– I agree, but on what terms?

After a hard bargaining, we came to the following agreement: profit sharing 20% for him and 80% for the hotel, after deduction of the musicians' and employees' wages and costs, the drinks, the advertising and the invitations.

The success was huge from the point of view of media coverage but also turnover. From ten pm onwards, drinks were sold at a single price of 100 francs, whether it was a glass of water or coffee, a glass of whisky or a flute of champagne!

The jazz bar became the darling of the jazz enthusiasts, so much so that one day Moustache showed up in my office and said:

– Michel, we need to go further, we should invite Lionel Hampton, the King of xylophone. What do you think?

– I agree but we should go even further. With Lionel Hampton, we're going to organize a big jazz parade in Paris on the Champs-Elysées, and we will go to the town hall.

– My friend, I love your craziness!

Lucia, Moustache and Gillot and I started to hatch an action plan over a delicious meal, because Moustache, with his hundred and fifty kilos, had to be fed. In May, we caused a mess in the city with fifteen open top deck Mercedes buses, each with a band from Europe and from New Orleans, with, at the helm, Lionel Hampton, Moustache, Gillot, Lucia and myself. The trip back to the hotel, passing through the Champs-Elysées again, was the highlight with all the musicians gathered together in the "Rendez-vous" bar, which on that day became the "Lionel Hampton bar", a new cult place for jazz in the capital.

Another interesting innovation: the creation of the "Maison Beaujolaise", in the basement, replacing a completely unproductive space. With Gillot, the boss, who later became the President of Méridien Europe zone, as well as a friend, we decided to make these premises profitable with a point of sale symbolising France. We came up with a flagship product known throughout the world: the "Beaujolais". For this to happen, a decorator, named Potier, agreed to play his part – five crates of Beaujolais against his artistic service. The Maison Beaujolaise product was based on a buffet formula with cold meats and cheeses, lentil *petit salé,* andouillette in a mustard sauce and typical regional desserts. All this served with nine Beaujolais vintage wines: Brouilly, Côte de Brouilly, Chénas, Chiroubles, Fleurie, Juliénas, Morgon, Saint-Amour and Moulin à Vent, served by waiters dressed as winegrowers.

It was such a success that the Compagnons du Beaujolais' brotherhood insisted on having their annual congress in our hotel, with the traditional inductions, of which I was an applicant.

Despite the significant work schedule, usually from seven in the morning to nine at night, but often stuck until ten or eleven pm, my passion for success had no limits. By my side, I had exceptional heads of departments, such as Maurice Brazier, head Chef and France's Best worker; Claude Monnet, pastry Chef and also France's Best worker, as well as a marathon runner; Jean-Pierre Kaspar, who had replaced me as Banquets Director; and other colleagues for whom I had a lot of respect, like Yvan de Pontcharra, Sales and Marketing Director; Bernard Lambert who had become Yvan's deputy; Christian Peyre, Rooms' Division Director; and my assistants, Bernadette and Daniel Boudet. The latter became Africa Managing Director and then General Manager of Méridien Montparnasse.

In January 1977, Méridien head office was looking internally for a candidate for the position of General Manager of Méridien Cocody in Abidjan. I immediately applied, without hesitation, with Daniel Gillot. He wasn't very keen to let me go, but in view of my explanations, he supported my application, accepted by head office that same day. Why leaving the "ocean liner"? For family reasons. Firstly, my wife Michèle and our young children would be able to take full advantage of the space offered by the hotel and the city's surroundings; and secondly, to see again our family residing in Abidjan. My brother-in-law was head Chef at Hotel Ivoire, legendary place par excellence, as previously mentioned.

Chapter 11

Abidjan, February 1977

A stopover to be visited again

Greeted at Abidjan airport by my brother-in-law, my sister-in-law and Mr. **Jean-Pierre Zimmerman**, Méridien Regional Director for Africa, and based at the Relais de Cocody hotel, considered as Méridien regional office for West Africa, there we were with bag and baggage and the entire family on Ivorian soil.

When the porters dropped off our suitcases in the apartment, one of them was quick to tell me:

– Boss, since you left, there have been successively five directors! I replied:

– Thanks for the information, but I am here to stay.

The very next day, I immediately got down to business with Mr. Zimmerman and Mr. Zilbenstein, respectively Regional Director Operations and Regional Director Finance, who tried hard to provide a detailed instructions' handover, as the last General Manager had left ahead of schedule.

Priority objectives: meeting with Mr. **Seri Gnoleba**, President of Sohico, company owning the hotel and also Trade Minister, and with **Koné Mamadou**, Minister of Tourism and member of the owning company.

My meetings with both ministers were extraordinary, warm, enriching, and supportive, with their wish to help, if necessary. Those two ministers were part of the new Ivorian elite under the guidance of **Félix Houphouet-Boigny**, affectionately called "the Old Man" or "Papa Houphouet". Married to Marie-Thérèse, he had been successively a traditional tribal leader, a doctor, a planter, a trade union leader, an Ivorian deputy in France, a Minister in the French government, Mayor of Abidjan and first President of Ivory Coast from 1960 to 1993. Houphouet-Boigny had played an essential role in the decolonisation process. Partisan of the "France-Afrique", whose authorship is attributed to him, he managed to develop Ivory Coast economically. Throughout the world, he was considered as the father of the Ivorian miracle, in view of the African continent's poverty.

The next day, I met the head of immigration at the Ministry of Labour, who received me very professionally, but no more than that, despite the customary recommendations expressed by Seri Gnoleba's secretariat. The usual questions were suddenly interrupted when, with a big smile, my interlocutor realised that I had slipped under his desk a plastic bag with two bottles of whisky and an envelope full of bank notes.

– Mr. Noblet, I am very pleased to welcome you here in Ivory Coast. I bid you and your family welcome. Don't hesitate to call me if you require my services.

He simultaneously stamped three copies of my work permit. To avoid a lengthy procedure, the method is very simple provided that you know the recipe and have the guts to do it.

With the exception of the head Chef and the Commercial Director, my team was practically the same, with Célestin, Sangaré, Quentin and Zoumana, which made it easier for me in terms of putting the new business strategies in perspective, redefining the product and positioning the hotel on the market.

Family-wise, the children found their bearings in their new environment, which they loved, with a lot of space, a sunny but humid climate and assimilation into the local and expatriate community, which was quite substantial.

"Costa do Marfim", Ivory Coast's original name, was so called by the Portuguese merchant sailors on their way to India. The country was considered as a flagship country on the African continent. It was much admired by Europe considering the positive transformations of the Ivorian economy, remarkable in agriculture: cocoa, coffee, wood, commerce and finance. All this was the result of a policy focused on private investment and foreign capitals.

The Ivorian society went through a deep mutation throughout that period: increase of the standard of living, of health, educational and social infrastructure. Ivory Coast had become the new Eldorado of the African continent. It was seen rather as a business destination than a tourist one, thanks to the development of high quality infrastructure. Destination directed towards an upmarket clientele and business tourism.

On Sundays, we organised picnics on Bassam beach with the family and Professor Brette from Abidjan teaching hospital, or, depending on the weather, we went to Yamoussoukro, the capital of Ivory Coast, located in an area of mountains and waterfalls. The dome of the Basilica Our Lady of Peace in Yamoussoukro has a distinctive feature, it is larger than Saint Peter's Basilica, in Rome!

Different ethnic groups characterise this country, true mosaic of four distinct groups, differentiated by linguistics criteria:

– The Mande group, also called Mandinka, divided between Malinké, Bambara, Dioula, and Dan.

– The Kru and Bete group.

– The Gour group (voltaic).

– The Akan group, also divided between: Baoulé, Anyi, Abron and Senoufo.

The relations between the Ivorian and expatriate communities were exceptionally good. Everyone respected everyone and both communities came together for official or non-official receptions, special invitations, etc.

Social life was extremely active. Every event was celebrated, like someone going or coming back from holiday, a promotion, a change of job, a new flat, a birth, a wedding, etc. Each celebration was marked with Laurent Perrier champagne. Ivory Coast was at that time the brand's number one customer.

The most exceptional reception of the year, which I had the privilege to attend, was undoubtedly the anniversary of Ivory Coast independence, on August the 7th, where "Papa Houphouet" and his wife personally welcomed their guests to the presidential palace.

I also enjoyed meals in private homes, usually with employees' families who wanted to honour me by introducing me to typical Ivorian dishes, such as foufou, the national dish (with plantain bananas and palm oil; kedjenou, chicken stew garnished with aubergines, onions, garlic, ginger and various spices; atieke, which has the consistency of couscous; mafé, cooked meat served with peanut sauce; and, the best of the best, agouti, a compromise between a rabbit and a rat, a luxury stewed dish, but with a disgusting aspect and smell.

Career lessons. Being associated with Ivoirians' life gave me great joy as it was giving me the opportunity to discover and go deeper in the local culture, and to become more integrated into the local community. This also facilitated my relations with the staff. Often, the mere fact of listening and understanding the reality on the ground unlocked doors, gateways and business opportunities.

I also understood that hotels play an important role within the economic fabric of a city, a region and a country. As an hotelier, I realised that we had to be visible on the market and popular with the people, the press, the politicians and the tourism industry. The hotel must be considered as a social place, a destination and a venue vouching for quality services, a faultless product and an overall ambiance where life is enjoyable.

Despite its small size, my hotel had unique assets: its restaurants, its salon and its park offering a panoramic view on the Ebrié bay and the Abidjan skyline. All through the year, we organised business lunches; dinners in honour of official delegations, chaired by one or several ministers depending on the circumstances; cocktails for about 500 to 1,500 people for embassies, etc.

Expatriation can sometimes be wearing. I remember one "exotic" cocktail. One evening, when the soirée was in full swing on the hotel lawns, with no less than 800 people, a storm broke and, within a minute, all guests and staff were drenched. But, in the blink of an eye, everyone cleared the lawns, taking dishes from the buffet with them, to continue eating and partying inside the hotel.

In the end, the party was magical, because the weather imponderable brought everyone together in an amazing atmosphere, with overjoyed guests dancing, singing and sipping champagne that flowed freely, in accordance with the ambassador's instructions. And how can I forget the "allegoric fresco" of the men, and especially the diplomats' wives and others, with their long dresses completely drenched and faded, and their ruined hairdos. No matter, they were ready to start again the following day for another party.

Another "exotic" story. One morning, I had an appointment with the Minister of Tourism to finalise the agenda for the next board meeting of the owning company. I went to introduce myself at his secretariat. While sitting down in one of the visitors' chairs, I saw coming out from the minister's office a young lady who could very easily compete with all the top-models on this planet. At the same time, the secretary urged me to meet the Minister. The latter received me, standing behind his desk, with a "Good morning Mr. Director, how are you?"

At that moment, I noticed his shirt-tail sticking out of his zipper. Without batting an eye, he tucked his shirt in, pulled his zipper up while asking the reason for my visit. In the end, the meeting was shorter than expected and the agenda was kept to the strict minimum. It is likely that, after the blowjob under his desk and my premature entry in his office, my dear minister regained his self-control by tongue-lashing his secretary for letting me in his office too early.

In the country of the thousand hills and never-ending spring. Six months before leaving Ivory Coast for a new destination, Paris head office rang to ask me to provide support at Méridien Kigali hotel, in Rwanda, until the General Manager's arrival. I also had to guarantee the hotel's pre-opening and the coordination of a dinner in the honour of an African summit, which was going to be attended by the French president, Valéry Giscard d'Estaing.

Head office had received instructions from the Ministry of Foreign Affairs in France, so we had to move fast, because the summit was taking place within four weeks.

Long live travels, yet another destination. The instructions received from head office stipulated that I was appointed "Head of Mission". I met four Méridien colleagues at the Charles de Gaulle airport: a Caribbean chef, a French head of reception, a German housekeeper and a Swiss engineer. So off we boarded an Air France plane, we were pretty much the only passengers on-board. In Kigali, we stayed at Hôtel des Mille Collines, as the Méridien was not operational yet.

I was in the heart of real Africa, an enchanting Africa popping up from my dreams: the country of the thousand hills and never-ending spring. Thousand and one unforgettable sensations in a timeless paradise.

The following day, a car from the French Embassy came to pick me up and take me to meet His Excellency the ambassador, who received me with great pleasure. From the start, he said that my mission would be very difficult. According to him, the Rwandans had no idea of the scale of the work that needed to be done to open the Méridien Umumbano hotel and to prepare the famous gala dinner.

He then informed me that a meeting had been scheduled, for the next morning, with the president of the Republic of Rwanda, Mr. Juvénal Habyarimana, whose policy, based on unity, peace and development, had made Rwanda the jewel of Africa.

The following day, wearing a suit and tie, I went to the presidential office where the president welcomed me with open arms.

– Mr. Noblet, what a pleasure to host you in Rwanda, you're welcome!

After the usual pleasantries, he didn't hide from me that my task wouldn't be easy and invited me to meet the Minister of Tourism, the following morning, who was in charge of gathering the future employees of the Méridien Umumbano hotel, with no hospitality experience!

As I thanked him for his warm welcome, he told me:

– Mr. Noblet, I've given instructions to the security and protocol services to give you free access to my office, at any time, so that you can keep me abreast of the evolution of your mission, and this until the arrival of the hotel General Manager who should be here within two weeks.

The next day, I met the Minister of Tourism who invited me to go to the back of the administrative offices in the Ministry's courtyard, where there were 500 to 600 applicants. The minister introduced me and told these good people, under a thunderous applause, that I was in charge, with my team, of selecting the staff for the future Méridien Umumbano hotel. I then spoke, thanking His Excellency the Minister of Tourism for giving me the opportunity to play a role within this magnificent country and inviting all candidates to apply the following day at the Umumbano hotel. Another round of thunderous applause.

During the evening and part of the night, I worked with my team on the strategy that we were going to adopt for recruitment, taking into account some selection criteria.

The next day, the whole of Rwanda was there, including families, to attend the event, covered by the press and photographers. With my colleagues, we had put in place a funnel system: first select employees who knew how to read and write, while keeping in mind that some illiterate candidates could be useful for cleaning or gardening.

In two days, we had selected two hundred people for a hotel of 85 rooms, with restaurants, bars, banquet hall, swimming pool and gardens. Among those two hundred people, we had identified all the necessary positions to guarantee service in all the hotel's operational departments.

The day after, we were in the active phases of training in a facility with no water or electricity, and without any food or equipment to explain to the future staff how to prepare a soup or a simple sandwich, or how to make the beds, etc. Five days later, the German housekeeper came to tell me that she was giving up the challenge, as it was impossible for her to work in such conditions. I had to ask head office for extra support.

In the end, I decided to go and see the president again, who received me straight away. I explained the catastrophic situation we were facing and I asked him to provide funding for staff training.

– Mr. Noblet, I'm sorry but we don't have a budget for this.

– But Mr. President, the Rwanda government owns the hotel.

– I'm aware of this, Mr. Noblet, but unfortunately, in the current circumstances, my hands are tied.

Upset, I decided to go to the local market to buy food and the bare necessities for the training course, using my own money.

Moreover, I requested an audience with the ambassador to explain how far we'd got.

– I'm not surprised by the president's reaction, so you're going to have to organise things differently, he told me.

I decided right away, in his presence and with his consent, to call the head chef of the Elysée Palace to explain the situation in great detail and the objective of my mission: namely to organise a super-dinner presided by President Valéry Giscard d'Estaing.

A week before the dinner, an air bridge was put in place between Paris and Kigali with, on board an Air France plane, all the necessary material and French products such as meat, fish, vegetables, fruit, cheeses, bread, champagne, wines, printed menus, etc.

Three days before D-day, my friend **Rudolf Jurcik,** a former Hiltonian, arrived, joined by Méridien executives, to take over from me as General Manager. Years later, he became Managing Director of the Méridien Middle East branch.

My mission ended with the customary expression of thanks from President Juvenal Habyarimana, who offered me two boxes of Rwandan cigars and a handicraft piece. I was also thanked by the Minister of Tourism, the French ambassador and, later, by **Henri Marescot**, president of the Méridien Hotels chain.

My Rwandan experience was enriching on a professional and interpersonal level: to discover different people, new popular traditions, but also the beauty of this country, considered as the Switzerland of Africa because of its climate (the temperature is between 22 and 25 degrees all year round) and surprising landscape.

Rwanda is landlocked between Uganda and Tanzania, who were at war. Hence the difficulty of leaving Kigali because of check points appearing everywhere. This forced me, before going back to Europe, to ask the president for a travel pass to go to Lake Kivu. As I didn't have a car I managed to make a deal with a local Lebanese man who let me a red Mercedes. For fuel, I had to do the necessary because there was an embargo. To this end, one evening, aware of the scheme, I bought fuel through bartering, a full tank against five crates of Primus (seeing as it was a former Belgian colony).

That specific evening, I found myself in a barn where the fuel seller had hidden his jerricans under a pile of jute bags…

One day later, with two of my colleagues, we decided to drive to Gisenyi, a little town next to a large park where mountain gorillas enjoy a protected environment. Very close to the famous Lake Kivu, we spent all day in a bungalow, rented out to us by the same Lebanese man. The place was magical by the beauty and serenity of the scene. We were alone in the world, in the middle of Africa's colours, surrounded by the Democratic Republic of the Congo, Burundi, Uganda and Tanzania. We did some fishing and grilled some tilapias, a kind of very tasty carp.

In the evening, as we were leaving Rwanda, the country of the thousand hills, I did regret the president, who, despite his inability to help me, had always been very respectful towards me.

On a politic level, the situation wasn't simple for him and his ministers, because of the cleavage between the Tutsi rebels and the Hutu tribes. His policy was centred on social justice and integral development, accessible to everyone. The president had an exceptionally good reputation throughout the world. Unfortunately, the Tutsi/Hutu conflict later led to the assassination of the head of the Rwandan state, as well as an actual genocide of the population.

Two days later, I was back in my hotel in Abidjan, which was giving me a lot of satisfaction and was allowing me to blossom within the Méridien Group.

At the end of February 1980, in my capacity of General Manager, I was invited by Mr. **Roland Ayme**, Vice-President Operations of the Méridien Group, to attend a global meeting of Méridien General Managers, which was to take place the following month at Méridien Sharjah hotel, in the United Arab Emirates.

At that moment, I became aware of how lucky I was to be part of an international group that enabled me to grow along my path of life, while discovering new horizons.

When the plane landed in Sharjah, I was overcome with the airport architecture, symbolising Bedouin tents and reflecting the local culture. That's the way I became immersed in the Arab world of the Middle East.

A personalized welcome was organized in one of the airport' salon by **Gianni Riatsch**, General Manager of Méridien Sharjah, who then drove us to the hotel, which included 220 rooms with balconies. A five-star hotel: view over the Persian Gulf, with a tennis court, swimming pool, restaurants, bars, nightclub and halls for conferences and weddings. As we entered the hotel, around seven pm, a Filipino orchestra was playing in the main bar. A few minutes later, after the usual formalities, a nice and pretty hostess showed me to my room. A VIP welcome: flower arrangement, a huge fruit basket and an open bar on one of the room's consoles (bottles of Martini, whisky, vodka and champagne).

How generous and how surprising. I thought alcohol was prohibited in the UAE. In fact, at the time, the Emir of Sharjah had no problem with such things, until the day when, for very specific reasons, he pledged allegiance to the Saudi Arabia King.

Mr. Henri Marescot, an outstanding man.

The second day of the General Managers' convention was livened up by a courtesy visit of the Emir, whom we had to call Your Highness, his staff, his armed guards, as well as the hotel owner, His Excellency Mohammed Al Massaoud. The convention was the opportunity to meet colleagues working around the world, Mr. **Henri Marescot**, the president of the Méridien Hotels

Company, and the directors of the different departments of Paris head office. The different meetings I attended, were fascinating, instructive and gave us the necessary directives for all the hotels. They were giving us a vision of the brand image, the bathroom amenities, the uniforms, the service standards, etc. The major interest for all participants was the information regarding the opening of new hotels around the world and the group's future perspectives. For example, during a chance encounter at a coffee break, I learnt that the senior management wanted to offer me the general management of Méridien Mohammedia in Morocco, in replacement of **Franco Cabella**, who had been approached to run Méridien Bujumbura. So to be continued.

Late afternoon on the third day, President Marescot closed the convention with exceptional panache and charisma. He was admired by everyone. Mr. Marescot, former Air France representative in Japan, was appointed, by the Air France board of directors, to develop the Méridien Hotels chain. His two predecessors were: **Mr. Jorger**, from the tax inspectorate and Mr. **Buichet**, from the multinational company, Thomson. Our president, Henri Marescot, with the rare off-handedness of hurried men, breathed at the speed of Boeings or Concords that he caught like I caught the subway. Medias branded him the "the hard-pushed man from Méridien". With his international experience at Air France, seven years in Japan and thirteen in the United States, he had succeeded in propelling the chain to a higher level. For him, each hotel of the chain was an export product of the French know-how. Whether it was the Congolese bush or the private rooms of Washington, he was always at ease. Henri-Georges Marescot was exhausting for his colleagues, but loved by all. He had the strength and the stamina of a bull, he didn't like to have people dawdling behind him. In appearance, nonchalant and absent-minded, he was aware of everything. Pleasant, if you didn't slow him down. He served his company like one serves their country. If he sometimes enjoyed a moment beside the pool, there was a good chance that he would talk business with you. He would, even under water! Leaving Roissy in the morning, he could have a second breakfast in New York, lunch in Boston, dinner in Montreal and be back in Paris the same evening. In the sleeping plane, the last lit seat was always his, with a file as thick as four or five phone books – a contract for San Francisco, Singapore or Douala… **In short, an outstanding man.**

Despite the short time, the UAE didn't leave me indifferent. I was fascinated by the success of the United Arab Emirates Federation, which consisted of seven emirates: Abu Dhabi, Dubai, Sharjah, Ajman, Um Al Quwain, Ras al-Khaimah and Fujairah – which was the result of the efforts of **Sheikh Zayed bin Sultan al Nahyan**, UAE's first president. He had been able to demonstrate his qualities of leader, enjoying prestige and respect on an international level. I already cherished the hope of coming back one day to this place.

In Ivory Coast, my hotel in Abidjan.

The Relais de Cocody, classified four-star, was becoming a happening place, as cultural and festive events were taking place almost every week. My goal was to bring a new energy to the local and expatriate community, because I have always believed that we had to make things happen and move out of the routine.

One morning, the phone rang in my office. The desk clerk informed me that a certain Ibrahim from Tambacounda – a former employee of Simenti – wanted to meet me. I couldn't believe my ears and I immediately asked that he be shown to my office. Incredible but true, Ibrahim, the man who was in charge of serving bread, ice for the drinks and cheese in Simenti was well and truly in front of me, in Abidjan. He told me:

– Boss, I've come by bike from Tambacounda to see you, I pedalled day and night. Boss, I want to work for you.

Once I'd got over the shock, I had to find a solution. Working in Ivory Coast meant a work permit, and priority was obviously given to Ivorians, because Ivorisation had been one of the government's priorities for the past few months.

The story came to a happy ending. My friend at the Ministry of Labour, in return for a free weekend with full board, with most likely his girlfriend, was sensitive to my request and, exceptionally, gave me a 6-month authorisation for Ibrahim, who became a kitchen porter.

Chapter 12
Mohammedia, June 1980
New Moudir on board

In April 1980, to my great satisfaction, head office gave me the opportunity to become General Manager of Méridien Mohammedia. My farewell party was a highly emotional moment: the staff, in liaison with the chief of a nearby village, honoured me by offering me a Baoulé blanket, traditionally worn by the honorary tribe's chief.

Mohammedia, City of flowers. In June, my first meeting began with an encounter with Mr. **Malterre**, representative of the Méridien Mohammedia owning company, belonging de facto to the Kingdom of Morocco. Mr. Malterre, very kind and pleased to welcome me, was a man in his sixties, very elegant, but also old fashioned. For two hours, and not withstanding the recommendations received from Mr. **Daniel Gillot**, my superior based in Paris, I had the huge privilege of listening attentively to Mr. Malterre as he focused on the habits and customs to be respected in Morocco, the ins and outs of the hotel by giving me detailed information on pretty much every head of department, the hotel's strong and weak points, its position on the market and most of all, the influential people I had to meet in the city: the governor; the chief of police; the president of the golf club, very close to His Majesty King Hassan II; His Royal Highness Prince Abdallah, the King's brother, based in Mohammedia; His Excellency Ahmed Alaoui, the Minister of Tourism, etc.

I received loud and clear this key information, which would help me get to know better the environment in which I was going to have to evolve. In that quality environment, I was feeling very motivated about managing my hotel and making it a favourite place for local customers and those from Casablanca, some twenty kilometres away. Working in Morocco, considered as a land of welcome, culture and traditions, where imperial cities competed in magnificence, along with the sumptuousness of landscapes, all meant a lot to me and my family.

Mohammedia, formerly called Fedala, considered as the city of flowers, was a large seaside resort with casino, marina, racecourse, skeet shooting and Royal Golf club.

In the seventeenth century, the port, under the name of Fedala, was mostly used as a temporary refuge for the light fleet of Salé pirates (city next to Rabat), chased by the King of France's frigates. Fedala was renamed Mohammedia on June the 25th 1960, by King Mohammed V, who restored Morocco's independence. The city's new name underlined the modern character that the Royal family wanted to impress on it.

Within the city and along the oceanic coast, Méridien was a true jewel of the Moroccan hotel industry, at the heart of an exotic park surrounded by palm trees and bougainvillea. At the clientele's service, a five-star hotel, with 188 rooms, including 10 royal and diplomatic suites, bars, restaurants, nightclub, conference rooms that could accommodate up to seven hundred people, meeting rooms, swimming pool, beach, four clay tennis courts, a putting green and privileged access to the Royal Golf club, of which the hotel was an active member.

Since our hotel operated quasi at 100% during the high season, between June the 1st and September the 15th, we had to be resourceful to have a sustained activity throughout the year. With my exceptional team of Moroccans, I decided to spare no expenses, because it was out of the question to disappoint the owner, the Méridien chain, the authorities, the local and international clientele, the staff and their families.

It was a big challenge, but in life, nothing is impossible. In my team, I had five direct reports: **Noureddine Hogga**, Sales Director; **Abel Masmoudi**, Rooms' Division Director; **El Jawouani**, Catering Director; Nabil the financier; and **Larbi**, head of maintenance. The latter, who was of a certain age, was bringing me incredible inspiration from the point of view of his methods and instructions' follow-up. He couldn't read nor write, but everything that I asked him to do, he would implement in the allocated time, without forgetting anything. His memory was phenomenal.

Masmoudi was the quiet force, I called him Mr. Public Relations for his management and coordination of actions with the authorities. Hogga, a smart man who infiltrated himself everywhere to find deals, either in Morocco or in Europe. El Jawouani, a man of action, always positive, working very hard and always ready for battle to implement large-scale gourmet events.

These executives, whom I considered as collaborators-friends, made, together with their respective team, the success of Méridien Mohammedia. Together, we organised exceptional events which made the hotel famous throughout the Kingdom.

We were inexhaustible regarding gourmet, sociocultural, sports and artistic activities. Our calendar of promotional events was extensive, which delighted my boss, Daniel Gillot, and Paris head office. Each week, we honoured Morocco by organizing on Friday evening a spectacular buffet, which highlighted the local cuisine, skilfully spiced and prepared by the hotel's Moroccan chefs. The whole range of Moroccan culinary arts was laid out on a multi-layered buffet: kemias, Zaalouk (aubergine purée), tabbouleh, stuffed peppers, pastilla, chicken tajines with confit lemons, prunes or peaches, tuna tajines, lamb and quince tajines, couscous, stuffed méchouis, and a festival of desserts with gazelle horns, baklawa, milk pastillas, and a variety of seasonal fruits. All this was accompanied by local wines, such as Ksar, Syrah, Guerrouane or the lively Boulaounae, and to finish off the famous mint tea, before the entrance of the Berber and Gnawa artists. Their magical dances enthralled the spectators, especially tourists, by their moves, their colourful typical clothes and the different musical instruments, with spellbinding sounds for guests.

The Moroccan folklore is of endless diversity and wealth, spread over the country's five regions: the Middle Atlas, the High Atlas, Sousse, Marrakesh and the Rif. The aforementioned diversity did not come accidentally but through the crossing of several civilizations who merged intimately to create an exceptional human interbreeding.

The crews. At the beginning of 1981, two business literally fell from heaven: the Air France crews, rotating every day for a year, and three Air Canada crews, mandated to ensure the flights to Hajj, Casablanca-Jeddah-Casablanca, after Ramadan.

These two deals enabled me to meet my budget target. As most of the flight personnel were usually women, this provided an additional attraction in the hotel. Managing a crew meant handling the captain with special attention, such as exclusive welcome with limousine at the airport, guaranteed suite and VIP treatment, with fruit baskets, bottle of local wine and pastries. As the captain is all-powerful and has to write a report on the stopover before taking off, it's better, as an hotelier, to offer the best possible benefits in terms of quality and service.

From time to time, we received requests from the royal protocol, informing us about the arrival of one prince or another from Saudi Arabia, with his suite, for an indeterminate period of time. Usually, when a prince was coming to stay, we literally cleared the decks for action as far as organization was concerned. For convenience and security reasons, the prince was getting the whole floor where the royal suite was located. VIP treatments had to be royal, with trays of fresh fruit, and no longer fruit baskets, which had to be renewed twice a day with different displays. The pastry chef had to excel in the choice and presentation of Oriental and French pastries.

For these people, naturally no alcohol, but all day long fresh juices: pineapple, orange, strawberry, pomegranate, and etc., orange blossom flavoured almond milk, oriental coffee with cardamom or saffron. The catering and housekeeping staff lavished attention, because the slightest request was rewarded with a royal tip.

The life of those princes and their circle, often difficult to manage, was virtually the same every day. Around one pm, breakfast served in the prince's suite with his tribe, right on the carpet, which we needed to protect with plastic tablecloths. Then an extended nap, and at around seven pm, the prince, in top form, had refreshments with his friends in his suite's living room. In the evening, we witnessed an endless ballet of young and charming Moroccan beauties introducing themselves to the prince's right hand. In his own special way, in a room near the royal suite, and in the presence of the lady supplying the young flesh, he selected the future little princesses for a few minutes or a few hours. The selected young women had to be bathed, carefully waxed and dressed in silky and transparent Kaftan, in order to be offered to his Royal Highness!!!

Two or three times a week, the prince ordered a special private soirée in the hotel's grand salon. A big buffet table, erected in front of the podium, included all dishes, skilfully arranged within reach of the prince and his guests. All these people didn't use cutlery to enjoy the abundant food, unfortunately subject to a lot of wastage.

These feasts, which only lasted for 20 to 25 minutes (natives of the Gulf don't usually stay for ages at the table), were interspersed by artistic activities: an Andalusian orchestra, one or two singers famous in Morocco. The highlight of the night was of course the belly dancer, who drove the prince mad. In particular, slow seductive progression, the playful looks, the moves' finesse, the hips' suppleness, and finally, the subtle eroticism, which most of the time ended in the nest, not to say the prince's bed.

What was interesting for the artists, was that each guest had, in front of him, a plastic bag full of large denomination bank-notes, and, at the instigation of the prince, who particularly enjoyed a vocal or instrumental interpretation or a specific move of a dancer, a shower of rolled-up notes was thrown at the artists, who naturally redoubled their efforts in their performance.

Doing business with the Royal Saudi family was naturally profitable, but it was also very nerve-racking, because their bills reached significant amounts in a short time. With regard to the Méridien procedure, we were systematically in an awkward position. In other words, we had to demand payment when the sum exceeded 1,000 dollars. With the prince, the 1,000 dollars were exceeded in two hours' time!!! Each time we presented the bill through the prince's right-hand man, the immutable answer was:

– Boukra Inch'Allah (tomorrow, God willing).

In the end, the full bill was paid on the day of departure, in rolls of bank notes. It was usually accompanied by watches and gratuities, for the staff.

During the first quarter of 1982, for the Méridien chain tenth anniversary, a meeting of all General Managers was organised at the recently opened Méridien Porto hotel, to develop the company's new and future directions. On that important occasion, my length of service was commended with all the honours and recognition, as one of the founding members of the company.

The hotel is requisitioned by His Majesty's Government.

One day, during the month of August, while my team and I were in the middle of work meeting, the phone in the room rang. The switchboard operator transferred a call coming from the Royal Palace of Rabat. It was Mr. Freij's voice, His Majesty's private secretary and the palace's representative in board meetings of the owning company, who told me, in a very detached voice:

– Hello, Mr. Noblet, how are you? I'm calling to inform you that your hotel will be requisitioned from tomorrow, for an Arab League Summit.

– But Your Excellency, that is impossible, we're in peak season and the hotel is fully booked with tourists.

– Mr. Noblet, do not worry, His Excellency the governor of Mohammedia will give you all the explanations in one hour, at your hotel. I wish you good luck, good bye Mr. Noblet.

Dumbfounded, I informed my assistants. An hour later, the governor and his entourage, including policemen, firemen, the city's land-management service, the army, etc. In short, around twenty people were waiting for me in the hotel lobby to hear the governor say to me:

– You have already been informed about the Arab summit. We need to use one of your conference room to coordinate the work.

Five minutes later, we were sitting around a large table presided over by the governor who announced from the outset:

– Sir, I inform you that your hotel is officially requisitioned from now on. Please take the necessary action to evacuate all the rooms and suites from six o'clock tomorrow morning.

– Your Excellency, I have well understood your request, but what do we do with our customers, mostly tourists who have come to stay with their families? What do I need to tell them?

– It is for reasons of State. All your clients will be moved to different five-star hotels across the kingdom, in Fez, Meknes and Marrakech. They will be the kingdom's personal guests and all expenses related to the Foreign Affairs Ministers' Summit will be borne by the Royal Palace. With all our respect and our gratitude, you may leave, Sir.

An hour later, the clients had been informed in writing. The reception and public relations teams were also in charge of calling everyone, without exception. For the most recalcitrant, I made contact with them personally. Although the hotel would be given financial compensation later, the consequences on a business level would not be very positive. But what can be done, when it is a royal decision?

The following day, at around five in the morning, an army of soldiers surrounded the perimeter of the hotel to secure it. Half an hour later, I saw big coaches parked near the main entrance, with on each of them, a sign stating the destination: Fez, Meknes and Marrakech.

At six am sharp, still apologizing, we bid farewell to our dear customers. Some of them were delighted of the opportunity to travel and discover the imperial cities of the kingdom, at the Royal Palace's expenses, if I dare to say so.

For others, it was hard to accept because they had their habits at the hotel. One of the resisting customers decided not to leave his room, which got the colonel riled up, who gave the guest 15 minutes to leave his room. The latter shouted like crazy, asserting that he'd sue the Moroccan government through his lawyer!

At seven in the morning, the hotel was empty of customers.

At eight am, a specialised team burst in with sophisticated equipment to badge all the hotel employees, including myself. According to the colour of the badge, some employees were not allowed to enter a particular zone.

At nine o'clock, three army officers asked me kindly to vacate my office so that they could use it as headquarters.

At ten o'clock, the concierge informed me that the kingdom's Foreign Affairs Minister wished to meet me in the hotel lobby. A minute later, I greeted the minister, accompanied by about thirty people, including the governor, representatives of the local security, firemen, military officers, Mr. Paccard, the Royal Palace architect, decorators, etc.

After having served refreshments to the group, the minister asked me to show him the suites, intended for the Arab Foreign Affairs Ministers. Reaching the floor in question, he asked;

– Mr. Director, how many suites do you have?

– Mr. Minister, we have one royal suite, nine diplomatic suites and ten junior suites.

– I'd like to see them all. For the royal suite, there's no problem, but carpet, curtains and bedspread need to be changed.

The architect and decorators were taking notes. The comments were coming one after the other. It got more complicated when we reached the junior suites, consisting of a large bedroom and a lounge area, i.e. a small sofa, an armchair and a coffee table. In a straightforward manner, the minister spoke to me:

– There's no way we can accommodate a minister in this room. Tell me, what's behind that wall?

– We have a standard room, Mr. Minister.

– Excellent. Mr. Architect, make a note to knock down the wall and do the same for all junior suites.

The architect's reply:

– I will bring in my teams today, Mr. Minister.

My turn:

– But, Mr. Minister, before work begins, I'm compelled to seek permission from the owning company!

The minister's scathing response:

– Mr. Director, his Majesty is at home everywhere in his Kingdom!

Mr. Malterre, aware of the situation, was very relaxed because he had received the green light from the president of the owning company, who was no other than Mr. **Karim Lamrani**, the Prime Minister. That very evening, Paccard's team were ready to get down to work in the hotel, with hundreds of workers who bustled about respecting the road map. I witnessed a total transformation and metamorphosis of the building, without having to spend a penny. Despite my repeated requests to the owning company to carry out such and such investment for months to no avail, I got it all within a few days! It was magic.

For the decoration of the premises, a true airlift was put in place between Paris, London and Casablanca. A renowned French perfume house supplied magnums of perfume for each suite occupied by a minister. Every day during the summit, a truck delivered fresh flowers to the hotel so that experienced florists could prepare arrangements for the suites, the public areas, the large plenary conference room and the sub-commissions' rooms. Since all this official community, including entourage, security and secretariat, was confined to the hotel, the catering department had to be operational from dawn to dusk for breakfasts, lunches, dinners, with different formulas every day, in conjunction with coffee breaks throughout the day.

At this exceptional occasion, I had the privilege to welcome **Yasser Arafat**, President of Palestinian Authority, Prince **Fayçal Al Saoud** of Saudi Arabia, and many more.

In spite of the responsibility and the fatigue, the entire organisation was perfect and acknowledged by the inviting power at the end of the plenary session. On the morning of the fourth day, each delegation had vanished, leaving behind gifts and generous tips for the staff.

Personally, I was glad to have achieved such an exceptional performance with my team, contributing to the influence of

Morocco, while meeting some of the world rulers and rubbing shoulders with a part of the Royal Palace's entourage. I got my office back, along with an empty hotel, which we had to revive with a new clientele. Satisfied to have a refurbished hotel and ready for new challenges. Two weeks later, the secretariat from the Royal Palace of Rabat gave me a large cheque covering the full bill of the summit and the lost revenue relating to the post-summit days.

Another day, Mr. Malterre called to inform me that the owning company's board of directors was to take place the following week, in the presence of Mr. **Henri Marescot**, my president. To this end, he asked me to be ready for a presentation about the hotel's marketing, activities, financial results and cash flow. Three days before the meeting, I received a phone call from Mr. Marescot informing me that he would be arriving the following morning with his wife on a New York-Casablanca flight. Incredibly enough, he asked me if he could spend the weekend at the hotel.

– Sir, it's your hotel and I would be honoured with your presence.

– Fine, that's very kind, but as I'll be arriving very early in the morning, there's no need to pick me up. Simply send the hotel's chauffeur.

The next morning, wearing a suit and tie, I welcomed the president and his wife at the Mohammed V airport in Casablanca, together with the Air France station manager. Mr. Marescot's first reaction was the following:

– I told you not to bother.

– But you are the president and I had to be there to welcome Mrs. Marescot and yourself.

– Fine, fine, but we won't talk business until the board meeting.

– Very well, Sir.

A few minutes later, we were in the car, on our way to the hotel, 40 kilometres away.

Once we'd exchanged the customary platitudes, the president asked me:

– Mr. Noblet, how's business? What's the hotel's occupancy rate?

– Ah, Sir, you're not playing by the rules, as you told me ten minutes ago that we wouldn't talk business.

And his wife to chime in:

– Henri, Mr. Noblet is right.

– Okay, I admit it, but still, just a little...

And so it was off for the requested information: occupancy rate, room average revenue, gross operating income compared to budget, customer segmentation, etc.

Once at the hotel, I escorted our distinguished guests to their suite, where a sumptuous VIP reception was waiting for them. The president told me:

– Mr. Noblet, my wife and I are off this weekend and yours will in fact start in a few hours so I don't want to see you until Monday, day of the board meeting.

– Very well, Sir, at your disposal if you need anything.

Friday went by without a call from the president; Saturday went by, no call from the president; Sunday afternoon, around three o'clock, I decided to call and invite him for a coffee.

– But with great pleasure Mr. Noblet, I'll be there in five minutes.

Knowing the fellow, I knew that he must have been bored to death. And so, after our mint tea, I suggested the following program:

– I propose a walk along the beach with your wife and my family (also including the dog called Fight) and then, because it's winter and night falls very early, we will go to my house for an aperitif, followed by a barbecue and then couscous. What do you think?

– Great, but my wife and I don't have the necessary clothes.

– Don't worry, I will send you the required items in five minutes and we'll meet here, in the lobby, in fifteen minutes.

A few minutes later, everyone was ready, dressed in tracksuits, hats and sports shoes. Even the dog was excited to go out with the president.

At that time of year, the beach was deserted, allowing everyone to enjoy the space, especially our children, Ralph and Nadège. I could see that the president was happy and that he appreciated this relaxing moment. The president was a charismatic man who loved Air France and Méridien Company. He was travelling all the time to meet owners, decision-makers, investors, financiers, politicians and the media. He was very active and could adapt to any situation, such as dancing the *French Cancan* with the owner, distinguished guests and the girls from the Moulin Rouge in front of Méridien Parker New York hotel, with its 850 rooms, who had just been inaugurated.

Around seven pm, after a long walk, we were home, where Khadija, the maid, was waiting for us with a nice fire lit in the chimney. The Marescot were over the moon, while appreciating the simplicity of the invitation with one of their directors' family circle.

The following morning, the president came directly to my office to assimilate the agenda and discuss the highlights that needed to be developed by the board members. At eleven am sharp, we went to the owning company's meeting room to take part in the board meeting, in the presence of:

– Mr. **Karim Lamrani**, president of the owning company, president of the Moroccan group OCP, world leader in phosphates, and Prime Minister;

– The Minister of Development, Mr. **Frejj**, His Majesty's private secretary;

– Maître **Barzilai**, the lawyer;

– Mr. **Ginié Gillet**, president of Hersent Group, and Mr. **Malterre**.

As one can imagine, my president received an extremely warm welcome. When opening the session, Mr. Karim Lamrani asked me to give my presentation, by now ready on a paper board, actually a flip chart. But before starting, I announced to all these high-flying people that I had a special gift for each board member, which was nothing more than a small foldable ball pen, which could be used as a key ring.

The positive reaction was unbelievable. The board members had fun, like 4-year old children, with this gadget embossed with the hotel's logo. President Lamrani was telling everyone, in a childish manner, that he really liked receiving small gifts, while he and the others handled millions of dollars every day. Finally, I gave my presentation, which only lasted for ten minutes, but was highly appreciated by the board members.

As I made a pretence of leaving while thanking everyone, Mr. Lamrani told me that I could stay. He then spoke to president Marescot, asking him what Air France's contribution was to promote the hotel and what were the opportunities to develop the

Méridien brand in Morocco, and finally, how we could increase the margin rate of the current operation.

President Marescot's answers were a work of art. He did an act worthy of the best politicians of this world, with, now and again, a tear in his eye. It was Marescot at his best. To conclude, President Karim Lamrani told Mr. Marescot:

– Sir, you are very good.

And all of a sudden he announced that the meeting was over, carrying on with: please come all to my house in Anfa where lunch will be served to us. Mr. Noblet, you also come with us.

Three quarters of an hour later, we arrived in the residential neighbourhood of Anfa where President Lamrani's daughter welcomed us. After the usual refreshments, we found ourselves in a dining room where two round table had been laid. One was presided over by President Lamrani, and the other, by his daughter. A woman of breath-taking elegance, and from what was said, are doubtable business woman who represented her father in about forty private companies. As required by Moroccan hospitality, guests were served by the father and his daughter…

One afternoon, I received a phone call from my friend Moustache, who informed me of his visit the following week with Johnny Hallyday and Michel Sardou, due to an invitation by the Royal Palace to hunt pheasants in one of the royal forests.

They stayed for a week, during which they were at my house practically every evening. We had the privilege of having dinner, together with part of the French artists' elite, while savouring the result of their hunt: roasted pheasant flavoured with herbs. Johnny, the heartthrob, must have had a few worries back then. Very jumpy and moody, which forced Sardou to act as a buffer to reason with him and advise him. Moustache, my mate, was happy with his hilarious stories and his "teddy bear" side that was liked by his circle. But in order for Moustache to be over the moon, and above all feel well, he had to have a full plate.

The Mohammedia Royal Golf. Méridien Mohammedia was the company's beloved hotel because it was the ideal place to organise promotional events with Air France. I was often requested to stage "Pro-Ams" (professional-amateurs), meaning golf competitions with major professionals and amateurs from the world of Parisian show business, business men and women in fashion, and artists. This type of events, which were taking place off-season, helped us have a sustained activity from the point of view of business, and, above all, establish our reputation on the market as a dynamic hotel.

One evening, while everyone was in top form after having enjoyed a méchoui, couscous and a *"gris de Boulaouane"* wine in one of the hotel ballrooms, one of the players challenged all the other players. To compete in three holes at the Mohammedia Royal Golf by only using the putter, with the obligation of drinking one whisky shot per stroke!!! Of course, under a thunder of applause, everyone accepted this crazy idea. Suddenly, half-drunk players and people accompanying them were on the golf course where the famous competition was over at the end of the first hole, before concluding in the hotel nightclub.

The spectacular soirées increased over the years and were renowned and prized by the Moroccan jet-set. Events that stuck in people's minds were:

- Those from the Moroccan Lions club soirées, which I was a member of, with an international production;
- The fashion shows with Nina Ricci; Brazil night with samba dancers and carioca orchestra;

- Peruvian soirées, with the famous Andean flute players;
- Seventeenth century themed soirées, with the staff in wigs and period costumes, with free-flowing champagne on the menu.
- Gourmet evenings, with traditional French products in the spotlight;
- Caribbean soirées with "Steel band" orchestras, etc., etc.

For my family, Morocco was the ideal destination, and more specifically Mohammedia and its peaceful environment, as opposed to Casablanca, the economic capital, noisier and overpopulated.

In Mohammedia, we were perfectly integrated in the community. Most of Ralph's and Nadège's friends were Moroccans, for instance the children of the Ait Mena family, who lived across the road from us. Anecdotally, Mr. Ait Mena who had made his fortune in construction, was an influential and respected man in the city. He could not read nor write in French, which obliged him to come and see me in my office to fill in his cheques, quite substantial, before signing them.

The people of Mohammedia were adorable and all had an exceptional sense of hospitality. As we had become part of the community, we participated in most events or celebrations, such as weddings, births, funerals, Feast of the Throne, Independence Day, anniversary of the Green March, Ramadan, Eid and Moussems (the gathering of tribes from a certain region, under the presidency of the governor).

In Morocco, the "Moussem" was part of the cultural heritage. It was a tribal, rural and popular tradition to celebrate planting and harvesting seasons. Richly adorned caidal tents were put up around a rectangular field, equivalent to the size of a football pitch, where the "Fantasia" took place at more or less regular intervals.

True equestrian show, it's an entertainment during which the riders, dressed in djellabas, hold long rifles pointed at the sky. The ride leaps forward in line until stopping dead in front of the dignitaries' tents and, at that point, they fire their weapons into the air in unison.

Discovering Hong-Kong, the Pearl of the Orient. On March the 9th 1983, I received an invitation letter from my colleagues **Michel Novatin**, General Manager of Méridien Hong Kong Airport and **Philippe Louie**, General Manager of Méridien Regal Hong Kong City, to take part in the eighth Méridien General Managers' meeting.

What a joy! During one week, I was going to leave Africa for Asia and meet General Managers from around the world, as well as senior executives from head office.

Three weeks later, I landed at the **Kai Tak** airport and discovered Hong Kong, "the Pearl of the Orient", under British mandate until 1997. The Méridien hotel was in the centre of Kowloon, a 15km² space occupied by sky-scrapers, from the seafront in Tsimshatsui at the end of the peninsula to Boundary Street in the North. At the tip of the Kowloon peninsula is located the tourist district of Hong Kong. On either side of the famous Nathan Road, boutiques, restaurants, pubs, hostess bars, snacks, photo and electronics shops were crammed.

Our Hong Kong hotels were chosen to organise the eighth conference of General Managers because Méridien development in Asia was one of the objectives of our chain.

The reception was extraordinary on behalf of the respective direction teams. The catering department of Méridien Regal Hong Kong City particularly distinguished itself with its themed coffee breaks, Chinese lunches with demonstration of Chinese noodles making and snake shows.

Méridien Hong Kong Airport organised a wonderful dinner where all participants had to wear Chinese costumes. What helped us better understand Asia was the presence of external speakers at our meeting, such as **John Pain**, Director of Hong Kong Tourism, who spoke about tourism; **Olivier Lacroin**, Director of the National Bank of Paris for Hong Kong and Macao, who talked about the relations between France and Hong Kong; **Dr. KS Lo**, President of the Regal hotels holding group, gave a very interesting speech about the relations between owning companies and hotel management; Mr. **Pakir Singh**, Managing Director of the Singapore Hotel Association talked about human resources; Mr. **Tat Soon Yam**, Secretary of the National Congress of hotel unions, spoke about hotel staff productivity; and Mr. **Edouard Chen Kwan Yiu**, Director of Studies at the Hong Kong University, gave a talk about economy in Asia and talked about the relation between China and Hong Kong.

During the short breaks we had, shopping was *de rigueur* at the end of the afternoon, and after dinner, we ventured into Hong Kong by night.

One evening, after having enjoyed the famous dim sum with two companions, we went to a girlie bar where we were welcomed by a doorman who shouted at us a "Just take a look." The note on the door announced drinks at only twenty five Hong Kong dollars, as well as erotic posters to stimulate the desire. We went inside. The waitress, bare breasted and wearing a scanty-panty, brought our drinks and started talking to us for a few minutes in a friendly way. That was the most expensive conversation in my life, because five minutes later, the bill amounted to four hundred and seventy-five Hong Kong dollars!! While protesting, they showed us a board on the wall behind a vase stating that there would be an extra four hundred HK$ for any conversation with the personnel.

If a customer was unwilling to pay, two bruisers were ready to beat him up. These practices seemed to be linked to the famous Triad, the Hong Kong mafia. As they say, travel broadens the mind!

"Méridien Leisure" hotels for tomorrow. During the conference, I was asked to make a presentation on the topic "the leisure hotels for tomorrow", which forced me to create something unusual, revealing on this theme.

After dinner, I asked the hotel General Manager's secretary to inform all participants to the conference to bring their pillows the following morning at the risk of being denied access to the conference, and to wear their Méridien Leisure polo shirt provided in their room.

In the morning, the dumbfounded hotel customers – mainly business men and women – saw in the lifts, coffee shop and hotel lobby, people carrying their pillow like a cuddly toy. Some must have been wondering about the exact nature of the hotel.

At nine o'clock sharp, the doors of the conference hall opened, revealing a dark room where you could only make out a U-shape table arrangement, without chairs, but topped at the four corners by a vague shape concealing something, and all of it with Creole music and a projection emblematic of holidays, sun, beach and coconut trees. Our participants were either seated or slumped on the pillow in the middle of the room. Suddenly, lights revealed the stripping of four Hong Kong nymphs in suitable clothes, suggesting sports, cultural, gourmet and recreational leisure activities.

The scene was set, and there I was, at the lectern, expanding on the subject about "Méridien Leisure Hotels of tomorrow". All this led, at the end of the session, to the official establishment of the Méridien Hotels Leisure division, which would include resort hotels such as Méridien Beachcomber in Mauritius, Méridien Seychelles, Méridien Guadeloupe and Martinique hotels, Méridien Mohammedia, Méridien Casablanca, etc.

This conference, important for the group's development was imbued with a sad note, namely that our president, Henri Marescot, was confined to his bed and therefore could not take part in the conference. In a telephone conversation in duplex, he had the strength to deliver a significant message on the success and the future of Méridien to all the people present. Unfortunately, a few months later, we lost a great president who left us after a serious illness. Mr. **Paul Bruyant**, the new president appointed by Air France, organized an extraordinary General Managers' meeting at Méridien Nice to solemnly praise the late Henri Marescot on his achievements. He then presented a particularly dense and substantial report on general policy for the future of the chain.

Back to Morocco. Forty-eight hours later, I was back in Morocco with a head full of ideas and the strong desire to have the opportunity to go back to Asia one day.

While waiting for a new professional transfer, I tried hard to develop the hotel so that it was recognized as "the place to be", while guaranteeing financial profits.

Morocco is a country well worth discovering, unique in terms of tourism, and internationally recognized for its welcome. For an unforgettable stay, you must discover the imperial cities of Marrakech, Rabat, Meknes and Fez. Each one has its own distinctive characteristic.

For Marrakech, it's about its palm grove, its golfs, its luxury hotels, its mythical square Djemaa el-Fna, its souk and its Koutoubia tower.

Rabat, listed as a World Heritage site, is both a historical and modern capital, where the Royal Palace and all the government authorities are located, along with the embassies.

Meknes, city of exceptional beauty, is the former administrative capital under the reign of the Alawite Sultan Moulay Ismaël. Being placed under the protection of the UNESCO, it is considered as the pearl of Central Morocco.

Fes, listed as a World Heritage site, with its huge medina considered as the largest in the world, is a must-see city for the tourist who can appreciate the rich culture stemming from the great tradition of Arabic-Andalusian art.

Two other cities also stand out: Agadir, city of renewal and easy living, sheltering, in an exceptional site, one of the most beautiful bays in the world; and the beautiful Essaouira, feet in the water, shelters, behind a wall meant to be impregnable, the Draa Valley on two hundred kilometres, from Ouarzazate to Zagora, the gateway to the desert.

But the ultimate for my wife Michèle, Ralph, Nadège and Fight, the dog, was to meet with our friends, Mazen, their dog Zouzou, Fight's brother, and the Mazzini, around a barbecue on Sunday in the Benslimane forest, located just a stone's throw away from Mohammedia.

May 1983, Mr. Christian Peyre, newly promoted Vice-President of Méridien Leisure Hotels, came to visit me to discover the hotel he didn't know. At a free and relaxed moment in the conversation, during lunch at the golf club house, he told me that the company needed my services to take over the management of Méridien Guadeloupe, because of the departure of my friend **Gianni Riatsch** who had just faced a general strike and who, after two years of good and faithful service, wished to see something else within the group.

The West Indies' hotels had a rather infamous reputation with regard to the unions, which, from time to time, voiced their grievances on the Island and this usually just as tourists were flowing in for Christmas, New Year's Day, Easter, etc. You need to know that our hotels in Guadeloupe and Martinique were considered as the flagship of the hotel industry in the French Antilles, and moreover properties and symbols of France through the Air France Group.

Nobody wanted to take over the management of one of these hotels, because it was a hazard destination. Well I accepted the challenge. In fact, the real challenge was to break the news to the owning company of Méridien Mohammedia.

Two days later, gathering up the courage, I went to see Mr. Malterre in his office. After having informed him of the situation, he was frosty, and while walking me back to the door, by way of reply, he said:

– See you tomorrow at nine am in the locker room of the club house for a round.

– Certainly Mr. Malterre, I replied.

The next day, in the locker room of the golf club house, in an awkward atmosphere, we laced up our shoes without exchanging a word, to find ourselves a few minutes later at the start of hole number one. As he was playing as badly as I was, his ball was thrown on one side of the fairway and mine on the opposite side, it was not promising. Finally, at the third hole, he decided to talk to me.

– Mr. Noblet, aren't you happy with us? Why does your head office suddenly suggest this transfer?

– It's part of the evolution of my career within the hotel chain. Of course, to replace me there will be a new General Manager with the required skills and the experience of Arab countries.

– I understand, but it will be different. The owning company and I, as well as the local community, appreciate you a lot.

– Thank you for your kind words and don't worry Mr. Malterre, I'll do my utmost to ensure a smooth transition and instructions' handover to the new General Manager, in a calm and professional way.

The ice was broken. This allowed us to finish our game at the fourth hole, painstakingly!

Two weeks later, Mr. Malterre summoned me to his office to report that, for my departure, I was given carte blanche to bid farewell to Morocco. In saying this, the owning company didn't want to lose face. They had to show the media and the community their gratitude towards me, while introducing the new General Manager, **Gerald Hardy**, from Méridien Damascus.

The party planned by me combined prominent citizens of Mohammedia, Mr. Ginié Gillet who had travelled from Paris, Mr. Malterre and his wife, my friends and venerable brothers representing the Moroccan elite, the Air France representative for Morocco, our important customers, the hotel's executive committee and, of course, Gerald Hardy, the new General Manager.

The event was enhanced by the presence of a jazz band, "the red beans", whose four musicians, old friends, were Air France pilots.

A month later, end of June 1983, my family and I, including the dog, embarked at Roissy airport, for Pointe-à-Pitre, the capital of Guadeloupe.

Chapter 13

Saint-Francois de la Guadeloupe, June 1983

Coconut punch for business class

June 29th 1983. Freshly arrived at Raizet airport, my friend **Gianni**, whom I was going to replace, greeted us with a huge bouquet and a "Kaou Fé?" (How are you?). The answer in Creole must be "Sakamaché" (all is well).

Guadeloupe, wonder of the Caribbean, distinguishes itself by its five different islands: Grande-Terre and Basse-Terre, which are one in the shape of a butterfly, La Désirade, Marie-Galante and Les Saintes. The Guadeloupe archipelago, lulled by the trade winds, tempered with an infallible sun all year long, lashed by the Atlantic Ocean and caressed by the Caribbean Sea, is undoubtedly a paradise. In short, a favourite destination for idleness, with its fine sand beach, sports, leisure, nature, hikes, etc. And to think I was going to be paid to discover it all!

Forty five minutes later, we arrived at Méridien Saint-François in Grande-Terre. The management committee was waiting for us, forming a guard of honour to welcome us and help us relax, we were served a coconut punch.

The hotel that I was going to have the honour of running, consisted of 271 rooms and suites in a four-star formula (most of them had a sea view), three restaurants, two bars, a nightclub, conference rooms, beach, swimming pool, tennis court, golf course and all water sports (canoe, kayak, pedalo, catamaran, jet ski, scuba diving and fishing).

Our apartment, located on the hotel's fourth floor, consisted of three bedrooms, living room, dining room and kitchen, all this overlooking the beach and its coconut trees. Delight for the eyes, first, in front of this incredible colour chart of blues from the Caribbean Sea. Next, a pleasure of the senses, imagining to be lying on the fine sand, feet in the water and then diving to explore the multi-coloured corals, while enjoying the relaxation, exhilaration, well-being ... and freedom!

In fact, I was dreaming, because the reality was going to be very different for the metropolitan that I was, and who was going to discover another aspect of the hotel business in a very peculiar social environment.

The next day, I got into the heart of the matter with Gianni, for the instructions' handover. Gianni, an Italian national, had been somewhat messed around during the last staff strike. He formalized with me everything I needed to know about the hotel, the financial situation, the yearly budget, my presentation to the staff and to the unions. Not to mention the courtesy calls to Mr. Lucien Bernier, the Mayor of Saint-François, Mr. Ernest Moutoussawy, the president of the regional council, and

Mrs. Lucette Michaux-Chevry, president of the general council. Then there was a cocktail party to celebrate both my arrival and Gianni's departure, to thank him and to wish him good luck. In fact, I was the one who needed the good luck!!!

A week later, I hosted my first morning meeting with the hotel department heads, which was revealing of the hotel circumstances, because the conversation was focused on the social aspect of the company. This made me think and compelled me, after this meeting, to meet Marius, the Personnel Director. I immediately understood that Marius, a native of Saint-François and graduated from a business school, was the key man in the company, with whom I would be in constant contact. During more than two hours, he provided an overview of the political, economic, social, and trade union situation (the UGTG, General Union of Workers in Guadeloupe) which was playing an essential role, under the guidance of the CGT, the central union in Paris. As such, he gave me a lot of details about who is whom, along with the staff's grievances.

In Guadeloupe, social work involves a political and strategic dimension.

Even though slavery had been permanently abolished in a Governing Council and formalized by Victor Schoelcher's decree on May the 27th 1848, there were still vague recollections within the local population, which had always found itself confronted with an identity problem. Namely, the fact that one day they considered themselves as Guadeloupian in their own right, another day as Caribbean, and the following day as French. Moreover, speakers from Guadeloupe, Martinique, Dominica and Saint Lucia can, for instance, understand each other in Creole without using either French or English. 95% of the Guadeloupians speak Creole as their mother tongue and French only as a second language, and 90% of them are black people or of mixed-blood.

While leaving my office, Marius added:

– By the way, Mr. Noblet, I must remind you of our meeting tomorrow at ten am with the members of the works council!!!

There's a first time for everything. As time went by, I knew that as General Manager I would spend almost 50% of my time with staff representatives!

But also as an hotelier, I had to play an important role in the hotel operations as regards to services, catering and entertainment. In a leisure hotel, we have to be active from dawn until dusk and offer customers the best in all the hotel's operational service modules. The customer usually comes accompanied, often with his family, and in addition, he pays his bill in contrast to the business hotel, where the customer signs his bill which will be later settled by his company. Important detail, when a woman travels with her husband and possibly the children, parameters change and expectations are paramount. The manager of a leisure hotel and his team must particularly pay close attention to the smallest detail, and this, all day long.

The day started at seven in the morning with breakfast service, which is – de facto – the most important meal of the day. In a four-star hotel, perfection must be the rule, together with a maximum amount of creativity, because the customer must be pleasantly surprised.

In the mornings at the entrance of the restaurant, we had set-up the "coco" take-off. Harry, as big as a basketball-player, a strapping guy always smiling, with a radiant complexion, knew how to get the customers in shape by offering them a freshly opened coconut, juicy with a shot of white rum.

Then, the customer was taken to his table by Eva, a faithful member of my team, who refused to join the trade unionists. She was, with her generous build, a strong woman who imposed her style with a lot of class.

The first customers were always the Japanese, very disciplined, who arrived in a group as the restaurant opened. Then, in order, the Germans, who were just as self-disciplined, around half past seven/eight o'clock, the Americans and the Canadians around nine am, the French around ten, and just as it was practically time to close the breakfast service, meaning around ten thirty, the Italians arrived, grumbling because the buffet was not sufficiently stocked.

Our buffet was simply exceptional. Different sections, different decorations and an unimaginable choice of food, satisfying all nationalities.

The fresh juice section, with Caribbean exotic fruit, full of vitamins: soursops, ambarella, papayas, pineapples, guavas, pomegranates, mangoes and passion fruits.

The bakery section with a plethora of croissants, pains au chocolat, brioches, milk rolls, baguettes, country breads, multi-grain breads, wholemeal breads, ciabatta, cheese puff pastries, Danish pastries, etc.

The Caribbean section, with Creole Black pudding, cod accras, chayote gratin (*gratin de cristophine*), pork stew (*colombos de porc*), fish *blaff*, *gumbos* salads, etc.

But also the egg section, prepared according to the customer's taste, in front of him; the waffle and pancake section, again prepared in front of the guest; the dairy section, with milk, soy milk, porridge, yoghurts of any kind, etc.

After breakfast, most of our guests took up deckchairs on the beach and lazed about. Amongst them, there was Mr. and

Mrs. Hart, regular customers of the hotel, who had been coming two to three times a year for years. To ensure the first beach newcomers didn't steal "their equipment", straw umbrella and the two deckchairs they had been squatting, they systematically padlocked the aforementioned deckchairs at the end of each afternoon.

Our famous Eva, with her outspokenness, and knowing that they were stingy, loved to tease Mr. Hart, despite her good relation with them. As a joke, she would tell him that she was expecting to receive, before their departure, a bottle of champagne, while adding "And a good one, some Dom Pérignon".

When they left, Eva always received a generous tip, together with a bottle champagne, but not a Dom Pérignon …

We had another regular, Mr. Frattini, of Italian origin, who, each time he arrived at the hotel, asked for a double safe to fill with wads of bank notes and, so, pay all his bills in cash. What is wrong!

On the beach, we had two retail outlets in beach huts: the beach bar, where we served fresh fruit cocktails, the famous *Ti-punch* with white rum (cane syrup and squeezed lime on crushed ice) and all the usual beverages, with snacks, sandwiches, cod accras, etc.

Then there was the Casa Zomar, a restaurant that was always full from twelve thirty to three pm. The menu was based on Caribbean cuisine, a reflection of the encounter of civilizations between European colonialists (the Békés) and African slaves, with exotic products, spices, seasonings and hot pepper.

The signature dishes that our clientele loved: grilled snapper served with its "*chien*" sauce (onion, herbs and chopped hot pepper, olive oil and lime); matoutou, made with crab and crayfish. And above all, the matété, the national dish: fish court-bouillon Creole-style, seafood, such as grilled or fricassee lobster, clams, etc.

For dessert, and for tourists seeking a gourmet emotion, we recommended the roast banana tart, enhanced with vanilla rum and raisin ice-cream.

Between four and seven pm, the hotel activity was calm, most customers preferring to nap.

At seven pm, the Lélé bar was the must-visit location and the place to be seen. The women came wearing elegant, flimsy outfits. All these high-flying people enjoyed the punch section that we were offering, with the Caribbean house band "Experience 7"in the background. For dinner, customers had a choice between a huge international buffet in the main restaurant and a service *à la carte* in the Saint-Charles restaurant, offering Italian specialities.

After dinner, the ritual was always the same: either the customers were looking for a more romantic atmosphere around the pool or at the Lélé bar, or an evening in the nightclub, always ending at daybreak.

In order to be much more creative and to avoid a conventional and predictable system, we had decided to develop a program of themed catering with a personalised event for each night, i.e.:

- Mondays: "Al dente" Italian night.
- Tuesdays: "Seafood" night on the beach, where the sea fishermen came to deliver their catches in front of the customers.
- Wednesdays: West Indian night under the coconut trees with the best of the local folklore, where square dancing had the place of honour. Anecdotally, square dancing was born in Guadeloupe from a melting pot of customs born from the court of Louis XIV. This dance is performed by two couples facing each other by forming a square. At the end of the evening, couples devoted themselves to the beguine.

- Thursdays: "Churrascaria" Brazilian night, its giant barbecues of marinated, grilled or roasted meat for meat lovers.
- Fridays: International night, "The World", offering the best of all five continents and a versatile orchestra.
- Saturdays: "Caribbean" night on the beach with filibusters celebrating a victory over the English by getting tanked up with old rum, and rhythms of percussions and Créole songs in the background.
- Sundays: "Romantic" night, seated dinner served in the hotel gardens.

These events had a very positive impact on the clientele, and for each of them, the staff was wearing a uniform related to the theme. These soirées were also meant to bring people together, like in a village, and to create a non-conventional atmosphere in the hotel, encouraging the staff to join in the day events in a laid back environment. That's how my employees-friends did their job, while actively participating in the themed nights as actors in the animation.

I had also understood that if we wanted to succeed by being better and different compared to competition, we had to interpret the hotel business like an everyday artistic production. In my imagination, the key word to make oneself known in the hospitality industry is "Passion", which must be conveyed at every level of the hotel. The customer who purchases a hotel stay, first of all buys a dream. To come to a hotel means to be welcomed and recognized by name. The customer will appreciate the doorman's smile, an elegant decoration, a floral arrangement worthy of the name, staff in an immaculate uniform, a perfect grooming, a sincere smile, a

positive and friendly attitude, good quality background music, being escorted to one's room, special attentions in the room, pleasant staff, capable to thank the customer when he pays his bill, etc. All this to bring comfort, satisfaction, which in turn builds customer loyalty.

This being said, I had to manage the hotel with the unions always on the verge of confrontation. My key-man, in his capacity as Personnel Director, was bringing me every month the book of grievances raised by staff representatives to which we had we had to provide answers. The staff representatives preferred to act like the lords of the manor at the negotiation table instead of bustling about their workplace. So to shorten these meetings, I had found a trick: firstly, to organize these monthly discussion at eleven in the morning; secondly, to expand at length each point raised in the issue. Moreover, as lunch time in the staff cafeteria was over, our friends started to show signs of tiredness and after a while, they couldn't take it anymore and asked me to adjourn the meeting so that they could go and eat.

Once the meeting was over, Marius and I officially answered in writing on what had been agreed on one or two issues, when initially we should have answered ten or twelve. If I answered ten or twelve issues in an hour, I could easily imagine that another stream of issues would have been raised in the following hour. When Marius and my secretary Olga sensed strong signs of discontent among the staff representatives, I summoned them to announce some good news, so as to unlock any potential conflict.

– Dear personnel representatives, I had an idea that I would like to share with you. I suggest that, on your initiative, we organise a giant zouk with the hotel guests, what do you think?

– Mr. Noblet, that's an excellent idea and the party will be great!

What they also enjoyed, was the organization of a picnic exclusively for the staff and their families on one of the Grande-Terre beaches. The service in the hotel obliged us to split the teams, and thus to organize two picnics over two weeks. These events had the advantage of bringing everyone together in an extraordinary festive atmosphere, where white rum was *de rigueur.*

One day, I used, as a wildcard, a familiarisation trip to mainland France for one of the staff representatives, who always showed unbelievable virulence against capitalism and Metropolitans coming to exploit Guadeloupe. It was the case of a certain Axel, purchasing manager and union leader who one day came to inform me that the staff would be on strike for the festive season, knowing that the hotel would be fully booked.

After my announcement that completely baffled him, he told me that, with his comrades, he'dreverse the idea of going on strike, and two weeks later, with his ticket in hand, Axel left Guadeloupe for two weeks to meet some relatives in the Parisian suburbs and, officially, take a familiarization course in the purchasing department of Méridien Montparnasse hotel.

The period of the festive season was, like every year, a real nightmare for our hotel, which inevitably displayed an overbooking of several rooms, and despite this situation, I personally received calls from mainland France to make additional reservations, particularly from our new president. One day he asked me to book a suite for a French minister.

On hearing my negative response, due to the context, he replied:

– You are the hotel's General Manager, sort this out to find a solution because I've already confirmed!

Another time, a regular customer, part of the Parisian jet set, asked me:

– I know that you are fully booked but, besides our friends who have already booked, thanks for finding an extra room for my friend **Solarro** and please, find a way to put us all together on the hotel's fourth floor with a sea view…

The Guadeloupe overbookings will remain etched in my mind for life.

Every morning, in peak period, the management committee scrupulously analysed the customers' list and each morning we set up a strategy to relocate such or such customer in one of the other hotels in Guadeloupe. For the customer, or I should say the "patsy" who needed to be relocated, the technique was always the same. Namely, when he reported to the reception on the day of his arrival, **Betty**, who was front office manager and also trade unionist, informed him, with her most radiant smile, that unfortunately we could not provide accommodate him in our hotel because of blah, blah, blah.

The motive changed every day: an official delegation, a problem with the computer, a problem with the water inlet in one side of the hotel, etc. If the client was recalcitrant, we had a plan B with **Marcel Levy** (Marcello for close friends), the Italian accommodations Director, a real charmer and looking like Omar Sharif. He introduced himself to the customer, taking him to the side, and looking him straight in the eyes, told him:

– Please come, I will explain to you, we'll work things out, blah, blah, blah…

If that didn't work, there was the plan C. Marcello called me from his office and said "Michel, it's your turn".

I then met the customer in question, usually a company director or a high-ranking executive of the civil society, in Marcello's office. Very often, the conversation started crescendo:

– What's your name? You're a gangster, a fraud, I'm going to have you fired from Air France, etc. You don't have the right, etc.

For my part, after my most sincere apologies, I tried to reason the customer saying that the situation should be sorted out within 24 hours (which was rarely the case), that we had planned everything in a nearby hotel with special attentions in the room, such as champagne, exotic fruits, pastries, a Mercedes car at the door and finally, that I was personally at his disposal during his stay in Guadeloupe, etc. We had to face this scenario several times during that week. At any rate, the first day of arrival in the West Indies was the most difficult to manage for a part of our well-off clientele, generally coming from mainland France and arriving stressed. Stress related to their hectic business lives, in their position, or other, which meant that at the slightest hitch we could expect atomic reactions. From the second day, in their beach wear by the lagoon and under the coconut trees, their smile was coming back as if by magic, and often, thanks to our teams' professionalism, we became best friends with these frustrated customers. I must say that for some high-ranking executives, even if everything was perfect with regards to reception, they had trouble disconnecting from their work environment when they were on holiday, especially if they were with their families and had to pay the bill themselves!

Speaking of bills, one day, my president called to ask me to make a reservation for the president of a large airline company who would stay with his family and it was necessary that,vis-à-vis the trade unionists, the stay was invoiced, while in the end the president in question would not pay anything!!! It was up to me and the financier to resolve the problem.

The originality of my president (a man respected by everyone and with whom I was on friendly terms) was that each time he called me from his Paris office, it was to ask something extravagant.

Another day, as the accrued financial results of the West Indies hotels, Martinique and Guadeloupe, had been crippled for years by bank interests and losses caused by social conflicts, exasperated, he asked me to sell Méridien Guadeloupe hotel for a nominal sum to one of the local institutions, such as the General Council, the Regional Council, the town hall, etc. These institutions, aware of the local social issues, kindly declined my president's offer. Another time, because he wanted to get rid again of both hotels, at his request I met Mr. **Leonard Lapi**, a well-known businessman from Paris. In a very direct manner, with his familiar cheekiness, he revealed in two minutes his strategy for the hotel takeover by an investor:

– Dear friend, it's very simple, you need to transform your 271 rooms into 130 or 140 suites, which would allow well-off customers, keen on discovering a unique destination, to arrive directly by private jet at Saint-François airport, located three minutes away from the hotel, and to benefit from utmost luxury accommodation with related services and high standing personnel. I'm meeting your president next week in Paris to follow up on this matter. Meanwhile, thank you for your hospitality and I'll see you soon.

We never saw each other again and there was never any follow-up to that episode.

I also had the opportunity to welcome Mr. **Christian Gérondeau**, better known by the general public as "*Monsieur Bison Futé*", through an advertising campaign that was a big hit and which, within the framework of his position as "Mr. Road

Safety", forced him to some important ministerial decisions. Quite a charming man, exemplary, who later became an important player within our group, and moreover, a friend of my family.

During the Guadeloupe adventure, I prided myself on not having experienced any social conflicts, which earned me adulation from the chain, however, the unavoidable happened one night with a bomb attack in the hotel, by a separatist at the instigation of the Caribbean Revolutionary Alliance. This organization campaigned for the break-away of Guadeloupe from mainland France. The customer in question, who had a booking in due form, had registered late one afternoon, paid his night in cash and, later, left the hotel leaving a bomb behind, hidden under the bed, which exploded around midnight.

Once the moment of panic had passed, all customers were directed to the assembly area pool/beach, with the exception of the Italians who left the hotel at once and are still running!!! An hour later, the hotel was fully under control of the police force and the fire brigade. There were only two slightly injured persons with burns. At two am, the area prefect, the town mayor, the president of the general council and the president of the regional council were in my office to show their compassion. At three am, I received the first phone calls from journalists who plied me with questions, particularly Paris Match (we made their front page), then from head office, then my colleagues in the hotel industry, etc.

This terrorist attack resulted in the closing down of the hotel, for six months, in order to do the necessary repair work. The hotel staff, who couldn't be dismissed, benefited from further training, compulsory and financed by the government, in a facility in the city of Saint-François, thanks to the support of the municipality.

My experience in Guadeloupe ended after two and a half years. A new challenge awaited me at Méridien Montreal in Canada.

Very excited by the opportunity to discover a new continent and new horizons, I enjoyed some relaxing moments with my family in our dear Pyrenees. Two weeks before our departure, there was a change of plan. Mr. **Gillot**, in charge of Europe zone, called me:

– Michel, I need you for a challenge at Méridien Porto in Portugal.

My reply:

– Sorry, I can't accept.

A quarter of an hour later, Mr. **Antoine Blavignac**, head of human relations at head office, was calling to ask me to accept this transfer because the situation was serious in Porto due to the owner's discontent. The latter threatened to break with the company because of the bad publicity of the hotel and the poor financial results.

My reply:

– I'm not the only one in the company, blah, blah, blah…

A quarter of an hour later, the group's president begged me to accept the job. Moreover, he was willing to certify, in writing, a transfer to North America after Porto.

My answer:

– I agree to make a return trip to meet the owner in the presence of the regional director, provided that I can come back to my holiday location for three more weeks.

He gave me a positive reply and so, during the month of May, I headed off to Porto via Lisbon, where I had to meet "O Signor Ingeniero **Moura Vicente**" again, former Minister and representing the owning company Hotelgal, for both Méridien hotels, in Lisbon and in Porto.

Chapter 14
Porto, May 1985
A Portuguese captain with a French accent

"Where the Atlantic meets Europe", that's the way this Southern country introduced itself to me, oceanic land by excellence, Portugal built there its history and its myths. My journey was going on: the discovery and knowledge of this country.

My interview with Mr. **Moura Vicente**, who had a perfect command of French, was courteous and instructive about the economic, social and political situation in Portugal. He insisted on the positioning of Méridien Porto, which needed to be rectified according to the sensitivity of the Northern community, conservative and traditional

Porto, Cidade Invicta. That same evening (May the 15th 1985) with my family, we found ourselves at Méridien Porto, which I already knew. We were given a warm welcome by the management team and I immediately got a good feeling. My apartment, located on the fourteenth flour, was spacious and very pleasant, with view on the Boavista Avenue, the city's main artery.

Porto, its name is on everyone's lips and on every table. Famous for its wines, Porto was also known for its past. Porto has as nickname "Cidade Invecta" (unconquered city) due to historical events.

Méridien Porto, located in a residential area, was a hotel with 223 rooms, 9 suites, a restaurant, bars, nightclub, health club, hairdressing salon, boutiques, business centre, convention halls, meeting rooms and a golf driving range.

Despite a rather difficult start, hardly indicative of a promising future, I gradually imposed my style by positioning Méridien Porto as "the hotel of the city".

It wasn't an easy challenge, because Méridien was the first hotel chain to open an international luxury hotel in Porto. Up until then, the city only had a classical, traditional hotel business, mainly consisting of small units. The creation of a hotel with more than two hundred rooms was bound to upset the market, which meant that we had to change people's habits. Moreover, in spite of a very intense economic activity, Porto remained a provincial city, a very withdrawn city, with very strong principles and traditions. Méridien Porto sparked mixed reactions at its implantation. So, as a true captain, I took the helm with much determination, firmly fixed on stirring my ship back to port, safe and sound. But before setting out to sea, I wanted to know who was whom in the community. That's how I met His Excellency the governor of the Northern region, the mayor of the city, the Bishop of Porto at the episcopal see of the diocese, leaders of the famous houses of Porto, decision-makers, the president of the Football Club of Porto, travel agencies and tour operators, the Air France representative, hotel customers, etc. Naturally, I tried hard to get to know my colleagues and the whole hotel staff, without whom nothing would have been possible.

One of my first decisions was to learn Portuguese, so that I could become far better integrated in the community.

Based on my review of the situation, I decided, together with my team, to set up a very specific policy aimed at giving a dynamic image to the hotel.

The main objective was to thoroughly play the integration card and to position the hotel as a "must", where there's always something going on. A hotel in the city is primarily a social place. To offer nice rooms, good service, it's the least that we can do, but it won't be sufficient to attract and gain the loyalty of our clientele. What is important is to bring an added value through various animations. In my mind, to organize events was indeed the best way to create a distinctive ambiance in the short time customers spend with us. And so, as part of a promotional event, as a welcoming friendly gesture, each customer was offered a glass of Porto on his arrival at reception, a simple but highly symbolic gesture.

In terms of catering, I had to reconsider everything because the menus, initially suggested, were based on the new French cuisine. In other words, a large plate with very little to eat, hence the frustration of the Portuguese who did not appreciate this style of cuisine at all.

We know that it was the Portuguese who discovered the precious spice route (coriander, pepper, ginger, curry, saffron and paprika), as well as many other exotic products that were unknown in

Europe up until then (rice, coffee, tea, tomatoes, potatoes from the New World and pineapple). Therefore, we also know that, on a daily basis, the Portuguese meal must be substantial, and inevitably include rice or potatoes.

A strategic U–turn was implemented in order to honour what the Portuguese and the visitors wanted to see on the tables, namely *bolinhos de baccalhau* as appetisers; the popular "caldo verde" soup; *cozido* (beef with cabbage, considered as the national dish); *cabrito*; *aors de pato* (duck rice); the *caldeirada* prepared with the best fish in the country, the *marisco* and the famous *bacalhau* (cod) – they said that there were as many ways to prepare it as there are days in a year. Not forgetting the *queijo da Serra* (goat's cheese), the *pao de lo* (a light charlotte), the *pasteis de nata* (small cream tarts), the *touchinho do ceu* (a cake made from crushed almonds), etc. The national wines: *vinho verde, Douro, Dao, Alentejo, Setubal* and *Algarve* and to end the meal amongst friends "uma bica", a sweet coffee, or a "garoto" coffee, an expresso with foamed milk; and to keep the pace, a "bagaça"!

This makeover, in line with market expectations, was praised by everyone within the Porto society. **Which goes to show that in business, everything is related to marketing. It's only marketing that identifies customers' needs and desires and, in fact, provides a way to ensure satisfaction in a profitable and more efficient way than offered by competition.**

In the same spirit, every Thursday, customers staying at the hotel were invited by the General Manager to a cocktail party, during which they could meet the hotel's executive management team. A good way to listen to our clientele and to connect while honouring customers and the people in charge of the hotel.

To promote the hotel, we regularly organised lunches with the press at Méridien, in collaboration with the country's most important national and regional newspapers. The central idea: Méridien, meeting place for the country's jet-set, politicians, artists, top athletes and business men.

Once a year, we organised the Top 50 cocktail party, bringing together, for one evening, the leaders of the top fifty companies in the country. The benefit of such an event was obvious, as this business clientele accounted for the bulk of our activity.

Each operation had to be well targeted and it was important not to forget anyone. For that purpose, we created the Secretaries' Club that met every month in one of the hotel's lounges. The purpose was very specific: these secretaries, in charge of booking the rooms, deserved quite naturally some special attention.

In the same spirit, every year, we invited all the city taxi drivers to a friendship cold buffet, coupled with a spectacular tombola. On one condition: the "I love Méridien" sticker had to be displayed on each car. Guaranteed success.

Since the textile industry amounted to 45% of the Portuguese gross national product, we organised twice a year, in collaboration with Air France, big fashion shows thanks to my usual contacts: Nina Ricci, Christian Dior, in order to present prestigious collections.

These events were the subject of gala nights, where evening dress was *de rigueur*. To these promotional activities could also be added the catering events with themed gourmet weeks: *bistrot* or romantic soirées, opening with a concert of classical music, followed by a candlelit dinner.

What the community really appreciated, were the plays and the operas with their international troops, which we produced in one of the hotel salons.

We also played a role of patron by presenting, as often as possible, exhibitions featuring local artists. These exhibitions were a huge success, so we transformed one of our boutiques into a "Café des Arts", which became a real artistic platform in Portugal.

Sports activities were also included in the hotel entertainment program, with three major events in the year: a golf tournament in April, the Vespa rally in July and the Méridien Squash Open in September.

On top of all this, there were two large-scale popular events, which associated the people of Porto for the St. John's Festival. The first one, an open-air dance with orchestra in front of the hotel, which turned into the centre of attraction of the city – a good way to show that the hotel was accessible to all.

The second event was the "Méridien Olympic games" that we organised at the city's Cristal Palace. Under the aegis of the Olympic Committee of Portugal and the Ministry of Sports, this very official sports tournament, intended for children aged seven to eleven, gathered twenty to twenty-five thousand people together. The revenue generated was donated to UNICEF.

All these events helped confirm our core objective: to get the staff, and indirectly their families and friends, involved so they become players within the company. This way, at Méridien hotel, we were able to develop a kind of symbiosis phenomenon within the hotel market.

"God is the artist and Rio his masterpiece". In 1986, a new General Managers' conference took us to Brazil for a week.

Upon reading the invitation letter, I closed my eyes for a second, thinking about the mixed colours, the music, the myths of Rio de Janeiro, the carnival and the football at Maracanã. Hosted at Méridien Copacabana in Rio and at Méridien Salvador da Bahia, we had a crazy week. Particularly during the excursions organised in mythical places such as the Corcovado, the Sugar Loaf, the favelas, etc.

"God is the artist and Rio his masterpiece" is the Brazilian saying! Salvador de Bahia, unique in its popular vitality and very colourful through its African origins, lives by the capoeira rhythms, the religious festivities and its fiery carnival of which we caught a fleeting glimpse.

The discovery and folklore aside, the theme of the conference was based on Méridien sales and team spirit. A major objective: "Succeeding together".

All these subjects were presented, commented on and discussed in plenary session and during workshops that were very lively. The development was also celebrated with actual openings in Vancouver, London, Paris-Montparnasse, Casablanca, Marrakech, Bangkok; contacts in Phuket, San Diego, and even others in the final stages of study.

On an operational level, we underlined that, in view of the big ideas, major advances, the computer and globalist management theories, there were the basic, the behaviour of the technician who knows the hotel business and who is aware that there are principles, gestures, and considerations that the customer will quickly perceive as the expression of a professionalism worthy of respect.

The owner, Moura Vicente, with whom I only spoke Portuguese, had a completely different opinion when he was with me. He realised that his hotel in Porto was playing a leading role in the prestige of the city and of the country. He made a point of taking part in all the hotel's major events and provided an unimaginable support with regard to the country's policies.

Every month, with **Jose Maria Soengas**, my colleague from Lisbon, we were facing the owning company in Mr. Moura Vicente's office to present the financial operating account of the previous month. Each time, it was an act of bravery because "O Signor Ingeneiro" wanted to discuss each line of the financial report, balance sheet and cash-flow… It was better to be well prepared for the discussion.

Apart from business discussions, our relationship was extraordinary. Mr. Moura Vicente and his charming wife considered us as members of their family and opened doors to help us develop our respective hotel's business.

Like everywhere, if you want to succeed, you need to be integrated, understand people and deserve their trust, while bearing in mind that you're not at home.

This country, Portugal, relatively preserved from the political turmoil that had shaken the continent, was for me a discovery.

Portugal surprises by its diversity and the wealth of its historical sites listed on the UNESCO World Heritage, and its beautiful landscapes that change from one region to another.

In the North, Porto, the regional capital, is surrounded by mythical cities: Gaia, Matosinhos, Braga, Guimarães, Vila Real, Bragança, Viana do Castelo, Barcelos and Sao-Joao da Madeira.

In the centre, Coimbra, the regional capital, famous for its university, is surrounded by important cities such as Aveiro, Viseu,

Guarda, Leiria, Castelo Branco, Covilhã, Figueira da Foz, Abrantes and Caldas da Rainha.

The Lisbon region. The capital, famous for the fado, is surrounded by cities worth visiting, such as Cascais, Setubal, Almada, Amadora, Queluz and Agualva-Cacem.

The Alentejo region on the Atlantic coast and its regional capital, Evora, is surrounded by very touristic cities: Santarém, Beja, Portalegre, Elvas and Sines.

In the South, the Algarve, and its regional capital Faro, usually attracts mass tourism. It is surrounded by seaside resorts such as Portimão, Lagos, Tavira, Sives, Ollao and Loule.

The independent island region of the Azores, with its regional capital Ponta Delgada.

And the independent island region of Madeira, with its regional capital Funchal.

Portugal has always been a popular destination, not only for its mild oceanic sun and the remains of its past, but also for the hospitality and friendliness of its people.

At that time, the President of the Republic of Portugal was called **Dr. Mario Soares**, and, unlike his predecessors, he preferred staying at Méridien Porto than in his presidential residence in Porto. When he was there, he obviously stayed in the presidential suite where we received distinguished guests that I welcomed personally, like **King Carl Gustav and Queen Sylvia of Sweden,** their **Royal Highnesses Prince Charles and Princess Diana**, or Brazilian artists such as **Gal Costa**, whom I received twice, **Simone Cristal, Gaetano Veloso,** etc. All of them felt at home in our hotel for different reasons. President Mario Soares particularly enjoyed our establishment because he was not dependent on an annoying and restricting protocol, and also because we could speak

French together and converse about the values and thoughts that we shared on philosophy and arts.

One day, Dr. Mario Soares' official car was late and he started to grow impatient. All of a sudden, the car arrived at full speed, with its sirens wailing at thousands of decibels, hardly bearable, and he said:

– You see, this is Portugal: lots of noise but no efficiency!

Another day, while we knew that he had to leave his suite at ten in the morning to attend a meeting in the political office of the Northern region, the accommodations Director, **Eric Lefèvre**, and I went up to his floor to greet him and escort him to the lobby. At ten o'clock on the dot, Dr. Mario Soares came out of his suite, greeted us and asked us: "where's my security?"

As nobody could reply, he asked Lefèvre: "Could you open the door with your pass?", showing the room next to the presidential suite, where his security service was staying.

Opening the door discretely, the sight was unique and surreal: both men from the president's personal security were watching television in their socks! When they saw the president's face, they literally dived in their shoes and fifteen seconds later, still apologizing, they were surrounding the president in the lift.

On February the 14th 1987, a historic event took place in Porto, as part of the 600th anniversary of the marriage between **John the 1st, King of Portugal, and Philippa of Lancaster, daughter of the Duke of Lancaster**, following the strengthening of existing family ties, expressed by the agreements of the Portuguese-English treaty of 1373. As such, the Royal Highnesses, Prince Charles and Princess Diana, representing the British Crown, were invited to this exceptional celebration. The protocol of the government, in connection with the English Embassy, had planned that the royal couple would be staying at Méridien Porto for a week.

Curiously, the Prince and the Princess arrived separately at the hotel, where a royal greeting awaited them by my staff who honoured them with an impeccable guard of honour. At around five pm, I had the privilege and honour of greeting the Princess, first, who told me in the lift that she was extremely tired and wanted to relax. A quarter of an hour later, while everyone was waiting for Prince Charles, I heard feminine exclamations coming from the service door leading to the kitchens:

– Signor Noblet, Signor Noblet, Princesa! Princesa!!

I arrived on the scene where I was told that the Princess, in sportswear, had used the service lift and had escaped through the kitchen to jump in a car that was waiting for her outside. I later learnt that she went swimming in the city fire brigade's pool, under heavy escort!!!

Half an hour later, to a warm round of applause, I welcomed the Prince who was quite relaxed, thanking me for the reception and greeting some of the staff. During their stay, Their Highnesses had complete discretion under the control of the protocol and the English security. Unlike our Portuguese friends, the protocol was from dawn till dusk, so we knew what was happening by the second. The head of protocol, who was in close contact with us all day long, gave us details of the different phases of the day.

Two days later, following an invitation from the British Embassy, I took part in the historic ceremony at the Sé Cathedral, built in the thirteenth century and located on the high side of the city.

On the day of the Prince and the Princess' departure, they asked to see me in their suite to thank me. As such, I was announced by the liaison officer who had clearly explained to me the protocol to follow, namely:

The security officer opens the door for me. I am announced, then I take three steps forward, then three to the left so as to find myself in front of the royal couple, three meters away from them. I bow with respect. I listen to them, I thank them and leave.

The Prince spoke, called me by my name and apologized for all the operational problems related to their visit, then he thanked me by involving all the staff for the excellence of the service and the thoughtful gestures that had been made during their stay.

In turn, I extended my sincere thanks on behalf of the owning company and the staff, and then said that we had been privileged and extremely honoured by their visit in our hotel. As I was leaving them, the Princess gave me an autographed portrait of the couple.

Virtually the entire city of Porto was gathered in front of the hotel to thank them for their visit and wave goodbye. As he stepped in his Rolls Royce, the Prince thanked me again:

– It was a great moment, Michel, thank you again for everything.

The next day, I received a letter of congratulations and thanks from His Excellency the Ambassador of the United Kingdom and from the governor of the Northern Province.

A week later, head office in Paris asked me to represent the company, with my colleague Myriam Riell, at **the celebration of the centenary of the International Herald Tribune newspaper** which was taking place at Méridien Paris Porte-Maillot in the presence of important personalities.

This celebration was also centred on an international conference on issues of concern to decision-makers at the level of democracies and industrialized countries over the coming decades.

That's how, over two days, I had the privilege to rub shoulders with and listen to these different speakers:

Russel Hogg, President and CEO of MasterCard, on the theme "Evolution of technology"; **Max Geldens**, Vice-President of MacKinsey, on "Manufacturing today and tomorrow"; **John Ashworth**, Vice-Chancellor of Salford University, on "Making education and work a lifelong couple"; **Elisabeth Dole**, Secretary of Transports in the United States, on "Relationship between government and the private sector"; **Wassily Leontief**, Professor at the Institute for Economic Analysis at the University of New York, on "New attitudes towards work"; **Alain Juppé**, the French budget Minister, on "Issues of governance horizon 2000";**Vita Zhurkov**, Director of the American and Canadian institute in Moscow, on "The outlook for economic and social cooperation between East and West"; **Toyoo Gyohten**, Minister of Finances for International Affairs in Japan, on "Global financial markets"; **Campbell Corfe**, Partner KPMG New York, on the theme "The capital explosion: a worldwide quest for money"; **Henri Martre**, Chairman of the Aérospatiale, on the theme "Aerospace markets"; **Karl Otto Pöhl**, President of the Deutsche Bundesbank, on "Are we moving towards a more stable international monetary order"; and **Helmut Schmidt**, former Chancellor of Western Germany, on the theme "Triangles, quadrangles or what else? Aspects of our immediate future".

Those two days together, between sessions, coffee breaks and lunches were very instructive about the knowledge and behaviour of these men and women, who were all both approachable and friendly. The climax of this important event was reached when, near the end of the closing cocktail party, the ceremony coordinator took the microphone and made an announcement:

Ladies and gentlemen, courtesy of Air France Company, we have a surprise for you, and kindly request you to head towards the hotel exit in five minutes where special buses will be waiting for you. Direction Charles de Gaulle airport, for a very special flight on board a Concorde plane, where dinner will be served. For your information, your ID won't be needed. We wish you a good flight.

Incredible but true! Three quarters of an hour later, the bus dropped us off in front of the plane where Air France Managing Director, surprised to see me, was welcoming the VIPs, of which I was a part. The supersonic flight lasted two and a half hours. A dinner including caviar, lobster, cheeses, pastries, sorbets was served, copiously washed down with vintage champagne and great wines, to finish off with Columbian coffee and white alcohol digestives.

The atmosphere in the cabin was very festive among the delegates who had magically become best friends. Most VIPs hadn't even realized that we were cruising at Mach 2 speed. We can say that we were tiddly when we landed at Charles de Gaulle airport!

On April the 7th 1987, the chain invited us to attend the General Managers' conference in London, over three days, at Méridien Piccadilly, the group's new jewel. Besides getting to know about the company's new directions, I had the privilege, along with the other managers of the chain, of having lunch one day with Mr. **Jean d'Ormesson**, of the French Academy, at the Brochet hall palace, where he gave a talk on the theme "Tradition". He started as follows:

"I am quite willing to speak ill of tradition, for example I know families of tradition, who are, for instance, idiots from father to son. You know the phrase of the father telling his son, who is a bit restless: stop reasoning and read your Descartes! Well Descartes is precisely the person who was opposed to tradition. If I had to choose between tradition and progress, I think I wouldn't hesitate for long and I'd choose progress. Tradition might be nothing more than a successful progress. I'll say that progress is an innovation in the experience. Always rely on principles, they will eventually give in. I fundamentally believe that traditions are made to be respected and, at the same time, to be shaken up and I believe that we must remember that progress must be respectful of the power of the past and of all that the past can bring. If we want to oppose tradition and technique, if we want to oppose memory and comfort, well we're on the wrong track but tradition, the past, memories are something that have a fundamental function I believe in your field of hotel business, like in all others, these are remarkable machines that allow us to dream. **"There is no future without the past and I am absolutely convinced that there is no project without memory."** And after a forty five minute talk, he concluded:

"It's memory that makes progress bearable and it's in the task of remembering and dreaming that you have such an important role to play".

Never in my life did I think that I'd share such a great moment with an "Immortal", whose mission is to promote the French language, according to the founding principles of the Cardinal Richelieu, in 1635.

At the end of 1987, Mr. Paul Bruyant, president and friend, retired and was replaced by Mr. Rodolphe Frantz, our new president. He was committed, with great determination, to develop the group profitably.

With the agreement of head office, I'd decided to improve my knowledge in economics, business and marketing by following a

6-month course at the *ESCP* centre (Paris business school). This was useful but demanding because I had to combine my professional work in the hotel, the lessons that I had to attend after work and, once a month, go back, for a week, to the ESCP academy.

Thanks to my wonderful team, which consisted of **Maria Joao Moreira**, Public Relations Director, who was senior executive in the hotel and central pillar since the pre-opening of the hotel and had greatly contributed to the hotel's success; **Alfredo Barretto**, Human Relations Director, "Mr Deixe comigo Signor Noblet" (I'll take care of it, Mr Noblet, in other words the person who facilitated all the situations with the authorities or the staff); **Georges Marchand**, Mr. diplomacy and member of the Portuguese aristocracy; **Carvalho de Almeida**, a strategist and an outstanding engineer; **Carlos Rosales**, the man who had the skill and style for maximizing the rooms' turnover: **Rolf Kettman**, Sales Director and an expert at selling congresses and seminars to foreign clientele; **Fatima Bulhoso**, also known as "Baixhinha", my assistant, motivated by a sense of responsibility; **Anna Maria Sapage**, executive assistant, the crucial link to coordinate all promotional actions with the press; **Palmira Diaz**, our guru in vocational training, etc. That team demonstrated every day its strength, its passion, its determination and its competence by wanting to be part of Méridien success and also be recognized by organising events that would stick in people's minds in the city of Porto and the Portuguese Nation.

We knew that to succeed, we needed a collective business vision by bringing together dynamic forces. Assuming that an employee, happy in his job, is a satisfied customer in the hotel, it was necessary that everyone, no matter what their level of responsibility in the company, gets totally committed

and feels completely involved. It was therefore necessary to establish relationships of trust and to work in a transparent world. Everyone had to be informed and everyone had to be able to express themselves.

To achieve this, we had implemented a real organization chart where different appointments were set. Each appointment matched very specific objectives on quality, business objectives, training, improvements of work conditions, innovation opportunities, etc.

A way as good as any to **never be outdone by everyday life, because we could never forget that we were a community of people aimed at serving the customer.** Every month, we celebrated the birthdays of all those who were born that same month. In terms of welcome, each newcomer was sponsored by a colleague with more seniority, allowing him to discover the hotel and its various components.

Twice a year, we got together outside the hotel, in a quinta (farm) for a day of relaxation based on arts. This allowed to connect beyond professional relationships, and moreover it gave everyone the opportunity to express their artistic talent under the supervision of seasoned professionals.

Customer or employee, life was good at Méridien Porto. **To succeed, you have to believe in people, love them and create what I call an emotional cohesion.**

To achieve this, we created the "success cocktail" which was in fact a virtual cocktail based on seven combined elements:

1. "Hygiene of the environment": when a customer walks into a hotel, he has to feel good.
2. Promotional events: essential to make oneself known and to be visible on the market.

3.   Quality catering: to better sell the hotel and be appreciated.
4.   Cultural events: to act serious and distinguished.
5.   Sports activity: shows the dynamism of the hotel.
6.   Animation for the general public: the hotel associates the city to its activity and, by extension, is within reach of all social classes.
7.   Staff event: to love and create an emotional cohesion with employees and their families.

The hotel continued to perform well and the owner was pleased with its reputation. It was considered as the best business hotel in Portugal by the media and the Ministry of Tourism. As for me, I loved my job, the relation with my team and my interaction with the local community.

At the beginning of October 1988, Mr. Rodolphe Frantz called to ask me to take over the management of Méridien Abu Dhabi, in the United Arab Emirates, while stressing that he would come and spend the following weekend in my hotel with his wife. I knew that he was aware that this transfer wouldn't be easy for the owner and for me.

Four days later, as scheduled, our dear president arrived with his charming Japanese wife. To show him that we had a sense of originality as far as reception was concerned, we organized the transport from the airport to the hotel by vintage car escorted by twenty or so classic cars, whose drivers were dressed in period costume.

This 1900 car parade was an amazing attraction between the airport and the hotel.

Late that afternoon, the president came to see me in my office to tell me the story of Méridien Abu Dhabi in great detail, insisting on the fact that the owning company, Abu Dhabi National Hotels, had given a formal notice to Méridien to take drastic measures to restore the hotel's image and profitability at the risk of losing the hotel.

With the further development of the Gulf region thanks to the oil windfall, the French government, the Air France Company and, of course, Méridien could not afford to lose Méridien Abu Dhabi, not to mention the new hotel openings in Saudi Arabia, Bahrain, Qatar and especially Dubai.

As the president's speech sounded very familiar with his predecessors', I explained to him my failed transfer to Canada because of Méridien Porto. He gave me a political answer: "Don't worry, we'll take care of you, blah, blah, blah".

From one dithering to another, we came to an agreement, but the hardest remained to be done, out of consideration for Mr. Moura Vicente who needed to be informed of our decision, which I did the next day to be told "eu gostaria que voce me dissesse isso no meu escritorio em Lisboa, obrigado!" (I want you to tell me this in my office in Lisbon, thank you).

That did not bode well.

On Monday morning, I'm in front of a livid Moura Vicente, who told me:

– The owning company is very happy with you. I have plans for you and therefore I ask you to take a few days to think about it before you venture to the Arabs!

Knowing myself and my loyalty to my company, I already knew the outcome. I waited a week before getting back to him to announce my decision.

Two weeks later, while I was already packing, as agreed, I introduced my successor to Mr. Moura Vicente. Three weeks later, with his consent, a Farewell party was organised in my honour with the Porto elite, in the presence of Mario Soares' representative, the Governor, Méridien Vice-President, Mr. Maurice Tapie, my successor, and my team. On this occasion, people gave one speech after another, including the one from Moura Vicente which was really special and full of praise.

I was happy and in my element in this country. I had to tear myself away from it emotionally for another destiny. But I cannot change, travelling is in my genes. Going into the unknown, towards a new challenge, this matched a deep desire to see something else and to surpass myself.

Chapter 15
Abu Dhabi, May 1988
Alert on board

Destination: Abu Dhabi, capital of the United Arab Emirates. An island of greenery in the country and a meeting point of two cultures: the modern business world and the Oriental tradition and hospitality. The extraordinary prosperity and development that the United Arab Emirates were enjoying were the result of one man's efforts: Sheikh Zayed bin Sultan al Nahyan, elected first President of the UAE Federation. He enjoyed a great prestige in the international arena thanks to his respect for humanitarian laws and his effort to maintain peace in the region. Under his influence and the black gold's (one million seven hundred thousand barrels produced daily), the UAE experienced an economic boom that enabled it to develop rapidly, becoming an essential partner in the region and the world.

Considering that every citizen has a role to play in the nation-building, Sheikh Zayed took the necessary measures to improve the status of women in society, by making access to education easier and by giving them a more prominent place in the country's political and social life. Taking advantage of the huge oil income, he had schools, universities, orphanages, and hospitals built in the Emirates and even abroad.

Abu Dhabi is the largest Emirate, taking up 87% of the country's total surface area, i.e. 67,301km². It is also the seat of the Federal Government, which includes six others emirates: Dubai, Sharjah, Ajman, Ras Al-Khaimah, Umm al-Quwain and Fujairah.

Of the five million inhabitants of the United Arab Emirates, 90% are from abroad, mainly the subcontinent of India and Pakistan, and the others from Arab countries, Iran, South-East Asia (Malaysia, Indonesia, Philippines), Australia, Africa, Europe and the United States.

Méridien Abu Dhabi – a five-star hotel inaugurated by His Highness Sheikh Zayed, the Emir of Abu Dhabi, and Mr. Valéry Giscard d'Estaing, the French President, in March 1979 – was located by the sea, in the heart of a residential area, a few minutes away from the business centre and the shops. It consisted of 235 rooms, including 25 sumptuously decorated suites, with a private beach, a swimming pool with a special cooling system, tennis court, water sports facility, restaurants (the "*Brasserie*"; the "Waka-Tua", a Polynesian restaurant; "the Oasis", a beach restaurant; "Al Berkeh", a Lebanese restaurant; "Al Finjan", a tea house), the nightclub "*Carrousel*", a business centre with an around the clock secretariat, conference and meeting rooms that could accommodate up to 600 people.

I paid my first formal visit to the owning company, where I met His Excellency **Nasser al Nowais**, the chairman, whose reception was lukewarm, as I felt that there was mistrust towards Méridien head office and the regional management. Apparently, there was litigation in the air. He made it very clear that the owning company expected a lot from me to straighten out the operation in terms of financial results and brand image in the city.

For my part, I thanked for the opportunity to work in one of his prestigious hotels, and that I was in this job to succeed. The meeting was fairly short, and as I was leaving, he wished me good luck.

A few moments later, I met Mr. **Abdallah Moussawi**, the Managing Director, and Mr. **Abdallah Al Saadi**, the Deputy Managing Director of the owning company, who received me in a very friendly way, and gave me some useful recommendations about what they expected from me. One of the specific advice that Mr. Moussawi gave me was revealing:

– Mr. Noblet, I know that you have a Maghreb experience, but here, in the Middle East, things are different. "Remember that everything you say will be repeated, and all that you think to yourself will also be repeated!!!"

A word to the wise…

The owning company was a real empire. First of all, by the impressive gold-coloured building that gave an impression of greatness and power, then by the structure of their business:

- Owners of Méridien, Sheraton, Hilton, Intercontinental hotels in Abu Dhabi and Al Ain, Sheikh Zayed's hometown;
- Fifteen or so Al Diar hotels in the Emirates, in Egypt and in Turkey;

- A travel agency with a fleet of taxis, 4 by 4 cars and buses for excursions and desert safaris;
- A catering company producing daily 140,000 meals for airlines, oil companies, multinationals, hospitals, schools and the palaces of the royal family for special events.

The United Arab Emirates is one of the most liberal countries within the Arab nations. Regrouping over 190 nationalities, everyone respects everyone here, whatever your nationality or faith. In terms of environment, this is definitely the place in the world where one feels most safe. It is the Arab country where women can work, drive and dress as they wish, in a decent outfit. It is the land of the Arabian nights, with its Oriental fragrances, colourful souks, cafés, bars, ethnic restaurants, nightclubs, boutiques, mosques and even churches…

Even though it was, at the time, the youngest capital in the world, Abu Dhabi wanted to position itself at the top of the list in terms of modernism, technology and new ideas to be harnessed.

In my hotel, we had a staff of 30 different nationalities, and from various social and cultural backgrounds, who worked in the hotel's operational departments.

My management team was also very cosmopolitan, with two Egyptians, one Lebanese, one Sudanese, one Tunisian, one Syrian, one Dutch and two French.

Considering the tense situation between the owning company and head office in Paris, we had to shake things up by finding ideas that would boost operations in terms of profitability. Three things:

- Firstly, restore trust towards the owners at every level of the Abu Dhabi National Hotels' organisation, by meeting them virtually every week, to fill the gap.

– Secondly, re-motivate the management team and the staff by listening to them.

– Thirdly, listen to the market and our traditional clients, such as Air France, Dassault, Schlumberger, Thomson, Matra, etc.

With a global vision of the situation and after having taking into account the hotel's strengths, weaknesses, opportunities and threats, I proposed to Mr. Abdallah Moussawi, the Managing Director, an action plan on business strategy, hotel repositioning, public relations and interest bearing investments. In particular, the creation of a second swimming pool, integrated in the site, would attract many more expatriate members in the hotel club, as well as four new restaurants in the disused premises on the hotel ground-floor.

The new proposed restaurants: an Indian restaurant, "The Maharaja", which would attract a local clientele interested in this type of cuisine; a Russian restaurant, "The Petrov", which would become the most select restaurant in Abu Dhabi; a steak-house, which would be positioned as a popular restaurant; and a Brazilian restaurant-bar, the "Casa Brasil", which would mesmerize customers looking for exoticism and lambada.

After having listened at length to my vision of positioning the hotel as the "Méridien Village" within the city, with a total of nine restaurants, Mr. Moussawi was delighted, surprised and, at the same time, distraught when I asked him to give me his agreement on the principle.

His answer was:

– Mr. Noblet, thank you for this presentation and I can see you're taking charge, but having said that, you must get the go-ahead from Mr. **Nasser al Nowais**.

At that point, I understood that, even in that mega-organization, the supreme decision-maker was the chairman.

Still, on the same day, I asked for an audience with His Excellency Nasser al Nowais, who received me the following day in his office.

Very determined to push my projects through, I told him that I had come to see him at Mr. Moussawi's request about the special projects for Méridien. He replied:

– Yes, yes, I am aware of this, please explain your strategy to me.

I thanked him and started by giving him my point of view on the way the hotel should be positioned in the future, and by talking about the idea of a second pool, which would enable us to register an additional 500 members in our club. His direct answer:

– I have no objections, please proceed.

I then went on with the restaurants. For the Indian restaurant, the "Maharaja":

– You don't have any experience in that style of cuisine!

– Mr. Chairman, looking at your hotel portfolio in Abu Dhabi, you don't have an Indian restaurant, and furthermore, Emiratis and the Indian business clientele will be drawn to this new product.

– I have no objection, please proceed.

For the Russian restaurant "Petrov":

– You don't have any experience in that type of cuisine!

– Mr. Chairman, as a former Catering Director for Méridien Paris, the new generation largest hotel in Europe, I've made a special deal with the Raspoutine restaurant in Paris, regarded as one of the most fashionable restaurants in the French capital. Furthermore, the historical links between Russia and France, and particularly the gastronomy, are real. In French cuisine, you can find Russian specialities such as beef stroganoff with paprika, pojarsky chicken, zakouskis, borscht, piroski, salmon coulibiac, blinis and caviar, etc.

– I have no objection, please proceed.

For the Brazilian bar-restaurant "La Casa Brasil":

– You don't have any experience in that type of product!

– Mr. Chairman, as you know, I've just moved from Portugal and the historical links between Portugal and Brazil are very strong. Besides, Brazilian cuisine stems from European, indigenous and African influences. I went twice to Brazil and I speak Portuguese. In terms of product, we will suggest feijoada, the national dish, bobo de camarao, churrasco, moqueca de camarao, pao de quejo, etc., and for drinks, cachaça, batida, caipirinhas, etc.

– I have no objection, please proceed.

For the steak-house, his answer was direct: "Please proceed".

At the end of the meeting, which had lasted for twenty-five minutes, I felt triumphant, but, as they say, now I'll have to get the work done.

The new profit centres generated a practical and efficient operation in the selection of consultants and the monitoring of each project, to which I associated the owning company, which de facto had to approve concepts and tenders.

Thanks to the efficiency and the professionalism of the Abu Dhabi contributors, the four new restaurants were soon operational. They were subjected to very special official openings for which we invited the ambassadors of the Russian Soviet Federative Socialist Republic, of Brazil and of India, Emirati dignitaries (including Mr. Nasser Al Nowais) and important customers.

For the Petrov restaurant, we organised a 17th century dinner, with musicians from Moscow. To impress our guests about

Russian gastronomy with original dishes I found a way to make a deal with one of the Russian Embassy's chefs, without the ambassador knowing about it! At the end of the dinner, after the usual toasts, the Russian ambassador stood up to congratulate us on the opening of the Petrov restaurant, on the exceptional quality of dinner, the authenticity of the food and for the chef! The chef and I came close to Siberia.

For the opening of the Casa Brasil, the party ended at four in the morning, in the company apartment with the ambassador. He was on top form, delighted that we were promoting his country in the Emirates.

For the opening of the Maharaja, we had to do things according to the rule book: to identify the most favourable D-day, in the most auspicious circumstances and to respect the "Puja", a ceremony of offering and adoration during which the officiating priest spreads flower petals, incense and breaks a coconut on the floor before the official opening of the restaurant door, and this in front of the press and television.

From April the 28th to May the 2nd 1989 I took part in a General Managers' meeting in Paris, on the theme "the Republic in motion", not in honour of the bi-centenary celebration of the French Revolution of 1789, but with regard to a meeting following the estates general of our convention initially held in San Francisco, and to know how Méridien was going to give itself a "Constitution" and on which values the Company would rely.

On that occasion, we enjoyed the presentation of **René Raimond**, an historian and renowned political analyst, who mentioned the notions of legislative and executive powers, of central power, all this in conjunction with the company's life.

Our agenda was quite substantial between the growing presence of Asia's economic power in the hotel business, the positioning of Méridien in the world, quality surveys, new technologies, new customer services, career management, the respective roles of the "head office, regions and hotels", the business and financial results, the company's policy, the short term objectives and instruments, the group's values, etc.

Four or five months after my arrival, the chairman paid me a surprise visit. Mr. Nasser Al Nowais was an amazing individual, who followed the company's evolution day by day and fulfilled his role in an exemplary way. A particularity: day or night, he never announced his visits, which meant that I had to be vigilant and have a well-informed and trained staff to follow the appropriate guidelines. So, when he appeared, I had to be informed immediately, or if I was away, my substitute would invite him to have a cup of coffee or something else.

Anyway, that day, while having some fruit juice, he asked me about my personal situation, if all was going well for me and how business was going, while being aware of everything. Then, a tricky question about my relation with head office in Paris and the regional direction. My answer was clear:

– Your Excellency, thank you for your confidence and thank you again for the privilege and the opportunity of working for your respectable company. My job is to manage this hotel to the best of my ability by positioning it as the best hotel in this city; to offer an attractive and profitable product and a good service; to contribute, with my team, to the influence of your company and of the Emirate of Abu Dhabi. Otherwise, in my mind, I must be loyal towards my company to which I'm proud to belong since its establishment.

He thanked me for my forthrightness and understood, at the same time, that I was not playing politics.

From one subject to another, there we were brainstorming about another ambitious project: a "health centre" including a gym, two squash courts, a spa fitted with a hammam in the Moroccan spirit, massage rooms, a cosmetology clinic and a hairdressing salon.

Four weeks later, I went to meet him in his office with a project draft, which I had discussed and studied with Shangland Cox Consultancy, as well as a feasibility study. The chairman, very interested, understood at the same time that this new centre would be the first of its kind, not only within the UAE, but also the Arabian Peninsula.

For the financing, which represented five million dollars in the initial assessment, he was very direct:

– Check with the financial department of the owning company, which will give you a cash advance, which will be reimbursed by hotel on basis of a schedule.

This exceptional centre became operational ten months later. During my three years in office, we developed a total of eighteen projects of varying degrees of importance, including an apartment hotel with eighty-four studios.

In Abu Dhabi, business evolved in the world of business society, surrounded by influential members. You had to be visible and available in cocktail parties, dinners, embassies, official events, or still in obligations related to the local community, such as weddings, funerals, births or religious celebrations.

Furthermore, the hotel stood out by its enviable financial results and our Méridien Village was very successful and therefore, the contentious situation with Méridien was being cleared up and getting back to normal.

The hotel was operating at full capacity with its nine restaurants, its tearoom, three bars, boutiques, two nightclubs – the "Carrousel" and the newly opened "Juke box", its four orchestras that performed every day, its club with one thousand two hundred members, its fitness centre, its banquet rooms and the catering service that we had developed on an industrial level to cater for receptions in the palaces, especially His Highness Sheikh Zayed's palace, where presidential dinners were organized and where I had the opportunity to greet François Mitterand and Helmut Schmidt for the second time.

Our slogan at Méridien Abu Dhabi was "Méridien, where the actions begin", because something was happening there every day: rock or classical concerts, tennis or squash tournaments, exhibitions of paintings, of pottery, of classic cars or of the new Lamborghini that we displayed in the hotel lobby, fashion shows, pastry demonstrations for children, games on the beach, or a new Brazilian singer, etc.

The Public Relations Department was operational non-stop, until the day Saddam Hussein invaded Kuwait, on 12th August 1990. Immediate reaction from the United States, under the leadership of President George Bush, who invited over sixty heads of state to join in his effort.

The operation "Sand shield" was set up under the leadership of the generals Colin Powell and Norman Schwarzkopf.

Overnight, my hotel fell to an occupation rate of 5%. What's to be done?

The French Embassy formed a crisis cabinet in which I was involved by finding myself community officer and responsible for the French community in one part of the city. My code name was "Bravo". The respective authorities and governments that had nationals in the Emirates feared the worst by imagining the invasion of Qatar, Saudi Arabia, Bahrain and the United Arab Emirates. We had to be organised by setting up evacuation plans by air, by road and by sea, under the authority of the Colonel Testard, the military attaché of the French Embassy. In front of the hotel's main entrance, two armoured cars were displayed. My apartment and my car were equipped with VHF transceivers by the Embassy. Every evening, in the middle of the curfew, the ambassador, whose code name was "Papa Charlie", was making contact with all the community officers, the consul and the vice-consul.

The code names were varied: Papa Charlie, Clover 1, Clover 2, Foxtrot, Alpha, Bravo and Echo. As Saddam Hussein threatened to use gas with his Scuds, a colonel of the French Army specially came from Paris to answer technical and specific questions related to the different scenarios about potential risks incurred. From a business clientele, my hotel was now filled with journalists who, for most, were writing their articles on the main bar's counter where they were gleaning information here and there.

Mid-August, the first American regiments and the famous Marines arrived in Dhahran, near Bahrain. In the UAE, under the control of the Americans, things were taking shape, which comforted the local population. One could say that Americans were everywhere.

Seeing this as an opportunity to boost the hotel revenue, and with the assistance of the American Embassy, I promoted the hotel and its services on American war ships having Abu Dhabi as destination. When the warships docked, I went on board with a special pass from the Embassy and, with the captain's authorisation, I made an announcement using the microphone, advertising the hotel's key points: two nightclubs with live music, the beach, giant barbecues with extra-large hamburgers or hot dogs, unlimited beer, for an all-inclusive package at 50 dollars per person.

In this way, I welcomed thousands of sailors, who had spent weeks at sea without drinking a drop of alcohol on board of mythical aircraft carriers such as the USS America, the USS Wisconsin, the USS John Young, the USS Prairie, the USS Tarawa, the USS Vandegrift, the USS Ranger, the USS Robert G. Bradley; and not to mention French ships, such as the Jean de Vienne and the Var frigates.

As far as the hotel was concerned, the rooms could accommodate up to six people, where Marines slept on mattresses directly on the floor. Room service was bringing huge daily takings by selling beers by crates of twenty-four cans, and the payment was done in cash. At that point, we didn't even look at the budget, because the turnover was speaking for itself.

Each time a ship arrived, I automatically invited the officers to a private barbecue in my apartment and the ritual was always the same: a welcome aperitif, mixed salads, grilled ribs and sausages, baked potatoes, French fries, frozen nougat with strawberries, wine, beer, Coca-Cola, and, to conclude, a cake in the shape of the American or French flag, depending on the nationality, that was sliced with a sabre, champagne and presentation of Emirati souvenir gifts for each officer, and family picture.

That's how I hit off with Douglas J. Katz, Admiral of the US Navy, who invited me for a meal aboard the USS America. I received the full honours, including the visit of the command centre connected to the Pentagon, with real-time explanations of all warships' movements, all nationalities combined, converging or moving around in the Gulf and the Indian Ocean. For weeks, we lived in a military atmosphere. Abu Dhabi had virtually become a city of singles, as most families had gone back to their countries of origin.

On August the 25th 1990, the UN Security Council voted a resolution allowing the use of force, and on January the 3rd 1991, President George Bush asked the American Congress to approve the use of force against Iraq, in accordance with the United Nations resolution. On January the 17th 1991, the operation "Desert Storm" started, to end on February the 28th 1991. In April 1991, the United Nations put a definitive end to the Gulf War through a resolution.

From then on, business with the traditional clientele was revived and life reclaimed its rights in Abu Dhabi. This new experience gave me the opportunity to meet people from another universe, Admiral Katz, with whom I kept in touch for several months; Admiral Gazzano, on the Var, in charge of the French Navy for the Indian Ocean; Major Girard, from the Jean de Vienne frigate; Major Kent W. Ewing, from the USS America; Major Paul D. Cash, from the Air Wing One, etc.

At the beginning of October, my friend **Bernard Lambert**, Deputy Managing Director and head of worldwide hotel operations for Méridien, gave me, with the approval of the Méridien board of directors, the opportunity to climb the corporate ladder by offering the job of **Vice-President Operations for the Middle East, based at the regional headquarters in Abu Dhabi.**

I accepted that promotion with great pleasure, which was the fruit of my labour, of my passion for the job and my determination to position the hotels I had managed as the customer's number one choice.

Besides, head office kept its word, which proved that the company had abiding principles towards its employees. During the farewell cocktail party, the owning company, in the name of the chairman, congratulated me warmly for this well-deserved promotion and for the huge work done at the hotel, while succeeding in restoring the trust and respect between Méridien and Abu Dhabi National Hotels Company.

The day after this event, Mr. Nasser Al Nowais received me personally in his office to thank me again, reward me with gifts and to say that I would always be welcome at Abu Dhabi National Hotels Company and that I could meet him at any time in case I needed advice.

Chapter 16
Abu Dhabi Regional office, November 1991
Full speed ahead

Vice-President Operations for the Middle East.

From General Manager, there I was, in command of a much bigger and far more complex ship, as VP Operations for the Middle-East. I became responsible for nine hotel operations: Abu Dhabi, Al Khobar, Cairo, Damascus, Lattakia, Heliopolis, Khartoum, Kuwait and the "Cruise ships on the Nile", under the name "Méridien Champollion".

I was based in Méridien regional headquarters, surrounded by extraordinary colleagues such as **Rudolf Jurcick**, Managing Director; **Ahmed Hassan**, Finance Director; **Ibrahim Sarwat**, Technical Director: **Raja Nasri**, Sales and Marketing Director; and the secretaries. Our team was quite cosmopolitan: ten employees, ten different nationalities. Nine hotels meant nine owners that I had to manage to ensure their satisfaction about the hotel and its profitability. I personally met them in their respective offices, to introduce myself and explain the overall objectives of the chain.

The Middle East, land of paradoxes. First paradox: in the aftermath of the Gulf War, there was a slight upturn and even a business recovery in this part of the world.

Second paradox: in a rather gloomy economic climate, we experienced an excellent performance of the hotel industry throughout the Middle East division. The crisis that had hit the Gulf countries triggered a new order. Upheaval in the balance of power, stabilisation of oil price, shifting of exchanges, of markets and of customers were the most visible signs. But in this turmoil, Méridien played its cards right. Not only did the hotels in this region record good results, but in addition, delivered results superior to those in previous years. I was lucky to manage and work with talented General Managers (most of them would later hold very important positions within the hotel industry). The hotels we managed were quite exceptional with regard to the products, locations and to the sophisticated owners traveling the world all year round, who had a very clear idea of what luxury, quality and service embodied. This forced us to always go higher in our standards to achieve excellence in our hotels in the Middle East, which was a central goal.

The constantly renewed quality of reception perpetuated the encounter inspired by France and the world. Our driving force was to consider that "Every bliss achieved is a masterpiece; the slightest error turns it awry". As hoteliers, we had to be perfect, as reception doesn't suffer from faux-pas. What would a hotel be if it did not make of each customer a guest, and of each stay a memory?

To be a point of reference in the city, our success rests on qualified and motivated staff. They alone can warrant the promise made to the client, they alone provide, through the services, a real art of living with a smile and human warmth, in contrast to the too serious.

The Middle East division, driven by great professionals, was usually marked out, within the company, by its management qualities and by the respect of head office's processes and guidelines.

In the Middle East, our way of working was based on principles of discipline and rigour, to develop the best in our respective hotels. The best means the respect for the group's brand image, for the standards in general, for quality communication within the hotel, market and owners; the latter paying us according to the achieved financial results and our fee structure related to the management contract. This meant that we had to be rigorous on the objectives to meet with regards to the annual budget.

The owners did not accept lightly a slippage of the results, which forced us to be creative, aggressive in terms of marketing actions, in brief, to be very business oriented.

With my friend and boss of the Middle East division, Rudolf Jurcick, we had the privilege of signing a management contract with Bahrain Prime Minister, His Highness Sheikh Khalifa bin Salman al-Khalifa, a member of the reigning Al Khalifa royal family, for the development of the five-star Méridien Bahrain hotel.

It consisted of 232 rooms and suites (including the royal suite, called "Amiri suite" that defied imagination in terms of opulence); an Indian restaurant, the "Nirvana"; a lounge restaurant the "Plantation"; a coffee-shop, "la Méditerranée"; a Mexican restaurant , the "Ranch"; a typically British bar with a fireplace, the "Burlington"; exceptional banquet rooms, which could accommodate 1,200 people (with a room exclusively reserved for the organization of Arab summits with ultra-sophisticated equipment); the Royal Sporting Club, competing with the one in Monaco, with pools, sauna, hammam, Jacuzzis, massage rooms, fitness centre, a beauty salon for men and women, and a private beach including all the possible and imaginable water activities.

Two months before the hotel opening, Sheikh Rashid, the Prime Minister's son-in-law and official representative of the hotel, with whom I had an excellent professional relationship, called to ask me to change the name of the hotel, because he believed that his hotel deserved the name "Royal Méridien", rather than "Méridien hotel". Surprised, I replied that this meant, for our company, the creation of another brand and therefore, I had to take advice from head office.

That day, I called Bernard Lambert in Paris, who hit the roof by responding negatively and by specifying that the development of another brand was out of the question. On further consideration, head office finally surrendered. A few hours later, I proudly informed Sheikh Rashid that, thanks to him, head office accepted not only his request, but also the creation of a new exclusive brand: "Royal Méridien".

The chain's forward march. In parallel to this prestigious development in Bahrain, Méridien kept moving forward with hotel openings in Chicago, Boston, San Diego, New Orleans, Vancouver and Dallas.

The development of the chain could only happen through profit to win the trust of new financial partners. We had to establish our credibility, and thus consolidate our results. Head office, divisions and hotels had to agree on a sustained management effort, or in other words, requirement of results.

Méridien was not a financial holding company, but a high-end company, committed to the quality of the service provided, the potential of its people and the improvement of its product. We had to push ahead to prepare the future.

That's how Méridien International Institute was created, for instance, with a view to developing and strengthening the training policy within the company. The purpose of the institute was to contribute to staff development and to ensure a high level of professionalism and expertise throughout all the hotels of the chain. And also to communicate a philosophy and values recognized by all: motivation, a sense of belonging, team spirit and the pride in the Méridien product and the service offered.

Different modules were developed to meet the objectives set by the chain and the hotels, such as:

- Institutional seminars aimed at the different management levels of the chain, to enable them to upgrade their skills and to improve their performance in the various hotel management disciplines.
- Field seminars intended for the divisions' and hotels' teams, led by specialists going in the field to be closer to local specificities and lead to action plans tailored to the economic, social and cultural environment.
- Support and advice actions provided at the request of hotels and regional divisions to cover fields as diverse as hotel openings, "Méridienisation", etc.

At Méridien, employees were welcomed into a universe where the dedication to excellence, mutual respect and constant improvement ruled. Our calling was certainly to offer to an international clientele the best services in over fifty luxury hotels, but also to share our ambition, namely that Méridien is a unique place where a special spirit blows, a subtle blend of French savoir-faire and of local tradition. And this, in all our hotels throughout the world.

Twenty years that we existed and were developing new establishments in perfect harmony with the commercial and tourist flows in the Air France stopovers. More particularly in the large international cities from Montreal to Rio, from Athens to New York, from Cairo to Singapore, from Dakar to Jakarta, from Bangkok to Melbourne.

Our development strategy was organised around three main poles: Europe, Asia and the United States. When the question was initially raised to find a new name for the chain, we opted for "Méridien" to underline its extremely international character – i.e. a true invitation to travel. The major objective was, in association with Air France, to bring good taste and refinement to the whole world, which are the image of France, to mix with it the local cultures to create a unique art of living that completely reassures the traveller.

Such is our job, perpetuating a tradition of services that dates back to the roots of the very word "hospitality". **Each customer is a guest and each stay a memory; that is our passion.**

We were conditioned to respect the promise made to the customer, i.e. ensuring his comfort and his full satisfaction, this had to be our constant worry. And to achieve this, men and women, who constituted the chain, had to activate all their talent and the whole power of their imagination.

Being a pioneer of Méridien, and to acknowledge my seniority within the group, head office, at the instigation of Bernard Lambert, offered me a week, full board, at Méridien Tokyo, trip included in business class for two. This superb and eye-opening trip was the prelude to a new adventure in Asia. Thank you so much again for your generosity, Bernard. Méridien was also about "the acknowledgement and respect of men".

One of the turning points for the company was to differentiate itself by adding the "Le" to our logo to become "Le Méridien", and thus redefine our brand image with Landor, international leader in brand development, and TBWA, advertising agency of worldwide renown. The latter developed a new advertising campaign for the group, illustrated by the artist Ken Maryansky.

With this evolution at the level of the brand, the objective was to be recognised within the club of the top five hotel companies in the world. In other words, that we were European with a French accent, that we respected the local culture whatever the latitude, that we focused on innovation, and that we took special care of our clientele. Our concern was also to adapt "green plans" in all our hotels: recycling, reduction, reuse and clean-up. Basic marketing reflex. We made the required efforts so that each hotel competed on creativity to better ride the green wave.

Unexpected "Trafalgar" in the company. End of 1994, there was a dramatic turn of events, or rather a "*Trafalgar*" in the company. **The English group Forte bought Le Méridien for 176 million pounds.**

Due to poor financial results caused by their agents' numerous strikes over the years, the national company Air France was forced to part with some of its sister companies, including Le Méridien.

Being bought by an English group caused a shock wave at the organization level of Le Méridien, but which was quickly cleared. In fact, this change matched an evolution in the company's positioning in the world; which allowed to secure, in time, opportunities for motivated and ambitious executives and employees.

Two months later, we were invited to Paris, then to London, for a conference where **Sir Rocco Forte**, with his exceptional charisma and class, spoke about his vision and industrial program for the Forte Group, which Le Méridien was now part of.

The Forte Group, listed on the London stock exchange, became the most important hotel group in the United Kingdom and a global leader, with 850 hotels and 600 restaurants in sixty different countries.

The hotels were divided as such:

- The exclusive and fully-owned Forte hotels, with hotels in London (The Savoy, The Waldorf, Grosvenor House, Hyde Park), in Spain: the Ritz in Madrid, in France: the Plaza Athénée in Paris, and in the United States: the Plaza Athénée in New York.
- Forte Heritage, consisting of a collection of hotels located in historical cities.
- Forte Posthouse, with hotels located on main highways.
- Forte Travelodge, with its two-star hotels established in the United Kingdom and in Ireland.
- Le Méridien, located in 50 countries.

As an independent company, Forte operated on different business levels, as far as the hotels were concerned: owner and manager, franchiser and administrator, which allowed them a maximum of flexibility in negotiation.

The chairman emphasized on development and synergies in marketing and commercialisation. For this, he had an aggressive sales force in the market, a network of 900 people and a centralised booking system connecting the world, offering a full range of services, but also career opportunities and a new organisation.

That's how Le Méridien regional office merged with the Forte regional office in Dubai.

Chapter 17

Dubai Regional office,
January 1995
With Sir Rocco on board

This situation allowed me to have a direct immersion with my colleagues from Forte, under the leadership of **Gerald Lawless**, Managing Director of the Middle East, who had become my new boss. Together, we were responsible for a network of eighteen Forte and Le Méridien hotels, which gave a new dimension to our group.

Gerald, who later became the chairman of Jumeirah International Group for the Dubai government, was a motivation for me, in the sense that I felt being welcome in the Forte team. With his charisma, his human qualities, his sense of duty and his respect for the company, he was a model of respectability. We have worked together on good terms, so that the integration and positioning of Forte/Le Méridien Group happened naturally.

Despite the culture change, there was never a gap in the language of the style "Us Forte" or "Us Le Méridien". We had perfectly understood that we needed to be complementary. The new deal: to work for the common good while taking into account the financial imperatives linked to the overall hotel performance, and more particularly of the fully-owned hotels, and by extension to protect the shareholders.

In this new organisation, I had to integrate in my mind that the main objective of London head office was to ensure that the share value was always attractive.

Things were also evolving at head office with the nomination of **Randolph Guthrie** as Group Managing Director and **Bernard Lambert** as Deputy Managing Director.

Unbelievable but true: one year later, we received a memo from Sir Rocco Forte announcing that over 50% of the shareholders had voted and accepted the takeover bid by **Granada Group**. In his message, he expressed his disappointment about the situation, acknowledged the efforts made by the teams to maximise the value of the market capitalisation of the group, he asked us to concentrate on our work, business as usual, and to provide the necessary collaboration to Granada Group.

The moral of this story is that we always have to work harder, so that the multinational corporations, listed on the stock exchange, get richer and that for the senior executives to continue working for the same group is not guaranteed on the long term.

Having said this, in my case, change was always positive. It allowed me to strengthen myself in terms of experiences, to discover new professional environments, to question myself and to face new challenges.

The disappointment was at its peaks within Forte Group and speculation started coming from everywhere because of the uncertain future. Naturally, the polemics were rife about the reputation of Granada Group.

That's how, following **Jules Prévost's** departure a few weeks later, I was appointed Vice-President Hotel Operations for the Asia-Pacific Group, based in the regional office in Hong Kong.

The Granada Group PLC, listed on the London stock exchange, consisted, in terms of business structure, of three very distinct sectors:

- Restaurants and services: Granada catering, Granada purchases, Granada road services on the motorways, Granada "Little Chef" restaurants, Granada special events, Granada vending machines, Granada fitness, Granada studio tours, Granada nightclubs, etc.
- Technologies: DVR, Granada business technology, Granada Media Group: Granada TV productions, YTTV productions, LWT productions. Brite programme, Granada Sky broadcasting, Granada films, Granada United-Kingdom broadcasting, etc.
- Hotels: fully-owned hotels, Le Méridien/Forte hotels under management, Le Méridien/Forte hotels as franchises, Heritage hotels, Posthouse hotels, Travelodge hotels.

Charles Allen, a talented man who played to win in business, was the mastermind of Granada Group. An exceptional man. For him, once everyone had agreed on the vision of a project, he set the direction and the management team had to achieve the specific objectives. He was convinced that to succeed in international business, the people in charge had to be autonomous and that the real buzz was to keep doing things differently.

Chapter 18

Hong Kong, January 1996

Supersonic speed

After a rock and roll landing, and a slalom skimming the Hong Kong buildings, here I was at the Kai Tak airport, therefore in Hong Kong, a huge international trade centre, one of the most important financial centres on the planet and one of the biggest container ports in Asia. Anecdotally, the annual volume in tonnage of Le Havre and Marseille ports was equivalent to ten days of port activity in Hong Kong!!!

I was fascinated by the idea of being in Asia, the largest and most populated continent in the world, where I was going to continue my path of knowledge through new horizons and cultures.

I was warmly welcomed by Mr. **Jean Gabriel Peres**, Le Méridien President for Asia-Pacific, and by his team. I immediately got into the swings of things with the operational responsibility for ten prestigious hotels: in Thailand, with Bangkok, Baan Boran in the Golden Triangle and Phuket; in Indonesia with Jakarta; in Singapore with two hotels (Orchard and Changi); in Australia with Melbourne; in New Caledonia with Nouméa; in Vanuatu with Port Vila; and finally in Japan with Tokyo.

Jean Gabriel, whom I had known for years, was an ESSEC graduate; he had started his career in Lagardère Group and EADS, before joining Le Méridien. Together, we worked in perfect harmony until the day he submitted his letter of resignation to head office, in April 1997, due to differences of opinion with the new leaders. He would later become CEO and Chairman of Mövenpick Group.

This combination of circumstances played in my favour, because in the wake of his resignation, I was appointed, by head office, President of the Asia-Pacific division, which meant that I was part of the board with my fellow presidents from the United States, Europe, Africa and the Middle East, under the supervision of **Bernard Lambert**, who became President for all Le Méridien hotels.

For my part, my new team was very cosmopolitan as I had, under my leadership, **Tom Barett**, Finance Vice-President, an Irish national; **Francis Killory**, Vice-President Development, an American, who spoke Chinese fluently; **Pierre Mallol,** Vice-President Technical Services, a Frenchman; **Frank Foster**, Vice-President Sales and Marketing, an Englishman; and the assistants and secretaries, who were all Chinese from Hong Kong.

Despite the transitions from Air France to Forte, and from Forte to Granada, I wanted to take the best from each experience, while creating a new dynamism to move forward; a dynamism made of openness, mutual respect, in which everyone worked to the best of their ability while making their contribution.

Three weeks after my nomination, **Charles Allen** called to tell me that he would be spending two weeks holiday at Le Méridien Phuket with his partner and that he'd like to meet me at Le Méridien Bangkok the day before he leaves for Phuket. On D-day, we met at seven pm in his suite, and after two or three minutes, he asked me about the evolution of business in Asia-Pacific, what my action plan was in terms of development, and my contribution to reach the group's objectives. Thank God I was fully armed with a useful presentation of our division's objectives and the potentialities in terms of expansion. On this last point, I explained that the existing method for development was quite restrictive, because we had to obtain head office's approval, which often caused a waste of time. To this, he replied:

– Michel, our new way of working is based on decentralisation, and, as Regional President of Asia-Pacific, it is your responsibility to bring business in compliance with the chain's standards.

Message well-received with delight. During that informal meeting, I felt confident and convinced that, with my team and my General Managers in the field, we were going to make things happen. I ensured Charles Allen of my full support, and we went for dinner in the hotel's Thai restaurant.

The next day, I offered to accompany him to Phuket. He replied:

– Michel, no formalities between us, I'm on holiday and I would be glad to see you again in London, within a month.

When he arrived in Phuket, the General Manager Rudolf Borgesius and his team were standing to greet him and show him, and his partner, the respect and consideration they deserved.

Ten days later, Charles Allen wrote me a letter thanking me for the arrangements made during his stay and re-confirmed his support for my mission.

In Asia, the request for a meeting with Chinese business men or women can be done over the phone or by fax, but you must avoid asking for a meeting during the Chinese New Year, which can fall in January or February; on this occasion, many Chinese take their holiday during that period, which is the equivalent of Christmas time for Christians.

The ideal way to meet business people is to benefit from a circle of influence with friends or asserted professional relations. It's called the "Guangxi". Meetings are always formal and professional, with no frills like in the Middle East. Business cards are always exchanged at the beginning of the meeting, with a nod of the head. To peruse the business card, printed in English and Chinese, is considered as a sign of respect. To make a hand gesture has to be done with the hand open and the palm towards the table and fingers should not point at your interlocutor. Never write with red ink, considered as unfriendly. Hong Kong professionals are sensitive to the length and the quality of the conversation, exclusively focused on business, which can sometimes be over in a few minutes. You should always wear formal clothes, dark suit and mandatory tie for men, and for women, a suit or a dress with a dark-coloured jacket.

I wanted to be fully integrated in the Chinese system and to have a hobby. Every morning, on the plaza of the cultural centre in Kowloon, whatever the weather, I devoted myself from 6 am to a Tai Chi session with my coach, whom I called Kun Shifo (Master). This ritual, practiced by many Hong Kong erson pavements or in parks, is a kind of choreography with extremely fluid movements, which allows the internal balance between the Ying and the Yang, in the mind and body alike, in order to relieve stress and improve health.

Taking into account the distance in Asia-Pacific, I had to organise and streamline my missions in a practical way, by grouping my trips together, from one point to another, except in special emergency. For example: Thailand meant a week-long mission during which I visited the hotels, met with the owners of hotels in Bangkok, Baan Boran, Phuket, and potential owners, with site visits. The owners of our hotels in Thailand were members of the high aristocracy, with **Khun Chalemband** (the word "Khun" replaces Mr. or Mrs. by mentioning the first name), owner of Le Méridien President in Bangkok and the Le Royal Méridien under construction; and **Khun Vinai**, owner of Le Méridien Phuket and the Baan Taling Nam hotel in Koh Samui and the Phuket Yacht Club.

In Indonesia, I was going directly to Jakarta to visit the hotel and meet **Mr. Bapak Probosutedjo**, owner and President Suharto's cousin, whom I had the privilege to greet twice. Mr. Probosutedjo, of Muslim faith, always received me with the honours, asking if I had a nice trip and if everything was perfect at the hotel; we had tea or coffee, then he invited me for lunch on his farm, a few kilometres away; we visited his tea and cloves plantations, which he exported as number one in the world. One day, he invited me to play tennis with him on an indoor court in the middle of his property. After Jakarta, I would take an Air Garuda flight, nicknamed "Air maybe" because of the company's bad reputation, to Bali, where we had a hotel under construction.

For Singapore, I needed two days to visit and meet the owners of our two hotels in Orchard Road and in Changi. The owner of

Le Méridien Orchard Road was called **Ong Beng Seng**, but for his circle and for some people, he was OBS, considered as a tycoon, because of his incredible wealth. The owner in Changi was **Miss NG**, who owned with her family part of the city of Singapore!!! She was punctual and polite, but always under pressure. Hardly seated, she bombarded me with questions about the hotel's performance and the meeting lasted, as a rule, about fifteen minutes, because for these Chinese, a minute of their time could represent several thousand dollars!

For the Pacific countries, I combined three destinations in one single trip: Australia, with Le Méridien Rialto Melbourne, where the owner was a local institution; Vanuatu, with Le Méridien Port Vila, whose owner was OBS; and Le Méridien Nouméa in New Caledonia, owned by the General Council. I visited Le Méridien Pacific Tokyo, with its 954 rooms, considered as the biggest hotel in Tokyo, quarterly, because of the nature of our contract, based on a franchise.

Besides these business trips, I was forced to attend meetings at head office in London, about every six weeks. The agenda was invariably focused on financial results, compared to our objectives, development and transfers, promotions of some General Managers, ideas to be developed and stock market indicators.

Often, after a hard day's work in the presence of head office executives, division Presidents and Bernard Lambert, Charles Allen invited us for dinner in one of our London hotels. The ritual was always the same: meeting at eight pm sharp at the agreed location for an aperitif that lasted half an hour; at eight thirty, we sat down to eat and once the first plate served, Charles opened the discussion such as: "Where do we stand in the United States?" And so on for each division, which meant that we had to be well prepared; at half past ten, after coffee and liqueurs, everyone said good-bye and see you soon. For my part, I set off again the following day for a twelve hour trip back to Hong Kong. Saying this, each month, I spent about 80% of my time travelling for the hotels, for the owners and to discover new opportunities for the Asia-Pacific division.

Over the following months, we had plenty to do with the construction and the pre-opening of:
- A second hotel in Bangkok, Le Royal Méridien Bangkok, with 350 rooms.
- A second hotel in Tokyo, Le Méridien Grand Pacific Tokyo, with 884 rooms.
- Le Méridien Jakarta Tower, with 103 rooms.
- Le Méridien Tahiti, with 150 rooms.
- Le Méridien Bora Bora, with 100 overwater bungalows.
- Le Méridien Isle of Pines, in New Caledonia, with 20 bungalows and 9 rooms.
- Le Méridien Nirvana Bali, with 278 rooms.

For all these hotels, we depended on a technical assistance contract, which consisted of bringing our hotel expertise in monitoring the work with consultants, builders, project managers and, of course the owners. Furthermore, we were responsible for the pre-opening and opening phases, for equipment selection, for staff selection which involves training and assessment of each candidate, for operational procedures, business strategy, marketing, pre-opening budget, etc.

When the hotel was ready for operation, a management contract became effective for the duration of the said contract, which was in principal 10 to 15 years, in the best case scenario.

The year 1997 was marked by the Asian crisis that had dramatic consequences on the economies in the region. The crisis was triggered in Thailand, with the devaluation of the baht, which caused a domino effect on the South East Asian countries. The cause of this crisis originated from a decline in exports and the lack of rigor on the government's part, as well as the actions taken by the banks. In fact, investors realised that Thailand's number of short term debts exceeded their stock of foreign currencies. Furthermore, the system highlighted the fact that there was no monitoring mechanism, which meant that a lot of decisions were made in private, without a trace in official documents! All of a sudden, the business market was extremely affected, with drastic decisions taken in all the countries concerned.

Early 1998, we signed Le Méridien Medan on the Island of Sumatra in Indonesia (230 rooms).

In what I call quick wins, I made an incredible deal by taking control of two prestigious hotels in Thailand, which were managed by a prominent Asian group.

The story goes as follows: one evening, I decided to call Khun Vinai, who was also the owner of the aforementioned hotels: respectively in Baan Taling Ngam on Koh Samui Island, and the Phuket Yacht Club. In a direct and relaxed manner, while apologizing for disturbing him, I asked him:

– Khun Vinai, I've heard that you've had some concern with the hotel management company that manages your two hotels. If that's the case, would you be eventually interested in offering us the management?

– First of all, you never bother me and secondly, could you visit both hotels incognito and, upon your return, come and see me in my office in Bangkok?

My answer:

– Thank you Khun Vinai for giving me the opportunity of visiting these two properties. I can make myself available from tomorrow.

– Fine, I'm taking care of your bookings and above all, be discrete.

I thanked him again. The following week, I went to his office to get the deal for both hotels. A month and a half later, both hotels became respectively Le Méridien Baan Taling Ngam and Le Méridien Phuket Yacht Club, which earned me the congratulations from Charles Allen, who had decided to come back to Phuket for a second stay with his partner.

Similarly, and in connection with my developer, Francis Killory, we signed an excellent contract in Taipei with **Mr. Chen**, the owner and the brother-in-law of the President of Taiwan, formerly Formosa, which was part of the four Tiger Nations, along with Hong Kong, South Korea and Singapore.

Le Méridien Taipei was a hotel that Mr. Chen was committed to renovating from top to bottom, which he did with the help of the technical service from our Hong Kong office. The day of the inauguration, in presence of President Lee, Philippe Morbelli, Pastry Chef of Le Méridien Bali and former Fauchon employee in Paris, made a truly exceptional cake in honour of President Lee. At the end of the meal, the latter made a very friendly speech to thank Le Méridien Hong Kong team for their enthusiasm, their professionalism and their support for the creation of a new flagship hotel in Taipei, and, of course, a special mention for the sublime cake.

In their way of life, the Taiwanese generally enjoy good food, good French wines and good company. Each time I went to visit the hotel, and the Chen owners, it was imperative to have lunch with them and to appreciate the dishes paired with French wines, previously brought at room temperature. These were always great moments, full of refinement and courtesy. Having said this, we had come a long way, because the negotiations of the management contract had been a moment of bravery, where for days and nights, we negotiated every word in the contract. It must be said that we had in front of us a Chinese Jew lawyer from New-York!!!

With all the openings in perspective, my team and I were often requested to bring logistic support to the General Managers who were, I must say, great professionals. Most of them came from other Le Méridien hotels throughout the world and we were joined in the passion and respect for our job, which inspired us.

For Le Méridien Grand Pacific Tokyo, whose investment amounted to a billion dollars, by our technical assistance contract, we had to visit the hotel under construction and submit an assignment report.

To perform this mission, I had to send a letter to the president of the owning company one month in advance to ask for permission to come and carry out our mission on such day… A written reply from the president confirmed the day of our visit, the reception at the airport, at the hotel and at the construction site.

On D-day, Steiner, Technical Director at head office in Paris, and I went to the site, with a car and chauffeur from the hotel, at three pm. We were welcomed by the site manager, who wore a dark suit, a tie and a hard hat. He received us by bowing respectfully and pronouncing our names in the Japanese way: "Noblet san" and "Steiner san". Then we were invited to go into a small room to remove our jacket and our shoes. In front of each of our seats, there was a wooden box with our name on it and with inside slippers, a spotless white coat and a brand new safety helmet – with our name on it– that we had to wear during the site visit. Each place we visited, hallways and aisles, were all protected by plastic sheets and when we came across workers, they stopped to greet us Japanese-style. I must specify that each worker wore a uniform of distinct colour that matched his trade, with tie, white gloves and hard hat!

After our marathon visit that lasted three to four hours, we came back to the small room to find that our shoes had been polished and our jacket placed on a coat hanger. When we got back to the hotel, we had to think about our report, because on the following day we had to meet the owners in a conference room to review the situation. Invariably, Steiner would tell me:

– Michel, I have a problem.

– Yes, what's wrong?

– I have nothing to report, everything is perfect in the conduct of the work!

Among the Japanese, I can say that there's no room for mistakes due to their perfectionism. The next day, we had an appointment at eleven am in one of the lounges of Le Méridien Pacific, located in the Shinigawa district. To be punctual, we arrived at ten forty five to note that the owning company was already there with the president, the General Manager and no less than a dozen senior executives who greeted us Japanese-style. After the usual courtesies, once tea and coffee had been served, at eleven o'clock sharp, the sliding door opened to reveal a boardroom consisting of a large table, fifteen armchairs on one side and two on the other side, two meters away, the translator being seated at the end of the table.

In Japan, even if your interlocutor has a perfect command of Shakespeare's language, the presence of an interpreter is mandatory. The discussion takes place almost exclusively between the representatives of the respective companies. If one assistant wishes to speak, he has to ask the chairman's permission. Generally, no response was formulated concretely, answers are made after a subsequent consensus between the Japanese executives, which are then confirmed in writing a week later.

After the meeting, which lasted no longer than an hour, we were invited for lunch in one of the hotel's Japanese restaurants, to enjoy delicious dishes of sushi, sashimi and the famous Kobé beef that we had around a Teppanyaki table. As I wanted to have additional information about the organisation and the hotel opening, scheduled for September the 8th 1998, I always made arrangements to invite the two president's direct assistants to have a drink at the hotel bar around five. This invitation was particularly appreciated, as for all Japanese, it is fashionable to get tanked up before heading home. The scenario was always the same. The ice-breaker was restricted to a beer, Asahi-style, then for the second, third and fourth drink, our Japanese friends could go from beer to port, to scotch on the rocks, via hard alcohol or otherwise, which meant that by the third drink, they were in tune to give me a maximum of details. I remained clear-headed, because, knowing the score, I was sticking to beer.

The opening of the hotel took place, as scheduled, on September the 8th 1998.

A fortnight before the official opening, I received an invitation stating the details of the ceremony, minute by minute, the dress code, namely a black suit, white shirt, black tie and white gloves!

At zero hour, I was welcomed by the president of the owning company, the hotel General Manager and hostesses, wearing a kimono, who escorted me to a seat, with my name on it, on a platform erected for the inauguration.

To the left of the podium, there were hundred or so photographers and TV cameras to catch this important moment. On cue, a hostess wearing a kimono spoke in the microphone in French, English and Japanese, saying that, prior to the official inauguration, we had to proceed with the rehearsal of the ribbon cutting and invited, by naming them, eight personalities to come and join her. We were all behind the ribbon, facing the media, to the right of our respective hostesses, who were holding a cushion with a pair of gold-coloured scissors on it. The hostess with the microphone told each of us the way to proceed: take the scissors with the right hand, then cut the ribbon held between the thumb and the index finger of the left hand. Then, the same hostess, and still in the three languages, asked us to do a second attempt by repeating her instructions word for word!!!

After the usual speeches, the famous ribbon, symbolising the official opening of the hotel, was cut according to the rule book, before we could enter and visit the hotel, ready to welcome customers.

Just like the Japanese reputation, all the hotel's departments were operating flawlessly, giving the impression that the luxurious five-star hotel had been operational for several years.

Next opening, Bali, the Indonesian pearl, a sunny paradise, combining beauty, spirituality, villages each more fascinating than the other, with its festivals, its temples and its religious processions occurring all year round. It is a unique tourist destination where a change of scene is guaranteed. In the middle of rice fields and surrounded by an 18-hole golf course (created by Greg Norman), Le Méridien Nirvana, overlooking the Indian Ocean and the famous Tanah Lot temple, consisted of 278 rooms, conference rooms, three restaurants, a bar and a magnificent swimming pool with waterfalls, a fitness centre and spa, where customers could treat themselves to hedonistic pleasures they dreamt of.

The hotel was managed by **Gérard Hôtelier**, aptly named, an exceptional hotelier by his professionalism and his charisma. Four days before the opening, while I was working with Gérard on the final details, we were startled by strange noises coming from outside. We left the office to find a dozen employees, armed with large bamboo, hitting the hotel walls and spraying them with water to ward off evil spirits from the establishment. When they saw us, they came to spray us to purify us, because everyone had to be purified, and, to top it all off, they sacrificed two sheep and chickens in front of the hotel!

Bali, a predominantly Hindu island, situated in the world's largest Muslim country, is focused on the practice of religion permeating all aspects of society, including superstitious beliefs. Unconditionally, every day, women leave offerings in the family temple and in public places. In Bali, gods, ancestors, spirits and demons are characters that influence everyday life and therefore offerings are made daily as a sign of respect, gratitude and to appease any evil spirit. The most usual offerings are flowers, rice, and/or small cakes, and incense sticks.

On the day of the inauguration, I wore the traditional batik shirt. After the recitation of the Quran's verses, I had to make a speech in which I praised Mr. **Aburizal Bakrie, owner and chairman of Bakrie Group**, for the completion of Le Méridien Nirvana complex, which would contribute to the tourist, economic and social development of Bali. The festivities for this event lasted the better part of the night and guests could enjoy a music festival, dances and songs, where several artists demonstrated their vocal talent. In another part of the hotel, in an open air amphitheatre, a cultural festival was taking place for the hotel clientele, with a full orchestra composed of twenty-five musicians. The percussions, mainly based on the Gamelan (the gong), accompanied the very choreographic traditional dances, such as the legong, the most graceful Balinese dance; the Kecak, known for its spellbinding atmosphere; and the Shanghyang and the Barong-Randga, representing the battle between good and evil.

On a culinary level, many specialities are influenced by India, Malaysia and China. They result from several centuries of migrations and trade with fearless sailors. Thus: curries, smoked duck or chicken, babi kecap (pork stew), babi (stuffed suckling pig and roasted on a spit), etc.

My favourite dish was the nasi goreng, a fried rice dish with spicy ingredients and served with small chicken skewers, called "sate", and a fried egg. When I went to Bali on a two-day mission, it meant, in terms of meals, four nasi gorengs, two lunches and two dinners!

The most singular hotel opening, besides Tahiti and Bora Bora, was the one on Isle of Pines in New Caledonia, located in Melanesia, 17,000 kilometres away from mainland France.

On Isle of Pines, time does not count. Called "the jewel of the Pacific" by some, and considered as the island closest to paradise by the Japanese coming to stay on their honeymoon. Being part of the French territory and linked to Nouméa, New-Caledonia's capital, Isle of Pines offers a pristine nature, with white sandy beaches, crystal clear water, without any building or billboard, in short, untouched nature. The inhabitants are Kanaks, French citizens.

Le Méridien Isle of Pines, located in the magnificent bay of Oro, a natural lagoon protected by a coral reef, is nestled in a coconut grove lined with a quasi-individual small beach for each client. The hotel offers luxurious bungalows with maximum privacy for wealthy customers, a restaurant, a tropical-style bar and a swimming pool.

The hotel was the fruit of an association between the Presidency of the Rally for Caledonia in the Republic, represented by Mr. **Jacques Lafleur**, and the owners of the land, on a 50/50 basis. The day of the inauguration, in the presence of official authorities, the Kanak land owners and guests, it was necessary to submit to the tribe's ritual by doing what is called **the custom**, a thousand year old rite, a proof of good manners (*"savoir-vivre"*)and a way to honour the hosts. It's about bowing down in front of the tribal leader, while offering him a pack of tobacco, a piece of cloth and a banknote. It doesn't have much value but it's a highly symbolic recognition and an obligation to express to the tribal leader the motives and intentions of the visit.

In French Polynesia, the two hotels we were developing with the *Compagnie Générale des Eaux*, as owners, were in Tahiti and in Bora Bora.

Le Méridien Tahiti, located at the edge of one of the most beautiful beaches of Pnaauia, with its 138 rooms and 12 bungalows, had a breath-taking view of the ocean and the Moorea Island, as well as all the sports and recreational activities of a seaside resort in its cultural environment.

Le Méridien Bora Bora, located 250 kilometres from Tahiti, found itself on the tip of a small Polynesian islet, in a lagoon with turquoise water, and was reachable only by boat from the airport.

The site was simply magical with its 100 bungalows on stilts, and in each room, a glass floor to enjoy the seabed. Bora Bora, the pearl of the Pacific (named "Pora Pora" by Captain Cook, becoming later Bora Bora), is a mythical tourist destination, marked by the presence of American troops during the second World War, who set up a military base and built a runway on the island.

The inaugurations carried out a few months apart were logistically based, more or less, on the same model as the Bali and Isle of Pines inaugurations. This said, the charismatic **Gaston Flosse**, President of the Government of the French Polynesia and authentic Gaullist (great friend of Jacques Chirac and a Freemason), spoke there with fervour and joy, surrounded by his courtiers and by women who covered him with the traditional wreaths of flowers each time he took part in an event.

For the Tahiti and Bora Bora inaugurations, we were treated to performances of sensual and frenzied Tahitian dances under the coconut trees. In the evening, Gaston Flosse invited us to his home residence for a small reception, with no fewer than 1,000 people! On that occasion, and as an aside during the evening, I asked him:

– Mr. President, what is your secret for always being in good shape and looking young?

– Mr. President (rolling his r's), firstly, every morning, very early, I go for a swim to the Venus Point of the island, and secondly, I'm lucky to have a young wife!!!

For the opening of the five-star Le Royal Méridien Bangkok – ideally located in the heart of the city, the business and financial centre and high-class boutiques, the 37-storey hotel consisted of 381 rooms and suites, a royal club, four restaurants with different themes, two bars, a fitness centre, boutiques and a convention centre that could welcome up to two thousand people. The owner, **Khun Chalemband**, had decided not to organise any events owing to a serious accident that had occurred on the building site and had caused the death of four workers. And so, as a sign of respect for those workers and their respective families, the opening took place in the strictest simplicity, benefiting from synergies of Le Méridien President, adjacent to Le Royal Méridien, belonging to the same owner.

What I remember from all these openings. They naturally contributed to the standing of the group in terms of expansion and optimization of financial results of the Asia-Pacific Division; our credibility vis-à-vis our owners, who, directly or indirectly, took advantage of a better market visibility and of the added-value inherent to global actions carried out by Granada Group. In general, the tireless efforts of our commitment to quality, service, adherence to standards and norms, innovation, passion for excellence, the passion of our sales teams, the desire to develop other operations in new markets, teamwork, the war on unnecessary expenditure and our refusal for mediocrity, have allowed us to rise by playing an essential role in our company, but also a role for the prestige and reputation of the countries in which we evolved.

Personally, I was working every day with determination and pleasure, either in my office in Hong Kong or through my travels from one place to another. I was galvanized by the desire to do well, to satisfy our owners who gave us their trust to manage their hotels representing tens or hundreds of millions of dollars, to meet, discuss and bring support to my teams in the field, who created the reputation and prestige of the company, to immerse myself in the environment and to meet diverse people, politicians, religious dignitaries, villagers or city people.

I always considered that the General Manager of each hotel was the most important person in our company. I loved visiting our hotels from top to bottom, which allowed me to appreciate the running of the hotel, to greet the staff I met on my way, to share a meal with these employees in the staff cafeteria. To fit in the social environment was for me very rewarding and motivating and helped to commit myself even more. Being in contact with the staff and listening to them was a pleasure for me, and often an emotion that enabled me to have my finger on the pulse of the operations, but also to reinforce my message on the role each person was playing, from the bottom to the top of the hierarchy. That's what we call complementarity. Employees often did the honour of inviting me into their homes with all their family members. Absolute and exciting pleasure.

One day, when I was in the Golden Triangle (meeting point between Thailand, Laos and Myanmar, on the edge of the Mekong river), at Le Méridien Baan Boran hotel, regarded as the best exotic hotel in Thailand, one of the employees invited me to his wedding, to be held in his village, located in the high hills of Chiang Saen.

After the ritual ceremony, we were treated to lunch in a long straw hut, raised because of the insects and snakes, in which all the guests were seated around a large table full of typical Thai dishes. Being a guest of honour, they insisted that I sat between the groom and the bride, who wore traditional clothes!

Apart from the groom who spoke English, the rest of the assistance spoke Thai, which didn't stop us from having fun, communicating through gestures, smiles, bursts of laughter and the translations done by the groom.

The meal I enjoyed eating with my fingers was varied and original: noodle soup with meat balls, papaya salad, fried grass-hoppers with chili and herbs, fried scorpions, chicken cooked in coconut milk, dried squid, sweet potatoes and corn on the cob roasted on a wood fire, sautéed vegetables, sticky rice served in a woven basket, and fried rice with vegetables and prawns.

Then followed the desserts of exotic fruits: mangoes, papayas, mangosteen, jack fruit, durian and bananas. All washed down with fruit juice and beer, and to crown the reception, before a series of souvenir pictures, I got to taste a whisky macerated in a bottle containing a snake!

I drank it and realised that I was still alive after having greeted and thanked the whole family. Incredible experience that I got the opportunity to renew when I decided to build and sponsor a school for the High Hills community, which was the subject of festivities during the inauguration, where this whisky was once again *de rigueur*!

As everyone knows, at that time, Hong Kong was the last Chinese territory occupied by Great Britain, a colonial saga, which had started close to a century and half ago, and ended on July the 1st 1997. On that day, I attended the official retrocession of Hong Kong to China. It took place at the Convention & Exhibition Centre, in the presence of President **Jiang Zemin**, of Queen Elisabeth's son Prince Charles, of Sir Chris Pattern, the last Governor of Hong Kong, and of Tung Chee Wa, the Chief Executive, appointed by the Chinese Government.

The most touching of the ceremony was to see, on one side, the British flag, the Union Jack, come down, and on the other side, the Chinese flag go up. By late afternoon, I saw sail past my balcony the Royal yacht, "The Queen Elisabeth", leaving the port of Hong Kong, greeted by thousands of boats, which escorted it to open sea. From then on, Hong Kong took the status of special administrative region of the People's Republic of China, under the concept "one country, two systems", and this for a period of fifty years, date when the concept would become "one county, one system"!

On November the 26th 1998, after 18 hours spent travelling, here I am in Louisiana, on the banks of the Mississippi River,

in New Orleans, birthplace of jazz, a city marked by French colonial heritage. I was invited to participate in the annual General Managers' convention. As luck would have it, I met there my son Ralph, who was working in the catering department of Le Méridien, before being transferred the following month to Le Méridien Dallas, as Catering Director.

To start the meeting on a good beat, we were welcomed by fifty or so members of a Gospel choir from the Catholic Church, who sang cheerful and rhythmic songs. Then there was the city mayor's welcome speech. The main topic of our conference was focused on the main directions to take during 1999.

The objectives? Permanently increase customer satisfaction and loyalty, but also the teams' capacity to attract the best employees in the hospitality industry and to create a partnership between the different functions at head office and employees in the field. All this was summed up in one sentence: "to introduce more passion in the business" which matched my belief.

To bring our three-day seminar to a close, the hotel management, in collaboration with local authorities, organised a special *Mardi Gras* style carnival, exclusively for Le Méridien participants with marching bands and all the folklore that went with it, not forgetting the traditional pearl necklaces that we had to throw at the crowd cheering us. The extremely festive evening ended very late.

Being in New Orleans as a Frenchman made me thinking in the sense that I was eager to discover and acquire memories. My son Ralph, as the perfect guide, took us to the historical centre, called the French Quarter ("*le Vieux Carré*"). There, I could admire architecture of Spanish-influence, with its wrought iron balconies, its inner courtyards and its patios with their fountains, all imbued with serenity. This peaceful atmosphere was completely different at night, especially on Bourbon Street, where cafés and jazz clubs got the upper hand. For jazz purists, the most typical place is undoubtedly Preservation Hall, where musicians are no less than 80 years old. But what a show!!! Having said this, you have to be patient to get in because, for each two-hour session, you have to queue. We did one excursion after another, with a two-hour boat ride on the mythical Mississippi River, with a paddlewheel riverboat from the Natchez Company. We carried on with the Arts District, the fashionable area, restaurants where gastronomy is characterised by a real festival of various Creole flavours: the Jambalaya, the crayfish, the gumbo, rice with sea food, etc. Served with the unmissable and famous Tabasco sauce, made in Louisiana, and found on every table.

Three days later, I left New Orleans for a stop-over in Las Vegas, before heading back to Hong Kong to negotiate two contracts: Le Méridien Sydney, with 350 rooms and suites in the heart of the city, near the Opera and Harbour Bridge, whose inauguration was scheduled two months before the opening ceremony of the Summer Olympic games in 2000; and the Le Méridien Kuala Lumpur, with 420 rooms and suites, with a unique location in KL Central, and whose opening was scheduled in 2003.

Beginning of March 1999, I suggested to head office to take over **Peter Cardnell's** position in Dubai, who had replaced **Gerald Lawless** at the head of the Middle East and Western Asia division.

This transfer was accepted not without difficulty by my hierarchy in London. This allowed me to move closer to Europe, to some extent, and to my daughter Nadège, who worked at Le Méridien Dubai Airport. And, the icing on the cake was that I was going to discover new territories, such as India, Sri Lanka, Pakistan and Iran, which had just recently been linked to the Middle East Division.

I left Asia-Pacific with other projects in the pipeline, for my successor.

Chapter 19
Dubai, May 1999
Cruising speed and turbulences

After the usual handover formalities with my colleague **Peter Cardnell**, there I was, in charge of the Middle East and Western Asia division. I was reunited with my secretary, **Shahenaz**, originally from Mauritius, and part of my former team. Spearheaded by **Ashock**, Vice-President Finance and Development, who had dual Indian and British nationality; **Russel Sharpe**, an Englishman, Vice-President Sales and Marketing; **Sarwat Ibrahim**, Technical Vice-President, of Egyptian nationality; **Robert Fadel**, Vice-President Operations, who had Egyptian and Swedish dual nationality. With the assistants and the inbound/outbound centralised reservation, we were eighteen.

Firstly, I listened to people around me, I visited all our operational hotels, and those under construction and I met every owner.

Secondly, I did a marathon at the double between Saudi Arabia, Iran, Oman, Jordan and Lebanon.

I had the product in mind, which enabled me to define, with my team and the General Managers, a SWOT analysis, which is a way of identifying the strengths, weaknesses, opportunities and threats of each hotel within the division. Consequently, we came up with a global action plan about strategies inherent to marketing, turnover, general expenses, operations, hotel pre-openings, workforce, owners, and in the end, our contribution to bookings of other hotels of the chain.

Our division employed 10,000 people, across all our hotels, representing 50 nationalities, mainly Asian, Australian, African, Middle-Eastern, European and American. A programme had to be structured to take all 18 operational hotels into account, split into four sub-regions:

- The Gulf: the United Arab Emirates (Dubai with three hotels and Abu Dhabi), Kuwait, Saudi Arabia (Al Khobar and Jeddah);
- Egypt (Cairo, the Pyramids and Heliopolis);
- Lebanon(Beirut); Jordan (Amman); Syria (Damascus and Lattakia);
- India (New Delhi, Pune, Bangalore).

In terms of pre-openings, we had a lot to do:

- Le Méridien Mina Seyahi in Dubai, 211 five-star rooms with its marina and its 1,200 meter long private beach. The hotel enjoyed an idyllic setting, while being close to the city.
- Le Méridien Makadi Bay in Hurghada with 918 four-star hotels, nestled between a mountain range and dunes on the

edge of the Red Sea, a region renowned for its aquatic life and its coral reefs.

- Le Royal Méridien Tower in Cairo, five-star, with 850 rooms and royal suites, two floors of restaurants and bars revolving on the roof; it was enjoying the best location in Cairo, by the Nile.
- Le Méridien Sharm el-Sheikh, with 440 five-star rooms, superbly located by the Red Sea, close to the shops.
- Le Royal Méridien beach resort and spa in Dubai, with 500 five-star rooms; situated along Jumeirah private beach and surrounded by lavish and beautifully kept gardens.
- Le Royal Méridien Mumbai, offering 171 rooms, located in the new shopping complex close to the airport, and Le Méridien Juhu beach, situated on the outskirts of Mumbai.
- Le Méridien Cochin resort and convention centre, in Kerala, with 151 rooms and suites, located in the heart of lush gardens, with a view of the picturesque backwaters.

In terms of development, our program also included negotiations in Doha, Muscat, Tehran, Beirut, Mecca, Medina, a second hotel in Jeddah with Bouygues Group, a second hotel in Heliopolis, Hurghada for the Sheraton takeover, Ain Sokhna, Alexandria, Goa, Kathmandu, Jaipur and Chennai.

For the latter, Ashock and I achieved a master stroke by directly meeting the owner who had already signed a management contract with an American hotel company, known and recognized internationally, and whose opening was scheduled two months later. But according to the information we had in India, we knew that the professional relations between the hotel company in question and **Mr. Periasamy**, the hotel owner, had become a source of conflict. With quite some nerve, we met the owner in his tiny site office, who, after some logical hesitation, agreed to listen to us. The atmosphere changed when he invited us to have tea, becoming much friendlier. Mr. Periasamy was respectively an Economics Professor at the University Of Maryland in the United States, and the owner of about ten universities in the State of Chennai. Interested by our offer, he realised that we already had three hotels in India, that we belonged to an English group listed on the London Stock Exchange, and, icing on the cake, that we had a sales service based in Mumbai. Forty five minutes later, he told us that, for him, it was OK, but that we would have to convince the members of his board of directors, which he convoked on that same day at five pm in a hotel lounge.

At the appointed hour, Ashock and I went straight to the lounge to find the board members already seated around a large table. Once Mr. Periasamy, the chairman of the owning company, had introduced everyone, he asked me to introduce Le Méridien Group. I stood up and did my little number to twenty or so minority shareholders, and Ashock, in his capacity of Indian from New Delhi, gave additional details, related to the synergies and economies of scale that we could achieve with our existing hotels and the upcoming ones. The deal seemed to be well underway until one of the shareholders asked a tricky question.

– Mr. President, what more can you offer compared to the American hotel chain, considered as a renowned operator within the hotel industry?

– Mr. Chairman, honourable shareholders, allow me to say that Le Méridien is a European hotel chain, with a French accent, that respects the local culture and is established in the biggest international cities from Rio de Janeiro to Los Angeles, from New York to Athens, from the West Indies to Africa, from Cairo to Dubai, from Singapore to Melbourne, and soon from Mumbai to Bangkok. Of French origin, Le Méridien is all about France at the instigation of Jacques Chirac, a great friend of your country. Le Méridien also symbolises, all over the world, good taste and refinement. Our job, as hoteliers, is to create a unique art of living, wherever we are, something that differentiates us from competition. Le Méridien here, in your hotel, would mean visits from great chefs and pastry chefs, organization of gourmet weeks, training modules, set-up of fashion shows with great French designers, classical music concerts, etc.

After twenty minutes, the chairman stood up, thanked me and said that he would get back to us at the end of the evening. At around eight pm, he called us to confirm that the board of directors was pleased with the prospect of being associated with Le Méridien. And, amazingly enough, he invited us to attend, the following morning at 3am, a pre-opening ceremony with his family and guests.

This ceremony, called "Puja", is a Hindu ritual that had to be done absolutely the following day, because it was set as auspicious by the Brahman priests. At three o'clock sharp, we were on the scene to attend to the aforesaid ceremony. Professor Periasamy invited us to sit near his family, opposite a rectangular hearth directly on the ground, while listening to spiritual invocations formulated by several priests.

There was also a sacred cow, richly adorned, representing divinity. The professor invited us to take part in the ritual, with his family, which consisted in offering freshly picked flowers and grains of rice to the divinity, while circling three times around the cow. Then, we escorted the cow inside the hotel, going around the lobby, the hallway, the restaurants, the bars and finally the coffee shop. There, the peaceful cow was milked and her milk was offered to us, served in small silver cups to savour it.

Then we went back to our initial positions. The ceremony lasted until nine in the morning, at which time we were invited to share a meal with all the guests.

By performing the "Puja", the professor and his family immersed themselves in this power, honouring the God associated with it. This way, they strived to identify with the divine principle by embodying it. As he thanked us for our visit, the professor asked us to send him the management contract, which he signed two weeks later at a press conference in Chennai, in our presence. While the "Puja" rites were going on, the American hotel company's logo, previously engraved in a granite block outside the hotel, was disappearing!

The day of the official inauguration, in the presence of dignitaries (including the CM, the chief minister of the State of Chennai, with its 65 million inhabitants), pompous speeches were made in a formal order. Each speaker received from Professor Periasamy, on an honorary basis, a traditional scarf commemorating the event. After the official reception, there was a giant banquet in the large lounge. Then there were the "bharata natyam" sacred dances done by a dancer who performed the "la nritya" rule contained in body gestures and facial expressions for the outbreak of emotions. A highly appreciated show, whose music is supported by a "nattu-vanar" creating a rhythm with small cymbals, by a percussionist with his "mridangam"and a flute player.

In the evening, a reception organised in the gardens, around the hotel pool, was reserved for family, friends and Le Méridien team. At the end of a copiously toasted meal and after the gifts' presentation to Mr. and Mrs. Periasamy, the atmosphere was so festive and joyful that the professor incredibly found himself in the pool, under thunderous applause!

Still today, when we meet in India, Paris, London or Dubai, Professor Periasamy never fails to tell those around him:

– Michel is the only man in the world who had the audacity to throw me in the water with my clothes on!

With my dream team, we were operating like a "Caterpillar", with our unchanging formula of expanding the boundaries.

Another funny event was the opening of Le Méridien Makadi Bay in Egypt, a huge hotel complex with a pool considered as the largest in Africa.

The owner was called **Mahmoud El Sharkawy**. He was aptly named, because he really was a shark! This man, who was the owner of the Mercedes assembly plant for Egypt, very friendly initially, would become red-faced when we asked him to approve the pre-opening budget, which amounted to one million dollars. This was fully justified in view of the hotel's size: 924 rooms, restaurants, bars, a nightclub, a marina, a sports club, the logistics, and last but not least, the 800 employees we had to train. At each of our meetings, it was rough and tumble, but as gentlemen, we respected and appreciated each other and we always made up in the end.

Alongside our daily duties, we kept the sacred fire alight at the level of the hotels' management by visiting them regularly, by galvanizing our sales offices to sell more, by developing strategies and synergies between hotels, and by identifying development opportunities on new markets. We were also very close to our owners, whom we met every month. It was about keeping them informed regarding the group's activities, about what the chain did for them, all this to maximise their hotel's return on investment. For me, an owner is like a child who needs to be advised, informed, pampered, and protected. He must fully realize that we are professionals and that we're taking care of his hotel and his personal reputation. The owners were, as one can imagine, influential men coming from governments, royal families, institutions, or wealthy individuals. The most original and eccentric owner was a member of the Gulf's royal family. He travelled around the world in his own Boeing 747. One day, when we were in a salon at Le Méridien Cairo, he found out that his butler had forgotten an envelope in London, in one of his private mansions. That put him into a fury and he demanded that his crew flew straight away, back to London to retrieve the letter.

Being attentive to the market, the owners, our customers and our workforce in general, we reinforced our image vis-à-vis the trade and the institutions. And so, for three consecutive years in a row (1999/2000/2001), we were recognised as the best hotel group in the Middle East, at the World Travel Market (WTM) Award ceremony in London.

In Dubai, in 2000 and 2001, we received the "travel intelligence trophy" for being the best hotel group in the Middle East and Northern Africa (MENA).

At the PATA conference in Kuala Lumpur in 2001, we were honoured by the World Travel Awards.

At the same time, our division won Le Méridien global challenge trophy, revolving around precise criteria: respect of deadlines for consignment of documents to head office, and respect of the chain's standards and procedures.

We saw ourselves as builders, with the desire to develop new hotels that would stand out and be distinct from competition, whether it be in our concepts, engineering, decoration, comfort or new ideas that we shared with the owners, architects and consultants. All this while keeping in mind that each development had to be profitable to contribute to our groups' expansion.

On May the 17ᵗʰ 2000, a second "Trafalgar" was announced within Granada Group, which was merging with Compass Group.

Compass Hospitality, listed on the London Stock Exchange, was the worldwide market leader in food service for concession contracts.

For the 1999 financial year, Compass had a turnover of 7.6 billion pounds and a profit of 914 million pounds. The objective of this merger was to allow Compass to focus on turnover (top line) and for Granada to maximise its net profit (bottom line) and share value. This merging thus promoted an easier development. It was officially announced in July 2000. The group became "Granada Compass-Hospitality & Media".

Being used to name change of the parent company, our vision was, on one hand, to stay on course by positioning ourselves as "the most efficient chain" in terms of quality and profitability in each market segment where we were in competition. On the other hand, we had the feeling that our new leaders and the high finance strategists would not stop there. The main objective was to develop new business opportunities, to maximise financial results and to show a positive balance sheet to increase the market capitalisation value.

Six months later, early 2001, the rumour was rife about a demerger-split between Granada Group and Compass Group, the latter becoming the parent company.

That is indeed what happened. Regarding this new change, **Bernard Lambert**, our boss, my colleagues **Jacques Motet** for Europe, **Hassan Adhad** for Africa, **Fabio Piccirillo** for the United States, **Michael Sagild** for Asia-Pacific, and **myself** for the Middle East and Western Asia, spontaneously decided to meet at Le Méridien Lingotto in Turin early September. Our objective: to define our position and a new strategy towards Compass Group and to brainstorm about another potential transition.

As one can imagine, all the changes and transitions that had taken place over the past few years had quite a disruptive effect on the people who were leading the group, particularly those in senior positions.

On January the 26ᵗʰ 2001, a terrible earthquake devastated the State of Gujarat in India with catastrophic consequences: 41,000 people killed or wounded, 900,000 houses and thousands of schools destroyed. The tragedy was both national and international. Spontaneously, our division organised a fundraising initiative at the level of Le Méridien. The solidarity and financial assistance were considerable, and this enabled us with our contacts, with the support of Mrs. Singh – the owner of Le Méridien New Delhi – and volunteer architects to go into action and build schools rapidly. We considered that this type of situation made the children terribly vulnerable. In addition to malnutrition, illnesses and shocks, they had lost the security of their usual landmarks: school and homes.

A few months later, the saga related to a potential buyer was going on. We were told that Compass was negotiating with hotel groups, as well as Nomura Securities, Japan's top broker. At that time, head office in London asked me to approach a **world-famous prince** in Riyadh so that he could make a potential takeover bid for our group. Thanks to my privileged contacts in Saudi Arabia, I managed to secure a meeting. On D-day, along with one of my General Managers in Saudi Arabia, I went to the place thirty minutes before the meeting. After having proved my credentials to reception and to security, I was received by the principal secretary who, very respectfully, offered us something to drink while explaining the attitude I had to have in His Royal Highness' presence, in other words, to be concise, precise in my questions, not to cross my legs and not point ... Ten minutes later, he invited me to present myself in front of the royal door. To the split second, the door opened revealing the prince, who received me cordially and invited me to sit opposite him. I was immediately caught and captivated by a strange atmosphere. Everything was dark: the walls, the floor, the furniture. On one side of the desk, a wall covered in television sets showing the world's stock exchange prices and, opposite me, the prince in his spotless "dishdash", whom I saw as a biblical appearance, if I dare to say so! After the exchange of business cards, the first thing he asked was:

– Are you mandated by your company?

– Yes, Your Highness.

I was about to show him a document when he replied that it wasn't necessary. At that point, I realized that before meeting me, he knew everything about me. I explained the purpose of my visit, namely that my group was looking for a buyer.

– Would you potentially be interested in this opportunity?

In two minutes, he showed me that Le Méridien was a respectable company with great potential, knowing that its portfolio, well spread worldwide, was clearly insufficient in the United States, with only 8 hotels. Therefore, he suggested that I take into account the contribution of his hotels, located in North America, which would allow synergies and a global reach by combining our respective reservation centres.

As an option, he suggested to consider another hotel chain that partially belonged to him, of lesser importance than Le Méridien, but complementary on European level. While continuing the conversation, he invited one of his experts to join us, so that his vision could be pursued between our two groups.

The meeting, initially supposed to last 20 minutes, went on for 40 minutes, which is an achievement because one hour can amount to a lot of money for the prince. Pleased with this exceptional meeting and the opportunity to derail the sale of the group, I got back to head office and explained in great detail the ins and outs. Confident about a positive outcome between the prince and Le Méridien, I was far from suspecting that I wouldn't be allowed to continue the conversation with him. Furious, I realised that, at the top level of the group, there were specific conflicting interests to ensure the transaction with Nomura occurred.

Before the announcement was made about the transfer between Compass and the buyer, the annual conference of Le Méridien General Managers took place in my area, at Le Méridien Dubai, whose owner is the government, represented by His Highness **Sheikh Ahmed Bin Saeed al Makhtoum**.

This meeting, which had an atmosphere of sadness, was characterised by a negative feeling about the potential buyer of the group, and some General Managers thought that this would be the last meeting in Le Méridien spirit. As far as I was concerned, I had to continue motivating my team, while ensuring them that this state of affairs is unfortunately very typical, when it comes to multinationals, and that, once again, we had to adapt accordingly.

Finally, Nomura won for a total amount of two billion two hundred millions pounds. At that time, Le Méridien alone accounted for 113 operational hotels under management and 37 fully-owned hotels globally, hence a total 150 hotels, not forgetting the twenty or so hotels under development

This new cycle of changes at the level of Le Méridien organization triggered quite a few important disruptions within the group, resulting in the discontent of some owners who considered that the successive takeover bids, which had occurred over a period of six years, disrupted the hotel teams and showed a lack of stability in the markets.

This new page of history for the group made me wonder about the repetition of strategies coming from the latest top brass in head office. New strategies meant: positioning, brand image, development, marketing, sales, public relations, human relations, financial objectives, etc.; in short, meetings in perspective, at the highest level, only to be told that next is now, by explaining the new definitions of objectives, etc., and often making fun of past experience, which is always shocking. Unfortunately, in most industries, the new leaders who take over a business are more comfortable in their arrogance and neglect to review their new company's background to better assess the future.

Since action is in my DNA and, at the same time, a motivation to move forward, while giving my best, I decided to leave Le Méridien ship.

I officially left Le Méridien Company on November the 29th 2001. And as a twist of fate, and of calendar, I had started my global journey on November the 29th 1971, and said good-bye on the same day, 30 years later! I learnt at the same time that my friend Bernard Lambert had also decided to leave the group.

I left Le Méridien without qualms, satisfied that, with colleagues and extraordinary friends from all backgrounds and all walks of life who deserved respect, I had contributed to the development of the French prestige, I had played a leading role in the hotel industry almost everywhere in the world, having developed, through my travels, 33 operational hotels and 20 in pre-opening for the group, hence 53 hotels.

During my hotel adventures, I sometimes encountered serious difficulties, sometimes chaotic, but despite this, I have always been driven by a consuming passion, which carried me and transported me to keep going further with the burning desire to discover and learn something new on the paths of knowledge and of discovery of new horizons.

I've always been driven by curiosity, which is for me is an absolute requirement, while trying to develop individual and collective talents and to search for perfection and refinement in excellence.

Chapter 20
Dubai, January 2002
MPJ stopover

Passion being my driving force, I decided to stay in Dubai for four reasons:

1. In accordance with my daughter, settled in Dubai.
2. Dubai is the perfect hub strategically, between Asia, Pacific, Africa, Europe and the Arabian Peninsula.
3. All my important contacts were there.
4. In reality, and despite opportunities offered to me to move to the United States, I wanted to discover business as my own boss. After 30 years of Le Méridien, it was time to face another challenge.

And so, I created a consulting company under the name MPJ, specialised in the search for hotel projects on behalf of operators /

hotel chains or of owners looking for the best suited operator for their project, market and profitability study, various business advices, etc.

My office was located in the Al Attar tower on Sheikh Zayed Road. Creating a company in this part of the world means that one has to be sponsored. I obtained my sponsorship thanks to the support of His Highness **Sheikh Ahmed**. Spontaneously, he generously offered the sponsorship through his principal private secretary, Mr. **Ali Mubarak Al Soori**.

In ten months, I reactivated many contacts, allowing me to do good business with international hotel companies and with an important group connected to one of the members of the Abu Dhabi royal family.

After the 11th September events in New York, my son Ralph, who was based at the Dallas Four Seasons, decided to join me in Dubai. Together we pursued our search for business, until the day I met an old acquaintance and friend from Le Méridien, His Highness **Sheikh Mohammed Bin Faisal Al Qassimi**, member of the royal family in the Emirates. He first solicited me for advice related to a spa concept that he wanted to create in his hotel in Sharjah. In the course of our meetings, one day, we came up with the idea of creating a hotel chain together. Why not?, we said. The next day, Sheikh Mohammed, very excited about this opportunity, said:

– I've been thinking and I agree to move forward. The only problem is that we need to convince my father, **Sheikh Faisal**.

The following week, I met H.E. **Sheikh Faisal bin Sultan Al Qassimi**, his son and his éminence grise, Mr. **Jean Dubois**, former boss of Société Générale in the UAE, acting as financial adviser.

After the exchange of courtesies, he offered me the traditional coffee and told me, in a very simple manner, "What can I do for you?"

I thanked him for receiving me and for giving me the opportunity to explain the idea that had germinated in the mind of his son and mine. Building on my hotel career, I explained in detail how to develop a regional hotel chain together. After listening to me for ten minutes without interruption, he said:

– Are you done?

– Yes, Your Highness.

He started by explaining that his hotel in Sharjah had been managed by an operator, Club Med, during a few years. Unfortunately, for different reasons, both parties had been forced to part. With a disarming smile, he added that he wasn't convinced. Seeing that the case was badly initiated, I decided to tackle the problem from a different angle.

– I understand your disappointment, Sheikh Faisal, and I respect your analysis. But, would you accept if I come back to you with a study, a business plan? This document would accurately detail the philosophy of the project, its concept, its positioning, its development, its organisation and its financial projection. I need fifteen days and, "with the grace of God", I think I might be able to convince you.

He smiled and said:

– I see that you are well integrated in our local community. I accept your proposal.

Two weeks later, I was back in his office, with only his advisor present. As agreed, I made a presentation of the project on my computer. After 15 minutes, he said:

– Are you done?

– Yes, Your Highness.

Then he got up and added:

– I am convinced, mabrouk (congratulations). But there is one condition: we won't serve any alcohol in our hotels.

In stride, my answer was clear:

– Sheikh Faisal, in business, you have to stand out, especially in our industry. Together, we are going to develop the first dry regional hotel chain in the Middle East.

– Bravo, aleq (perfect). Get organised with my son.

From then on, a new adventure was taking shape and my journey was going on again.

Chapter 21
Sharjah, December 2002
New flight plans

The following week, we created a partnership, formalised by a notary in Sharjah.

I offered to manage their hotel in Sharjah (Coral Beach Resort), because the position of General Manager was available. This enabled me to simultaneously create our hotel company.

At the time, some false friends didn't hesitate to say "From a position of President for a multinational, Noblet is now a mere General Manager." It is true that, for some people, it is difficult to be humble, but having said this, I said to myself: "Let it go, leave it be, time will tell." In fact, to be back in the field, to challenge myself and be busy with real people was extraordinary and rewarding. The hotel I was managing, consisted of 156 four-star rooms and suites, four restaurants, conference hall and a beach resort with two pools and a fitness centre.

Two months later, I sealed an extraordinary deal, in the centre of Dubai, for Sheikh Faisal. It involved the purchase of an operational five-star hotel with 150 rooms and suites, for 60 million Dirhams. Because of the real estate boom in Dubai in 2002, the hotel was evaluated at 150 million Dirhams six months later!

The previous owner never spoke to me again and for good reason!!! Following a prior agreement with the initial owner, the operator (Safir, a Kuwaiti company) left the hotel a month after the transaction. And so, after appointing **Imad Hussein**, an Iraqi graduated from a Belgian hotel school, as General Manager of Coral Beach, we moved to Dubai, to Coral Deira Dubai. In this new hotel, I appointed a new Tunisian General Manager, **Mohammed El Khala**, and we set up there the offices of our hotel chain named "**Coral International Hotels and Resorts**". We obtained our licence from DTCM (Dubai Tourism Commerce Marketing) and had the brand "Coral International" registered for intellectual property.

Chapter 22

Dubai, March 2003

New destination

The Coral International head office was located in the Coral Deira hotel, our second property. In the front line, my team was composed of:

My son **Ralph** (operations), **Fadi Mazkour** (sales and business development), **Hina Bakht** (communications and marketing), **Hatem Gasmi** (finance and development), **Fouad Nohra** (technical assistance), **Mohammed Jalil** (administration and government relations), and **Ann Mascarenas** (secretary).

My challenge, with regards to my partners, was to develop a hotel company with limited working capital! And since our turnover was solely linked to the fees collected from our first two hotels, we had to control our cash-flow very carefully. We also had to create our own standards and procedures, which amounted to a Herculean task, while having to find new hotels.

In September 2003, we organised a press conference at the Coral Deira hotel, with the media and TV channels.

Hina Bakht, with her degree in political science, coming from corporate business, and thanks to her professional contacts with the media, brought together two hundred people, 30 journalists and three TV channels!

In the presence of **Sheikh Mohammed Bin Faisal Al Qassimi** and my executives, and as Managing Director, I made a presentation of our company. Points elaborated on: partnership, philosophy, our first hotels, our integration in the local community, the hotel concept we wanted to develop and the presentation of my colleagues. Then I officially announced the creation of the first alcohol-free hotel chain in Dubai. Our goal: a portfolio of 25 hotels within five years!!!

Most of the guests probably thought I was a visionary living in a utopian world… After about ten interviews with journalists, radio and TV, we made the front page of the main newspapers the following day.

We were on the launching pad. Therefore we had to hurry to find new hotels. For that purpose, we had to become increasingly visible on the market, with attractive and powerful marketing tools, and so enter the UAE market in priority, and the Gulf. At the same time, we increased our PR actions in our hotels: cultural exhibitions, concerts, operas, fashion shows, culinary demonstrations, etc. Our goal: to draw attention so that people would talk about us by all means.

A few weeks later, I took the risk of signing a two-year lease for a hotel in Ajman, with 95 rooms. Thanks to the good economic climate, this deal enabled us to generate a substantial amount of money. Off plan, I invested it in the purchase of offices in

Jumeirah Lakes Tower, on the prestigious Sheikh Zayed Road, which would be operational three years later.

Our operational manuals were becoming increasingly fine-tuned. They related to administration, management and technical service contracts, marketing, sales, management, human relations, hygiene and security, guidelines for decoration and equipment, small tools, uniforms, etc.

Taking my pilgrim's staff, I met potential owners in all the Gulf countries, including Saudi Arabia, considered as the most important market in the GCC countries (Gulf Cooperation Council). This organization includes six Arab and Muslim petro monarchies of the Persian Gulf: Saudi Arabia, Kuwait, Qatar, Bahrain, the United Arab Emirates and Oman.

In four months, under the name Coral International, we managed two hotels in Oman, four in Dubai (Coral Deira, Coral Oriental, Coral Boutique Hotel Apartments and Coral Boutique Hotel, with its 32 luxury villas) and Coral al Khobar in Saudi Arabia

The latter, belonging to the multibillionaire (in US dollars) banking group Al Rajhi, represented a bravura moment to get the signature of **Sheikh Mohammed al Rajhi**, the **chairman**. At first, we were in competition with big international hotel groups, such as Intercontinental, Hilton and Mövenpick. Between my initial contact with the owner's representative and the signing of the contact, there were four different owner's representatives, forcing me to systematically repeat my presentation and to be convincing each time. This first hotel in Saudi Arabia, with 160 rooms, was the major reference and the basis for our future.

As part of our development, I expanded my team with an IT manager, **Hari Haran**; a webmaster, **Hani Nazmi**; a corporate chef, my friend **Michel Miraton**; a corporate housekeeper, **Necla Toprak**; a second secretary, **Sabine Iran**.

A bigger team meant additional office space. For this purpose, I had the second basement of Coral Deira fit out into offices. We became cave men, while waiting for our new office on Sheikh Zayed Road, which we were to occupy 18 months later.

The atmosphere within our team was exemplary. The wish to live together, where everyone fully played their part to contribute to our company's growth. The team spirit was magical between us, but also with the hotel teams. In other words, head office, which we represented, General Managers, heads of department and staff were one. I have always considered that our job, at head office, was to beat the service of our hotels in the field, by providing them our logistical support, our expertise and by being totally transparent. Our General Managers played the part of our group's ambassadors, enabling a potential owner to appreciate our style, the quality and professionalism that we all embodied.

In accordance with business trends and market needs, we set off on new paths. On top of the Coral International brand, positioned as 4/5 star, we wanted to develop three other brands, which was ambitious.

And so were born ... the **Corp Executive Hotels** brand, four-star, targeting international business men and women; **Ecos** brand as a budget hotel; **EWA** brand, an apartment formula, particularly appreciated by Gulf customers when travelling with family.

With our four brands, we could satisfy any demand, depending on the potential owners' budget, but also the different customer segments (5, 4, 3 and 2-star).

In order to no longer be dependent on a major international marketing agency and to avoid delays, interpretations, translation mistakes, etc., we decided to create our own marketing, advertising and event communication agency, under the name of MPJ, headed by Hina Bakht as Vice-President.

This agency allowed us to have our own hotels as clients, but also to be suppliers for other clients, such as institutions, hotel chains, multinational companies, governments and foreign tourism organizations (Monaco, Malta, Malaysia and Ajman); also creation of stands for Arabian Travel Market, launch of the latest luxury Mercedes, special events such as operas, fashion shows, etc.

To be more efficient in hotel management, we invested in an ultimate centralised reservation system with **Trust International**, equipped with all the corresponding technological systems.

In terms of training, we created our own academy, the **Dubai Training Centre**, in conjunction with DTCM in Dubai and AHLA in the United States, and in parallel a team building centre and related activities.

In order to unite all our products, we created a holding under the name **Hospitality Management Holdings** (HMH) with a logo recognisable by its design and colours: a mosaic of the world, also symbolising the rainbow nation of South Africa, on account of the hotel we were developing in Cape Town.

To be more visible internationally, strategic alliances were forged with the hotel group Husa in Spain, with one hundred or so hotels in Europe, with which we had trade agreements; with the American group HMC, specialist in customer loyalty (marketing programs for catering on the local market and rooms on the international market); Emirates Airlines, with their Skywards program; Visa card international; and Aramco in Saudi Arabia.

May 2008, our first convention to celebrate our group's fifth anniversary.

I wanted to organize it at Coral Beach Resort in Sharjah, on the date our group was born in 2003. For the occasion, there were non-stop presentations and speeches for two days. What were the results? 26 operational hotels (our initial objective of 25 hotels in five years had been achieved), 10 under construction and 20 in negotiation. Then it was the improvised speech of Sheikh Faisal bin Sultan Al Qassimi who was very pleased with the success of HMH. After having thanked all participants for the work achieved in five years, to my surprise, he announced my new appointment, while congratulating me. I was promoted from Managing Director to CEO and Group President.

Sheikh Faisal, in his capacity as former head of the Armed Forces of UAE, had been for many years the right-hand man of Sheikh Zayed, the father of the nation. Then at some point, certainly at the time of his retirement and with the agreement of Sheikh Zayed, he decided to no longer be involved with the affairs of the state, and to devote himself exclusively to business.

Each time I met him, either during a courtesy call at his office in Abu Dhabi or Sharjah, he called me "**Michel Ibn Battuta**" (the traveller, in Arabic), because he knew that I was travelling a great deal. He was extremely courteous, always apologizing when he called me, rarely after five pm. Despite his wealth through his numerous companies (factories, bank, hotels, real estate, super-markets and others…), he was always perfectly simple and humble.

After the crash of October 2008, resulting from the 2006 and 2007 subprime crisis in the United States, like everyone, we had to face a recession and, consequently, an economic stagnation. Despite this situation, we stayed on course with regards to development. And so, in Sudan, although we already had two hotels in Khartoum and in Port Sudan, we signed three new contracts with a government agency, The Social Security, with 21 million members, respectively in Port Sudan, Khartoum and Nyala in Darfur, which I had the opportunity to visit three times. Nyala is the capital of the state of South Darfur, with a population of 600,000 inhabitants. We were the first hotel in the region, which was a major event during the official opening. Our revenue came from the Khartoum government, from local authorities, from NGOs delighted to have us, and from traders coming from Chad.

The only constraint for travelling to Darfur was to get a pass from the Ministry of Interior and to have a seat on a plane because air traffic was very busy every day, and this despite the large aircrafts.

To do business in such regions seems paradoxical because of the risks taken, but as far as I'm concerned, I always followed my instinct and my desire to discover, to meet locals and to become integrated in the local reality, because even in a hostile environment, something positive always emerges, especially in business.

For the anecdote, while taking a picture of a huge baobab, I met a Bedouin, living frugally, with whom we sympathised and enjoyed tea and dates with his family in his shack, surrounded by goats. As I was leaving, I told Abdallah:

– From now on, you are the Ambassador of France in Darfur!

We saw each other a second time. I was glad to bring him, and his family, small gifts and a small French flag.

I also had a strong desire to develop a hotel in Bagdad, a mythical city, whose ancient name is "Madinat al Salam" (City of Peace!!). It was the capital of the Abbasid Caliphate.

After making several trips, I signed a management contract for a five-star hotel with 90 rooms, for which we were responsible for

technical assistance before the opening, and the management of
the operation. Being the first new hotel to open in Bagdad, and
symbolising the new flagship of the hotel business in that city, all
eyes were on us.

This new hotel, decorated by a South African, was perfectly well
situated in a secure area near the University of Bagdad. When I
say "secure", you must imagine a tank at the corner of the hotel
and the small adjacent road. This led to a private house. An Iraqi
senior official lived there and a group of armed men, deployed in
front of the main and the service entrance, not to mention the
walk-through metal detectors.

For each visit, the owner, Mr. Yasiris, a Shiite, had an
armed chauffeur, Abou Khaled, driving a four-ton armoured
Land-Cruiser, meet me at the airport! We left the highly-secure
airport to go to the hotel, and every two kilometres, we had to go
through check points. That said, the hotel was always full. The
average income per room flirted around 350 to 450 dollars because
business, despite the political instability, continued unabated.

One evening during Ramadan, around ten pm, Ahmed Yasiris,
with whom I'd dined, said:

– Michel, come with me, we are going to express our respect
to Prime Minister Maliki at his private residence by the Tigris
River. Needless to mention the security checkpoints to go through
before reaching the front door. De facto, I realised that my owner
was a close friend of the minister. He received us cordially, in a
casual local outfit, as it was Ramadan. He invited us in the majlis
(reception room), where about sixty people were savouring oriental
pastries, dates and sipping tea or coffee. Pleasant atmosphere and
open conversation with anyone who will listen. After half an hour,
Yasiris signalled that we had to get up and thank our host for his

hospitality. While thanking Prime Minister Maliki, I took the liberty of asking him for a favour, as a joke:

– Your Excellency, it's always a pleasure to come to your country, however the difficulty in coming over here, is to get a visa!

I hadn't even finished my sentence that he was calling for a henchman.

– Mohammed, taal, taal!!! (come here)

Presenting my passport to Mohammed, he said:

– For this gentleman, I want a two-year residence visa and an ID card before he leaves the country!

The next day, Mohammed came to pick me up in a Land-Cruiser and, in accordance with the governmental procedure, he took me to a hospital for a blood test. The hospital in question was partially dilapidated by the bombing. We climbed the three flights of stairs, because the lifts were out of order. We were welcomed in a clinic, in fact quite Spartan, and I gave my passport to an employee who invited me to sit down on a dirty sofa. Meanwhile, Mohammed went to an adjoining room, coming back two minutes later with his left arm folded.

– What happened to you?, I asked.

– Yalla Abibi. Let's go, I gave my blood for you!

That's Iraq, in all its splendour. As I was about to leave the hotel to go to the airport, Mohammed gave me my passport, stamped with the residence visa, and my ID. In return, I gave him a 100 dollar bill, which he did not expect.

To go to the airport, it's wise to leave practically four hours before take-off because of the road traffic and the endless check points. Especially close to the airport walls where cars and luggage were systematically searched and sniffed by dogs; then they went through a first scanner before being put in a second scanner, and were searched again before going on board.

My colleagues, devoted and eager to play a part in our group's success, agreed to follow me regularly in my marathon trips by car, from Jordan, via Beirut and through the Beqaa Valley to reach Damascus. Then, towards Aleppo, along the dangerous roads to Homs: potholes in the road, cows and goats crossing the motorway, not to mention the road hogs. We had two hotels in Aleppo, one of the oldest cities in the world. One was close to the mythical souk and the big mosque, with a view on the citadel, historic site where Saladin (his name meaning "the Righteousness of the Faith") reigned as absolute ruler; and the other hotel was close to the airport.

Setting off on the Lattakia road, we went through Homs, Hama, Tartus, past the famous "Krak des Chevaliers" fortress, dating from the eleventh century. Lattakia is a seaside city. We had a significant project there but, unfortunately, it didn't come to a successful conclusion.

Our other epic journeys, by car, day and night, took us to Al Khobar, Al Assa, Jubail, Damam, Dhahran and Riyadh. We even visited, during Ramadan, a hotel under construction at three in the morning, starting from the roof. The following day, we were flying to Jeddah, and then to Dubai. We were full of zeal and had no fear.

Unfortunately, in 2011, because of the war in Syria, the two hotels we were managing, were plundered and destroyed by the loyalist forces? By the rebels?

Similarly, a century-old hotel – belonging to the national company EGOTH – that we managed, located next to the Cairo stock exchange and close to Tahir Square, was also the scene of clashes. This historic hotel, part of the Egyptian heritage, was meant to be completely refurbished, under instruction of "raïs Mubarak", for a total cost of about fourteen million dollars. From hearsay, King Farouk was particularly fond of this hotel, where he would stay, for a couple of hours, with a lady friend!!!

At the same time, we opened hotels in South Africa, Cape Town; in Lebanon, Beirut; in Jordan, Amman; in UAE, Abu Dhabi, Dubai (3 hotels), and Fujairah; in Bahrain; in Saudi Arabia, Jubail, Dhahran, Riyadh (3 hotels) and Al Assa; and finally in Oman, with Muscat. And to end all, we moved into our brand-new offices on the prestigious Sheikh Zayed Road.

As I was keen to reactivate my contacts in India, I made three trips to different states, such as:

- The state of Maharashtra with Bombay (Mumbai), India's commercial capital, where misery mixes with splendour, with its favourite cities, such as Bollywood and its cinema productions, and Pune, India's ultimate cultural city, with its university and its faculties of famed education .

- The state of Rajasthan, commonly called the Golden Triangle, with New Delhi and other magical and important cities such as Jaipur, the capital of Rajasthan, Udaipur, Ajmer, and Jodhpur. It is a culturally very rich state, showing the India of bygone days, with its palaces and majestic forts.

- The state of Uttar Pradesh, with the city of Agra, inseparable from the Taj Mahal mausoleum, a monument symbolising the greatness and beauty of eternal love. It was designed under the instructions of Maharaja Shah Jahan in memory of his wife Mumtaz Mahal.

- The state of Tamil Nadu, with its capital Chennai, formerly Madras. Dozens of kilometres away, Pondichery ("new village" in Tamil) is a creation of the French colonisation of India.

– The state of Karnataka, with its capital Bangalore, considered as the Indian Silicon Valley, is the example of a centre of excellence of global importance for computer software, biochemistry and aerospace.

– The state of Kerala, with its capital, Cochin. This state has a literacy rate of 97.5%! It's easy living India, with its backwaters, the Venice of Kerala, an ultimate tourist destination.

– The region of Goa, former Portuguese colony, where tourism is the main source of income.

Why go back to India?

Simply to meet up with old friendly acquaintances and owners with whom I had the opportunity to work, but also to prospect due to the strong existing potential for business and tourist hotels.

India only receives four million inbound (international) tourists per year, very little for such a big country (while Dubai, for example, welcomes 14 million visitors per year). However, in terms of domestic travel, whether for business or tourism, it adds up to four hundred and fifty million customers for India's hotel trade. So, internally, the opportunities are real, especially as the existing hotels are ageing and no longer match international norms, except for the big luxurious hotel chains in cities such as Delhi, Mumbai, Cochin, Chennai, Bangalore, Pune, etc. But we still have a long way to go in terms of quality reception and of standards, especially in the mid-range hotels.

Having said that, eternal India, fascinating with its stunning scenery, its megacities, is an incredible mix between the Middle

Ages and modernity. Its riches cannot be confined to a single trip...

I'm still a resident of Dubai, in partnership with Sheikh Faisal and Sheikh Mohammed, who inspire respect, have principles and deserve to be known.

As one of the witnesses to the expansion of the United Arab Emirates (particularly Dubai and Abu Dhabi) I tend to think that this is where everything happens.

Thanks to the visionary genius of His Highness **Sheikh Mohammed Bin Rashid al Maktoum**, Dubai, not an oil producer, stands out by its dozens international universities; its infrastructures, unique in the world; its airline companies Emirates Airlines and Fly Dubai; its airports with five terminals, which have become number one in terms of volume of travellers; a wide range of hotels, which can fill every customer segment in budget, 2,3,4,5 star and super-deluxe; its hundreds of restaurants, fast-food, ethnic, brasseries or gourmet; its bars, clubs, nightclubs, coffee shops and tea houses... And also every conceivable leisure activities, massage parlours for men, cosmetics centres, shopping-centres equivalent to cities within the city, souks, its financial centre, its art district, knowledge village, congress centres, sports city, museums, ports, its marinas, yacht clubs, golf courses, historical centre Bastakiya, its ski resort, leisure centres, pure white sand beaches, clubhouses, sophisticated clinics and hospitals, parks, aquatic wonderland, mosques, churches, temples, the underground, the tram, horse races (the most important one in the world being the "World Cup"), golf and tennis competitions with the best players, desert or sea excursions, spectacular fountains, the shopping festival, "The Palm" – an artificial island in the shape of a palm tree... And not forgetting "Burj Khalifa", the highest tower in the world, over 828 meters high…

All this development is due to the Ruler His Highness Sheikh Mohammed Bin Rashid Al Maktoum, who manages Dubai like a company head. He recently said: "how you see Dubai today, only represents 5% of my vision". Thanks to him and his government, Dubai has expanded at supersonic speed, in an environment where 190 different nationalities co-habit. Competing with other big cities (London, Paris, New York, Hong Kong, Kuala Lumpur and Singapore), Dubai is considered as a major gateway for trade, tourism, hotel industry, real estate, international economic, social, cultural and sporting events, the Gulf's gold and financial market. All these factors contribute to making the United Arab Emirates a favourite destination, attractive and secure.

For Dubai, development can only be achieved through the human factor, which contributes to the influence of future generations. For His Highness "MBR" (**Mohammed Bin Rashid**), "the future belongs to those who dare dreaming and find the courage to pursue their dreams".

One of his premonitory dreams was the organisation of the World Expo 2020, with this fundamental message: "Connecting minds and creating the future". The Dubai government's business model is to attract superior talents, to be efficient, to develop quality systems and services in general, and, in the end, to give to citizens the opportunity to grow their collective energy.

Today, for a young person, the city of Dubai is, by itself, a great university to grow, learn and start a business.

Chapter 23
Dubai, February 2015
Smooth landing

After 13 years of good and faithful services, during an HMH board meeting in 2014, I announced my desire to retire from business operations early 2015, to dedicate myself to personal activities.

Being still the company's President, I took part in board meetings and representation assignments until April 2015, when I completely withdrew from the company. I sold my shares to my partners, for both HMH Holding and MPJ.

After 50 years of travels across the world, I left the hotel operations for good.

In this magical journey, I've met some remarkable people, whether it be in the bush, on construction sites, in hostile environments, in presidential and royal palaces, in hotels, in glamourous sphere, in refugee camps, in ghettos, in tribes, in religious and secular places, or in the middle of the desert, etc.

When my mother Odette showed me the way to the Toulouse hotel school in September 1962, she could not have suspected that my holiday around the world would last so long, despite the regular stopovers I made in the Comminges region, to spend a few hours with my family.

At the end of my internship at Café de la Paix in September 1965, I left for the unknown, but with the determination to move forward, in search of the Holy Grail. For me, it was the light, the wisdom, the knowledge of humanity and of its conscience, while considering passion as the driving force behind action, allowing the achievement of major projects.

I can say that my life has been an everyday adventure, a journey of perpetual discoveries, with the universe as sole guide. My happiness is not a state of mind but an adventure, in which I challenged myself every day. It was also a need for utopia, to surprise myself and to surprise others through sensible approaches regarding innovation, with sometimes quirky ideas.

A hotel is like a theatre, with a director represented by the General Manager who must enact a new play every day, with artists who must perform, and are represented by the staff, and finally the audience, embodied by the customers. "Hotel business is show business", which is produced on the hotel podium to surprise, seduce, respect and love through professionalism, quality of the reception, subtle fragrances, floral decorations, background music, smiles, make-up, sophistication, elegant uniforms, femininity, top-quality events, special attention, positive attitude of the staff, excellence in catering, kindness, irreproachable services, etc. In conclusion, for a hotel

manager to be proud of his work, he must enjoy what he's doing and must learn to indulge himself so he can tactfully sell dreams to customers who do him the honour of visiting him. Simultaneously, it is important to be integrated in the local community by positioning the hotel as a humanistic enterprise.

In terms of self-fulfilment, the hotel industry is a fascinating and rewarding job/vector for your own development. On a personal level, if I had to start again a life project, I'd do the same.

The hotel trade is also the industry of the future. For example, in 2014, it amounted to 2,200 billion dollars in the global economy, with one billion international travellers.

The emergence of China, India, Africa, Russia and Brazil, and the rapid expansion of the middle class, will lead to the arrival of a new generation of hotels, adapted to the needs of this demand. We must already take into account the Gen Y, or Millennials, (generation born with the technology) who is looking for convenience, meaning 3 fundamental elements in their requirement: a good bed, a good shower, and highspeed Internet to be connected 24/7. The size of the room doesn't matter, as long as it's comfortable. In terms of price, the Gen Y has a smart attitude, by saying why pay 200 or 300 dollars for a room if I can buy a simpler but modern and functional product for only 50 or 60 dollars! The reality of low cost flights perfectly connects with low cost hotels. With an estimated one billion six hundred million international travellers within 10/12 years, not everyone will be able to pay for a 1st or business class plane ticket, and, by extension, not everyone will be able to afford a luxury, 5, 4 or 3-star room, hence the future of low-cost hotel is becoming a growing and promising reality.

Throughout my long career in the hotel industry and still today, I've always considered that without the sound basis of my parent education, of my academic career (especially at the Toulouse hotel school), of my first years of apprenticeship in major institutions with France's Best Workers who taught me the science of the sacred in excellence, of usually my superiors, and of my respective teams who played an important role in my professional life, I would not have been able to play the missionary role of world citizen in the hospitality industry.

In my professional career, I've always felt that I was an eternal apprentice. When getting up every day, I knew that by the end of the day, through my achievements, my mistakes or specific situations, I would accumulate more knowledge. All this, to improve myself or to hone my professionalism, whether it be in the formulation of a new strategy or a new product positioning.

Depending on where we live, we have the duty to adapt by respecting the habits and customs, while leaving an impact on management and leadership. Generally speaking, expatriation is a logistic and psychological challenge. The initial image is an attractive facade: to live a new experience, to have a better salary, tangible benefits such as accommodation, hardship, etc.

In actual fact, we experience constant adjustment troubles, like emotional absence of relatives (father, mother, brother(s), sister(s), friends, colleagues), the distance of one's country or region; but also the ongoing effort we have to make to fit in the new environment, the paperwork to be in order with local authorities, children's enrolment at school, the spouse who leaves his/her job to follow husband or wife.

Besides the hazards of life: the temptations of becoming infatuated with someone else (which can lead to marital breakdown), the spouse who can't find a suitable occupation, or who sinks into lethargy, contracting a serious illness or

having to undergo a risky surgical procedure, the high cost of living, the distance with the country of origin.

We often live in a climate of political, economic and social upheaval, of insurrections and provocations in which we have to remain in control in all circumstances. We shouldn't wallow in ease. We shouldn't make unflattering comparisons with our country of origin because, in that case, why not stay home? We should ban arrogance and forget where we're coming from, etc.

In short, being an expatriate is a job.

A young person who finds himself or herself in Dubai for a first expatriation, it's the icing on the cake. The attraction of the city can go to one's head, with the illusion of success. In the end, money, prestige, fame or being number one at the box office is not what success is all about. The real success is to be inwardly fulfilled and not be afraid of anything.

Throughout my career, I have always thought that I was having a new adventure every day, with my instinct and my determination as guides. My main objective? To succeed in the day's challenge and to build a reputation in the company that inspired me. For me, work has always been a source of satisfaction and pleasure, by being associated with exceptional colleagues, men and women of different conditions, origins and faiths, who have allowed me to discover their world and their environment, which are a vehicle for cultural and intellectual enrichment. Especially as our world needs both diversity and variety.

My international experience has allowed me to create my own philosophy for team management. In terms of leadership, I believe that we must be consistent and logical with ourselves.

Each manager has his own leadership style and his own method to convince, motivate and lead. My leadership was built on my observations and my attentiveness.

My 25 basic principles of leadership?

1. Leadership = to love what you do, but also to know how to translate your passions into actions.
2. The leader must be inspired to lead and manage his men and women for a precise purpose. To do this, together with his team, he will define **the company's mission and vision**.
3. True leadership is not a matter of prestige or power, it's about responsibility, with the obligation of **liking the people you work with.**
4. The good leader, while being at the heart of the business, must **encourage the development of everyone**.
5. Keeping your distance with your colleagues is the best breeding ground for rumours and unproductive criticism.
6. I've always chosen to be in control and to **regularly engage with each colleague**, in order to assess their performance against their respective objectives, to advise them and to establish a trusting relationship.
7. As a leader, **be vigilant and ready for a fight** in front of the ongoing challenges of the harsh reality of business.
8. **Never neglect a simple detail** as it can lead to negative consequences.
9. **Abolish the court and courtiers**. Ensuring that all your direct reports are like you is a sign of mediocrity and weakness.
10. All idea-generating concepts have no value if they are not implemented quickly and efficiently. The permissive policy of **procrastination is a heresy** as it's already too late.

11. Never wait for someone's blessing or authorisation. A true leader decides which actions to take, while protecting his product. **If you don't go forward, you move backwards.**

12. Only surround yourself with the best on the market, because in a market economy, where everything is tactical and strategic, where you need to move fast, **the best added value, is your workforce's professional quality.**

13. For me, everything related to pretentious titles in flowcharts does not mean much. What is important is to **lead a team in order to carry forward a common project.**

14. **Personal ego has no place in an organisation.** The ego is often destructive in a team.

15. Optimism and passion are multipliers of force and energy. One of my former boss at Le Méridien once said: "Michel Noblet's weakness is his optimism and his enthusiasm". Meanwhile, you must decide to be happy every morning and **play the emotional cohesion's card with your team.**

16. **Apply the principle of recognition and satisfaction**, which leads to personal or collective appreciation.

17. The first wealth is above all **health** and to have a leader's position means nothing if you have to make yourself sick as part of your professional activity.

18. Where possible, and to eradicate stress, it's good and relaxing to visit natural sites, such as parks, garden, beaches, etc. and to **meditate through introspection** or still to practise a gentle sport.

19. Blaming others with an apology is a weakness and a rejection of responsibility and authority.

20. In today's world, we must be **multifunctional and embrace diversity in any organization** if we want to have a range

of views and perspectives and thus, better perform on the markets.

21. Improve yourself by always **learning more**.

22. For any project **the roadmap must be clear** and answer three fundamental questions: Where are we? Where do we want to go? How do we get there?

23. The basis for success for a leader is to **produce reports and financial results consistent with the defined objectives, in conjunction with the teams in the field, head office and shareholders**. And this on time and accurately.

24. Being a leader means to occasionally disrupt habits, even if it upsets some people. **Being a leader is also to put things into perspective with a sense of humour.**

25. Finally, to be efficient, the leader must have a balanced life, he must be happy and in harmony with himself and to that end, he must make an effort to dedicate as much time as possible **to his family.**

When I play back the movie of my personal adventure, despite successes, failures, hardships and humiliations, I see that I have always been privileged in view of the distress and suffering that happen every day across the world.

I've been around five continents. While being paid, I've had fifty exceptional years, 50 Years of Vacation that no tour operator or travel professional could have offered me, considering that we only live actively a part of our life, because the rest isn't life, but simply time flying by.

And all this to reach a priceless promotion, called RETIREMENT! Before a new beginning … Of course!!!

The great Colombian novelist **Gabriel Garcia Marquez** once wrote:

"What matters in life is not what happens to you but what you remember and how you remember it".

Pictures

A 17th century dinner at
Le Méridien Porto

Their Royal Highnesses,
King Carl Gustav
and Queen Sylvia
from Sweden

His Royal Highness,
Prince Charles

Her Royal Highness,
Princess Diana

Her Royal Highness,
Princess Diana

His Highness
Skeikh Ahmed
Bin Saeed Al Maktoum

His Highness
Skeikh Ahmed
Bin Saeed Al Maktoum

His Excellency
Mr. Suharto,
President of Indonesia

His Excellency
Dr. Mario Soares,
President of Portugal

Their Excellencies
Sheikh Faisal
Bin Sultan Al Qassimi
and Sheikh Mohammed
Bin Faisal Al Qassimi

Signatures for hotels
in Mecca and Medina

Dr. Palani G. Periasamy,
Le Méridien Chennai

Special event
in New Orleans

Reception for Mr. and
Mrs. Bernard Lambert

Welcome at
Le Méridien Bangalore

Meeting of the
Asia-Pacific General
Managers in Bali

The Middle East
Le Méridien team
at a seminar in
Le Méridien Phuket

The Middle East
Le Méridien team
with Sir Rocco Forte

The world presidents
of Le Méridien
at a meeting in Turin

A pharaons' party
in Cairo

Relaxing moment
on the Nile

Trophies of the best
hotel group in the
Middle East in 1999,
2000 and 2001

The new builders
in the Middle East
and in Western Asia

Admiral Douglas J. Katz
from the US Marine

The US Marine

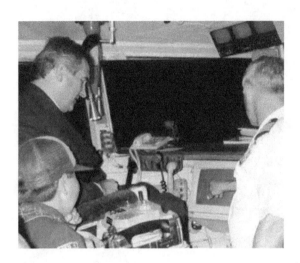

A new commanding
officer for the US America
with 6,000 men on board

Lunch in a village in
Northern Thailand

Viva America!!

Imprimé en France
ISBN 978-2-36252-688-6
Dépôt légal : 4ᵉ trimestre 2016

CPSIA information can be obtained
at www.ICGtesting.com
Printed in the USA
LVHW06s0100030718
582582LV00008B/16/P

9 782362 526886